Competition Law in Spain

Competition Law in Spain

Mauricio Troncoso
Patricia Pérez Fernández

This book was originally published as a monograph in the International Encyclopaedia of Laws/Competition Law.

Founding Editor: Roger Blanpain
General Editor: Frank Hendrickx
Volume Editors: Francesco Denozza & Alberto Toffoletto

Wolters Kluwer

Published by:
Kluwer Law International B.V.
PO Box 316
2400 AH Alphen aan den Rijn
The Netherlands
E-mail: international-sales@wolterskluwer.com
Website: lrus.wolterskluwer.com

Sold and distributed in North, Central and South America by:
Wolters Kluwer Legal & Regulatory U.S.
7201 McKinney Circle
Frederick, MD 21704
United States of America
Email: customer.service@wolterskluwer.com

Sold and distributed in all other countries by:
Air Business Subscriptions
Rockwood House
Haywards Heath
West Sussex
RH16 3DH
United Kingdom
Email: international-customerservice@wolterskluwer.com

Printed on acid-free paper

ISBN 978-94-035-0290-8

e-Book: ISBN 978-94-035-0175-8
web-PDF: ISBN 978-94-035-0255-7

Printed in the United Kingdom.

The Authors

Prof. Dr Mauricio Troncoso is Associate Professor of Commercial Law at the Universidad Autónoma de Madrid (since 1996), where he teaches Competition Law, Company Law and Contract Law. He has over two decades of experience in Competition Law. He has written two books and several articles on competition company and patent law. He has been visiting professor at the *Humboldt-Universität zu Berlin* and lecturer in many universities of Europe, America and Asia, among them the Hong Kong University, National University Singapore, Chicago-Kent University and *Università degli Studi di Padova*. He holds degrees from the Universidad Complutense de Madrid (LLB, Bachelor of Law, 1989, with major honours) and Universtità degli Studi de Bologna, 1993 (Juris Doctor, *Summa Cum Laude*), where he wrote his PhD on Predatory Pricing. He won the First National Award in Law Degree (1988–1989), the Universidad Complutense de Madrid Award in Social and Legal Sciences (1988–1989) and the Universidad Complutense de Madrid Faculty of Law Award (1989). He has been Alexander von Humboldt Foundation Scholar, foreign professor nominated to carry out research in Germany (2007–2008) as well as Visiting Researcher at Max Planck Institute for Intellectual Property, Competition and Tax Law, Munich (2007–2008). He has been Coordinator of the Project 'E-Learning on Patent Litigation' of the European Patent Academy (European Patent Office) (2013) and has participated in the working group on the Patent Declarion of the Max Max Planck Institute for Intellectual Property, Competition and Tax Law, Munich (2011–2014). As of 2013, he is Of-Counsel at Baylos Abogados, where he advises clients in matters related to Competition Law, Patent Law, Company Law and Contract Law. He has contributed General Introduction, Part I Chapters 1, 2, 3 and 4, Part II Chapters 2 and 3, Part III Chapter 2 of this monograph.

The Authors

Dr Patricia Pérez Fernández is Associate at Cleary Gottlieb Steen & Hamilton LLP (since 2014) in Brussels, where she practices European and Competition Law. She also teaches EU and Competition Law at the Catholic University of Lille (undergraduate and master courses). Prior to that she has been a scholarship holder of the Spanish Ministry of Education (as of 2010), the German Academic Exchange Service (DAAD) and the Max Planck Institute for Intellectual Property and Competition Law in Munich, where she spent two years researching and writing her PhD in private enforcement of competition law. She was born in Stuttgart, Germany, in 1986, where she went to school and high school. She holds a degree in Law from the University of Castilla-la Mancha (2009, with major honours), as well as a Masters in Fundamental Rights and Public Liberties (2010). She was finalist with honours in IX Young Lawyer Award, Garrigues (2009) and won the second prize of the *Centro de Estudios Financieros* 2013 award. During the elaboration of her PhD she has been teaching competition law and company law, publishing regularly articles in academic journals and participating as a speaker in conferences in Europe and America. She has completed an internship at the Legal Service of the European Commission in Brussels. She is regularly attending conferences as speaker (Queen Mary University London, University Carlos III Madrid, University Rey Juan Carlos, etc.) and teaches EU and Competition Law in Master programmes at the IE University and Centro de Estudios Garrigues, both in Madrid. She has been a Visiting Professor at Sciences Po, Paris. She speaks German, Spanish, English and French. She has contributed Part I Chapter 5, Part II Chapter 1, Part III Chapters 1 and 3 of this monograph.

Table of Contents

Table of Contents

List of Abbreviations

CE	*Constitución Española* (Spanish Constitution)
CNC	*Comisión Nacional de la Competencia* (former Spanish Competition Authority)
CNMC	*Comisión Nacional de los Mercados y de la Competencia* (current Spanish Competition Authority)
LCD	*Ley 3/1991, de 10 de enero, de Competencia Desleal* (Spanish Unfair Competition Act 3/1991, of 10 January 1991)
LDC	*Ley 15/2007, de 3 de julio, de Defensa de la Competencia* (Spanish Competition Act 15/2007, of 3 July 2007)
LOPJ	*Ley Orgánica 6/1985, de 1 de julio, del Poder Judicial* (Spanish Judiciary Act 6/1985, of 1 July 1985)
RDC	*Real Decreto 261/2008, de 22 de febrero, por el que se aprueba el Reglamento de Defensa de la Competencia* (Spanish Competition Regulation 261/2008, of 22 February 2008)
SDC	*Servicio de Defensa de la Competencia*
TDC	*Tribunal de Defensa de la Competencia* (Spanish Competition Authority from 1963 until 1989)
TFEU	Treaty on the Functioning of the European Union
TTBER	Commission Regulation (EU) 316/2014 of 21 March 2014 on the application of Article 101(3) of the Treaty on the Functioning of the European Union to categories of technology transfer agreements

List of Abbreviations

General Introduction

§1. General Background of the Country

I. Geography and Climate

1. The Kingdom of Spain is located in Southwestern Europe, where it occupies 80% of the Iberian Peninsula (while Portugal accounts for the other 20%). In addition to the peninsula, it comprises a series of archipelagos, including the Baleàric Isles in the Mediterranean Sea and the Canary Islands in the Atlantic Ocean, as well as two cities, Ceuta and Melilla and other small enclaves in Northern Africa. It is the fourth largest European country by area (504,645 km^2) and the second most mountainous after Switzerland.

2. Spain owes its extraordinary diverse climate to its five large mountain ranges and its position between the Atlantic Ocean and the Mediterranean Sea and its proximity to Africa (the Strait of Gibraltar, which separates its coasts from Morocco, is only 12 km wide). Its three main types of climate are: Mediterranean, continental and Atlantic. The first, which affects all of southern Spain and its south and east coasts, is characterized by high summer temperatures, mild winter ones and scant or moderate rainfall. The central plain has a continental climate with very warm, dry summers and cold and moderately humid winters. The country's north and northwest have an Atlantic climate with moderate winters, relatively warm summers and heavy rainfall year-round.

II. Population

3. Further to January 2016 data, Spain has the fifth largest population, 46.4 million, in the European Union. Its population density (92 people/km^2) is perceptibly lower than in most of western Europe, however. Moreover, its population is unevenly distributed, concentrated primarily in Madrid and on and around the coast. The country's two largest metropolitan areas are Madrid (6.6 million) and Barcelona (5.2 million).

4. Spain has traditionally been characterized by emigration, first to Latin America (in the nineteenth and first half of the twentieth centuries) and then to

Western Europe (last third of the twentieth century). In recent decades, however, immigrants have been drawn to Spain, mostly from Latin America, Morocco and Eastern Europe.

5. The official national language is Spanish, while certain regions have co-official languages (Catalan, Basque and Galician).

III. Government and Politics

6. Since the ratification of its 1978 Constitution, Spain is a parliamentary monarchy. Article 1 of that charter defines Spain to be a social and democratic State subject to the rule of law which advocates freedom, justice, equality and political pluralism as the highest values of its legal system. National sovereignty belongs to the Spanish people.

7. The 1978 Constitution embraces the principle of separation of powers. The legislative power lies in *Las Cortes*, a two-chamber parliament consisting of the lower house or Congress of Deputies and an upper house, the Senate. Both are elected by universal suffrage every four years unless previously dissolved by the Head of State.

8. Executive power is wielded by the Council of Ministers. The Council is headed by the President of the Government, elected by the lower house and appointed by the King. The President of the Government designates all the other members of the Government, subsequently appointed by the King.

9. The judicial power is vested exclusively in judges and magistrates (*see* paragraphs 20 et seq.)

10. Regionally, Spain is a quasi-federal state. It is divided into municipalities, provinces and seventeen regions denominated autonomous communities (*Comunidades Autónomas*), vested with considerable local autonomy. All these institutions are self-governed, and the regions have executive and legislative bodies of their own.

11. Spain has been a member of the European Union since 1 January 1986.

§2. Economic System

12. Further to the World Bank statistics, in 2015 Spain was the fourteenth largest economy worldwide and fifth Europe-wide. Spain's gross domestic product (GDP) that year was USD 1,199,057 million, and its gross national income per capita was USD 28,520. By sector, GDP is distributed as follows: 2.5% farming and fishing; 17.1% industry and energy; 5.5% construction and 74.9% services.

13. In its most recent history, the Spanish economy underwent uninterrupted expansion from 1996 to 2008, primarily on the back of the construction industry. The international financial crisis, in conjunction with the bursting of the real estate bubble, ushered in a five-year recession. Initially, the various levels of government raised spending in an attempt to jump-start the economy with economic stimulus programmes. That raised national debt from a historic low of 36.3% in 2007 to a likewise record high of 93.4% of GDP in 2013. In light of the failure of these policies, beginning in 2010 governments began to implement drastic spending cuts, which concurred with a decline in private spending, prompted by the steep rise in unemployment and the downturn in personal income and investment. That slide in the domestic market has given way to export growth and improved productivity in recent years.

§3. Legal System

I. Legislative Hierarchy

14. Spain's is a civil law system, as opposed to common law systems in which the intellectual framework is based on court-based decisional law.

15. Relevant sources of law are EU law, the Spanish Constitution (CE), statutory law, and secondary law. While not a source of law *de iure*, Spanish case law carries considerable weight de facto.

16. EU law and the Spanish Constitution are at the top of the hierarchy of laws. Ranking second in the hierarchy are acts or statutes, i.e., laws enacted by national or regional parliaments. Administrative legislation (*Reglamentos*), which may be adopted by national or regional executive branches to apply and enforce acts, stand on the third rung and take a number of forms: royal decrees, decrees or orders (*Reales Decretos*, *Decrétos*, *Órdenes*).

17. Further to the principle of the supremacy of EU law, legal provisions, including constitutional provisions, in effect in Spain that counter European legislation are not applicable.

18. Sub-constitutional legislation that infringes the CE is null and void. A Constitutional Court decision must be forthcoming to nullify acts, whereas regulations can be repealed by a Supreme Court judgment.

19. Administrative legislation is subordinated to acts (*see* Article 97 CE).

II. Judiciary

20. The institution that governs the judicial power, the General Council of the Judiciary (*Consejo General del Poder Judicial*), was established under Article 122.2 of the Constitution (CE) to guarantee the independence of this branch of government.

21. The judges comprising the judiciary are mainly professionals whose appointments, obtained by competitive examination, are indefinite, subject only to removal, suspension, transfer or retirement as provided by law (Article 117.2 CE). They are independent, impartial and accountable under the rule of law.

22. The principle of jurisdictional unity is the basis of the organization and operation of the courts (Article 117.5 CE) and the Constitution explicitly prohibits any special jurisdiction, outside the partial exception of military courts.

23. The four branches into which the judiciary is divided are: civil, criminal, labour and administrative, each with its own hierarchy. The Supreme Court is the highest judicial body in all branches of justice, except the provisions concerning constitutional rights and guarantees (Article 123.1 CE). The Constitutional Court, in turn, hears cases dealing with alleged unconstitutionality of acts or regulations, individual appeals for protection against violation of fundamental rights and conflicts of competence between the Central and Regional Governments.

§4. Historical Background on Antitrust Law[1]

24. Spain adopted its first Competition Act in 1963 (*Ley 110/63 de 20 de julio, de Represión de las Prácticas Restrictivas de la Competencia*). Whether its adoption was a purely domestic initiative or more probably a response to outside pressures, mainly from the US (given the provision in the 1953 bilateral Agreement on the desirability of an antitrust policy), is not entirely clear. While the act reflected the principles laid down in the 1957 Treaty of Rome, it apparently drew its inspiration for the institutional framework more from German and British than European Community arrangements.[2] Its enforcement was entrusted to two bodies: the Competition Court (*Tribunal de Defensa de la Competencia* or TDC), a quasi-judicial body competent to adjudicate, grant exemptions, impose penalties and publish reports and studies; and the Competition Service (*Servicio de Defensa de la Competencia* or SDC), an administrative body under the aegis of the Ministry of Trade responsible for preparing proceedings and conducting investigations. The act had

1. *See* García, F., 'Fundamentos del Derecho de la libre competencia', in Bello, Mª.P. – Hernández, F. (coord.), *Derecho de la libre competencia comunitario y español*, Thomson Aranzadi, Cizur Menor, 2009, pp. 51–53.
2. Borrell, J.-R., 'Spanish Competition Policy: A Case of Government's Response to Domestically Perceived Problems', *The Antitrust Bulletin*, 1998, p. 454.

scant impact on the Spanish economy, however, and remained virtually unimplemented and unenforced for over twenty years,[3] probably because the power to impose penalties was vested in the Council of Ministers, acting on a proposal from the TDC, and the control of mergers was confined to voluntary registration in the Registry of the Competition Restraints.

25. The situation changed in 1986 with Spain's membership in what was then the European Economic Community (today the European Union, EU), for competition policy was one of the institution's pillars, not only to strengthen competition in Europe but also as an essential tool for effectively building a single market.[4]

26. The result was the adoption in 1989 of a new Competition Act (*Ley 16/1989, de 17 de julio, de Defensa de la Competencia*). This new act defined competition policy as one of the key elements in the economic model established by the 1978 Constitution. Its new provisions included:[5]

- prohibition of agreements of any nature that might stifle competition, even if never implemented;
- possible authorization of restrictive agreements in certain cases;
- prohibition of abuse of dominant market positions;
- creation of a system for the voluntary notification of mergers, repeal of the former registration system and assignment of decision-making in this area to the Government;
- regulation of state aids;
- entrustment of the TDC with the furtherance of fair competition policies;
- vesting of the TDC with the power to fine (formerly reserved to the Council of Ministers, further to TDC proposals).

27. That act was subsequently amended by *Real Decreto-Ley 6/1999 de Medidas Urgentes de Liberalización e Incremento de la Competencia*, which introduced a system of mandatory notification for concentrations exceeding certain thresholds and *Ley 52/1999, de 28 de diciembre, de Reforma de la Ley de Defensa de la Competencia*, which straitened control over state aids by enabling the TDC to institute proceedings ex officio to determine whether the subsidies granted by public authorities distorted competition.

28. The legislative framework for antitrust in Spain underwent major change in 2002. Whereas the Constitution was initially interpreted to vest the central Government with exclusive competence in this area, Constitutional Court Sentence 208/1999 of 11 November acknowledged the regions' executive competence in

---

3. Borrell, J.-R., *The Antitrust Bulletin*, 1998, p. 448.
4. *See* European Commissions brief 'Spain: Anniversary of the Spanish Competition Act' available at *ec.europa.eu/competition/ecn/brief/01_2013/es_anniv.pdf*.
5. Borrell, J.-R., *The Antitrust Bulletin*, 1998, p. 460.

competition law. In response to that sentence, an act was adopted to coordinate Central and Regional Government competences (*Ley 1/2002, de 21 de febrero, de Coordinación de las Competencias del Estado y de las Comunidades Autónomas en materia de Defensa de la Competencia*).[6]

29. The adoption of Regulation (EC) No. 1/2003 on the implementation of the rules on competition laid down in Articles 81 and 82 of the Treaty (now Articles 101 and 102, TFEU), together with a demand for more independence for competition authorities, drove further reform of the Competition Act. The process began with the publication of a White Paper in 2005 and ended after two years of public debate with the adoption of the third Competition Act (*Ley 15/2007, de 3 de julio, de Defensa de la Competencia*) or LDC.[7]

30. The most prominent differences between the LDC and the 1989 Competition Act are listed below:[8]

- The authority responsible for applying the competition rules was restructured with the creation of the National Competition Commission (*Comisión Nacional de la Competencia*) or CNC, which replaced and integrated the bodies formerly entrusted with investigating (*Servicio de Defensa de la Competencia*) and ruling on (TDC) competition files, with two separately administrative units (*Dirección de Investigación and Council*). In addition, the CNC was vested with broader decision-making and investigative powers and greater independence.
- The application of the provisions of competition law were decentralized, providing for application not only by the CNC but also by the regional competition authorities, further to the criteria on distribution of competence laid down in the LDC and in aforementioned *Ley 1/2002, de 21 de febrero, de Coordinación de las Competencias del Estado y las Comunidades Autónomas en materia de Defensa de la Competencia.*
- The reference to the exploitation of economic dependence as illegal antitrust conduct was removed.

6. *See* García, F., in Bello, Mª.P. – Hernández, F. (coord.), *Derecho*, p. 53. For an in-depth study of the regions executive competence *see* Guillén, J., 'La descentralización del Derecho de la Competencia en España', in Garcia-Cruces, J.A. (dir.), *Tratado de Derecho de la Competencia y de la Publicidad*, Tomo I, Tirant lo Blanch, Valencia, 2014, pp. 751–885.

7. *See* European Commissions brief 'Spain: Anniversary of the Spanish Competition Act' available at *ec.europa.eu/competition/ecn/brief/01_2013/es_anniv.pdf.*

   The White Paper is available at www.minhap.gob.es/Documentacion/Publico/SGPEDC/Libro%20Blanco.pdf.

   See *about this Paper,* Pérez, J.I., *et altri*, *Diagnosis of the White Paper for the Reform of the Regulatory Scheme of the Power Generation in Spain*, Instituto de Investigación Tecnológica (IIT), Universidad Pontificia Comillas de Madrid, 2005.

8. *See* Signes, J.I., 'Fundamentos del Derecho de la Política de la Competencia', in Signes, J.I. *et altri*, *Derecho de la competencia*, Civitas Thomson Reuters, Cizur Menor, 2013, p. 44; Ortiz, L. *et altri*, *Manual de Derecho de la Competencia*, Tecnos, Madrid, 2008, pp. 27–28; Alonso, R., 'Lección 14. Derecho de la Competencia', in Menéndez, A. – Rojo, A., *Lecciones de Derecho Mercantil*, Volumen 1, Civitas Thomson Reuters, Madrid, 16ª ed. 2016, p. 299.

- The former system involving individual authorization of restrictive agreements was replaced with one based on legal exemptions, similar to Regulation (EC) 1/2003.
- A leniency programme was established envisaging full exemption from fines or reduction of the amount thereof for undertakings which, while having participated in a cartel, report its existence and provide sufficient proof to initiate an investigation.
- The regulations on mergers control were amended: the market share threshold was raised, a new simplified notification system for certain operations was introduced and Spanish legislation on takeover bids was adapted to European rules. Decision-making independence was also reinforced by attributing the final decision to the CNC, while acknowledging the Government's veto right where the general interest is at stake.
- The CNC and regional competition authorities were granted a more substantial role in the prior analysis of public subsidies and assessment of their effects on competition.
- Jurisdiction over any extra-contractual liability stemming from infringement of competition law was assigned to the Mercantile Courts.
- The procedures for conventional termination and interim measures were elasticised.
- Infringement brackets were defined, and the mechanism for calculating fines clarified, with a ceiling based on the last reporting year's profit.

31. Subsequent provisions for implementing the LDC were laid down in the Competition Regulation (*Reglamento de Defensa de la Competencia*) or RDC, enacted under Royal Decree 216/2008, in turn supplemented with the National Competition Commission's by-laws, approved under Royal Decree 331/2008.

32. Spain's institutional framework has recently been overhauled. Under *Ley 3/2013, de 4 de junio, de creación de la Comisión Nacional de los Mercados y la Competencia* the market supervision and regulation provisions formerly force were remodelled in-depth and a new supervisory body was established, the National Markets and Competition Commission (*Comisión Nacional de los Mercados y la Competencia*) or CNMC. This new body integrates the former CNC and five other sectoral regulators.[9]

33. It is important to point out, however, that while this overhaul has affected the institutional framework set out in the LDC, the act's substantive provisions remain unaltered. Thus, the functions of investigating and ruling competition files, formerly performed by the *Dirección de Investigación* and CNC Council, have been entrusted to the new *Dirección de Competencia* and the CNMC Council. The regulation of this new institutional framework has been completed with the Royal Decree 657/2013.

---

9. Namely: *Comisión Nacional de la Energía, Comisión del Mercado de las Telecomunicaciones, Comité de Regulación Ferroviaria, Comisión de Regulación Económica Aeroportuaria* and *Comisión Nacional de Sector Postal.*

Part I. Structure of Antitrust Law and Its Enforcement

Chapter 1. Sources of Antitrust Law

§1. National Sources

34. The core sources of Spanish antitrust law include the Competition Act (*Ley 15/2007, de 3 de julio, de Defensa de la Competencia*) or LDC, informed like its predecessors by the antitrust provisions of the TFEU (previously the EC Treaty), and its relating implementing regulations.

35. In addition, other statutes contain provisions related with the antitrust offences or with the LDC. The most important are, on the one hand, the Penal Code, whose Article 284.1 regulates the offence traditionally known as 'seeking to alter the price of things'.[10] On the other hand, the LDC and its related legislation contain a set of rules that regulate the administrative proceedings that can be raised to the CNMC (*see* especially Articles 36–70 LDC). For all matters not envisaged there, the provisions of *Ley 39/2015, de 1 de octubre, del Procedimiento Administrativo Común de las Administraciones Públicas*, which repealed *Ley 30/1992, de 26 de noviembre, de Régimen Jurídico de las Administraciones Públicas y del Procedimiento Administrativo Común,* apply (*see* Articles 45 and 70).

36. Lastly, two other pieces of legislation govern private antitrust enforcement: first, the general rules on the attribution of jurisdiction among judges and courts set out in the Judiciary Act (*Ley Orgánica 6/1985, de 1 de julio, del Poder Judicial* or LOPJ), to determine how jurisdiction is distributed among judges (*see* in particular Article 86*ter*.2.f, LOPJ); and second, the Civil Procedure Code (*Ley de Enjuiciamiento Civil*), which govern the respective proceedings.

10. Article 284 of the Penal Code envisages prison sentences for anyone who: '1. Using violence, intimidation or deceit were to attempt to alter the prices that would arise from free competition of products, merchandise, securities or financial instruments, services or any other movable assets or real estate that is subject to contract, without prejudice to the punishment that may be imposed on them for other felonies committed.'

§2. INTERNATIONAL SOURCES

37. Like other Member States, Spain is bound to apply the provisions of European Union competition law. Consequently, Articles 101–109 of the TFEU and their implementing legislation are directly applicable in Spain.

38. Among the secondary sources it is necessary to highlight:

- Council Regulation (EC) 1/2003 of 16 December 2002 on the implementation of the rules on competition laid down in Articles 81 and 82 of the Treaty of the European Community (presently Articles 101 and 102, TFEU), together with Commission Regulation (EC) 773/2004 of 7 April 2004 relating to the conduct of proceedings by the Commission pursuant to Articles 81 and 82 of the EC Treaty (presently Articles 101 and 102 TFEU).
- Council Regulation (EC) 139/2004 of 20 January 2004 on the control of concentrations between undertakings, together with Regulation (EU) 1269/2013 of 5 December 2013 amending Commission Regulation (EC) 802/2004 implementing Council Regulation (EC) 139/2004 on the control of concentrations between undertakings.

§3. SECONDARY SOURCES

I. Regulations

39. Further to the authorization to do so contained in prior competition acts and presently laid down in the Second Final Provision of the LDC, the Government has decreed a series of regulations to implement and apply the latter. The most prominent include *Real Decreto 2295/2004, de 10 de diciembre, relativo a la aplicación en España de las normas comunitarias de competencia*; *Real Decreto 602/2006, de 19 de mayo, por el que se aprueba el Reglamento de exenciones de* determinadas *categorías de acuerdos de intercambio de información sobre morosidad*; and *Real Decreto 261/2008, de 22 de febrero, por el que se aprueba el Reglamento de Defensa de la Competencia* (hereafter RDC).

II. Guidelines

40. Before its integration into the present CNMC, the CNC issued a series of notices or *Comunicaciones*:

- *Comunicación de 6 de febrero de 2009, de la Comisión Nacional de la Competencia* on the quantification of fines imposed for infringement of Articles 1, 2 and 3 of *Ley 15/2007, de 3 de julio, de Defensa de la Competencia* and Articles 81 and 82 of the Treaty establishing the European Community.
- *Comunicación de la Comisión Nacional de la Competencia, sobre terminación convencional de expedientes sancionadores* (October 2011).

- *Comunicación de la Comisión Nacional de la Competencia, sobre los supuestos a los que resulta de aplicación el formulario abreviado previsto en el artículo 56 LDC en los procedimientos de control de concentraciones económicas* (October 2011).
- *Comunicación de 19 de junio de 2013, de la Comisión Nacional de la Competencia, sobre el Programa de Clemencia.*

§4. Sources' Relation and Hierarchy

41. The highest ranking legislation is found in European Union law and the Spanish Constitution. Further to the principle of the prevalence of European Union law over Member State legislation, any national rules that counter the former are not applicable (for the Union provisions would apply). If a provision of a national act or regulation counters the Spanish Constitution, that provision is null and void.

42. The following rung on the legislative ladder is occupied by acts, in particular the LDC. They are followed by regulations (*see* Article 97 CE), which are void if they counter the provisions laid down in an act.

43. The legal nature of notices or *Comunicaciones* is controversial. Insofar as they can be likened to *instrucciones* and *circulares internas*, they would traditionally be denied legislative status, the argument being that they are of an internal nature and not binding on third parties. At the same time, however, they might be regarded as 'internal rules', but not regulations. From that perspective, they would have intra-governmental efficacy and would be binding on the lower bodies for which they are intended. Externally, they would neither have legal efficacy (i.e., they would not be enforceable with respect to, or binding on, third parties) nor vest authority (power with any effect on third parties' legal affairs).

44. Such lack of effect on third parties infers that non-compliance in itself has no impact on the validity of administrative acts (*see* Article 21.3 LRJPAC), although non-complying public officials may incur disciplinary liability. Where citizens believe that they have been the object of singular and unjustified non-compliance with *instrucciones* or *circulares*, they may allege that the principle of equality has been breached or the principles of legal certainty, legitimate expectations or estoppel have been violated.

§5. Role and Authority of Precedents

45. Both Spanish competition authorities and courts must base their decisions first and foremost on the provisions of positive law. Precedents may only be invoked when such provisions are ambiguous or leave room for interpretation.

46. Precedents may nonetheless impact future decisions on the same issues. Judicial precedents take preference over administrative precedents.

Chapter 2. Scope of Application

§1. Territorial Reach

47. While the LDC makes no specific mention of its geographical scope, its content clearly infers that it is applicable nationwide, for its provisions apply to practices '... in all or part of the national market' (*see*, for example, Articles 1, 2 and 10).[11]

48. The LDC is the sole applicable legislation when a restriction on competition involves the Spanish market only, with no possible effect on trade between European states.

49. Moreover, whether or not the effects of such conduct are confined to a single region is only pertinent for determining the competent authority for applying the LDC: the CNMC or the regional antitrust authorities.

§2. Special Sectors

50. As a general rule competition law applies to all sectors of the economy.

51. Community law provides for certain exceptions to this general rule, however. The TFEU itself, for instance, envisages 'attenuated' application of antitrust legislation in agriculture (Article 42) and the military or defence industry (Article 346.1(b)).

52. Spanish competition law makes no such distinction: i.e., the legislation is applied equally to all sectors of the economy. That interpretation is supported by the reiterated application of the LDC by Spanish competition authorities in sectors such as agriculture (*see*, amongst others, the TDC Resolutions of 3 June 1997 (Proceedings 352/94, conduct, *Dairy industries* case); 23 November 2004 (Proceedings 569/03, conduct, *Beet seed* case); 25 April 2005 (Proceedings 583/04, conduct, *Oil* case); and 28 September 2010 (Proceedings S/0011/07, conduct, *Citrus* case)).

53. Certain statutory barriers to entry are still in place on the Spanish market, however, most in connection with the need to meet a series of legal requirements to practise professions such as law or auditing.[12]

11. This is borne out by the fact that in the explanatory statement, the LDC refers to the CNC as the 'body responsible for applying this act, promoting and protecting the maintenance of effective competition in all the production sectors and throughout the national territory'.
12. Regarding the application of Competition Law to regulated sectors, *see* Calvo, G. – Ramos de Molins, A., 'Derecho de la competencia y sectores regulados', in Loma-Osorio, D., *Tratado de Derecho de la Competencia*, Aranzadi, Madrid, 2013, pp. 589–654.

§3. State-Owed Enterprises and Public Utilities[13]

54. The key provision in this regard is Article 4 LDC, which reads as follows.

> Article 4. Conduct exempt by law
> 1. Without prejudice to the eventual application of the Community provisions regarding prohibition, the provisions of this chapter shall not apply to conduct those results from the application of an Act.
> 2. The provisions of this chapter shall apply to situations restricting competitions which are derived from the exercise of other administrative powers or are caused by the action of public authorities or public undertakings without this legal protection.

55. Further to that premise, a distinction must be drawn between activities conducted by State-run undertakings pursuant to statutes or acts and all other activities conducted by such undertakings. The former are exempt from the LDC while the latter are not: i.e., any possible anticompetitive conduct on their part would be subject to the LDC.

56. That general rule must be qualified, however, in connection with undertakings engaging in 'public' or 'official' business. Although nothing in this regard is written into the LDC, the competition authorities have interpreted Community doctrine that limits the application of antitrust law to such enterprises when engaging in 'essentially economic' activities to be applicable in Spain.[14]

57. The competition authorities have instituted proceedings against a number of public bodies, including:

- Port authorities: TDC Resolutions of 18 October 1999 (Proceedings r352/99, appeal, *Tenerife Port Authority* case); and 4 July 2000, (Proceedings r395/99, appeal, *Santander Port* case); and CNC Resolution of 26 September 2013 (Proceedings S/314/10, conduct, *Valencia Port* case).
- Fishermen's organizations: TDC Resolutions of 29 July 1993 (Proceedings 329/93, conduct, *Fishermen's organization of Cariño* case); and 8 June 2004 (Proceedings 564/03, conduct, *Fishermen's organization of Santa María de Sabada* case); and CNC Resolution of 2 December 2010 (Proceedings S/0265/10, conduct, *Fishermen's organization of Sant Pere de l'Atmella* case).
- Airport authorities: TDC Resolutions of 16 November 1998 (Proceedings r296/98, appeal, *Spanish airports* case); and 2 August 2007 (Proceedings 621/06, conduct, *CST/AENA* case); CNC Resolution of 4 June 2013 (Proceedings S/0387/11,

13. *See* García, F., in Bello, Mª.P. – Hernández, F. (coord.), *Derecho*, pp. 57–61.
14. As it has been pointed out, the instances where the Government engages in 'official' or 'public' business through a company should be differentiated from others in which a State-owned company conducts business consisting of supplying the market with goods or services. Antitrust law is applicable to the latter, but not to the former (García, F., in Bello, Mª.P. – Hernández, F. (coord.), *Derecho*, p. 60).

conduct, *AENA* case); and CNMC Resolutions of 2 January 2014 (Proceedings S/0404/12, conduct, *AENA commercial services* case); and 6 February 2014 (Proceedings S/0420/12, conduct, *AENA 2* case).
- Public broadcasting authorities: TDC Resolution of 12 June 1998 (Proceedings R291/98 and R292/98, appeal, *Regional televisions* case).
- Professional organizations: TDC Resolution of 19 November 1999 (Proceedings 446/98, conducts, *Arquitectos de Madrid* case; and CNC Resolution of 14 April 2009 (Proceedings 639/08, conducts, *Colegio Farmacéuticos Castilla-La Mancha* case).
- Governing Councils for the designation of origin; CNC Resolution of 28 July 2010 (Proceedings S/0091/08, conducts, *Vinos Finos Jerez* case).
- Public postal service: TDC Resolution of 2 April 2001 (Proceedings r417/00, appeal, *Postal service* case); and CNMC Resolution of 21 January 2014 (Proceedings S/0373/11, conduct, *Postal service 2* case).

§4. Sensible Effect and *De Minimis*

58. Application of *de minimis* doctrine in the Spanish system has inspired much debate and posturing; regarding not only its acceptance but also the criteria whereby 'minor importance' and the reach and effects thereof are defined.[15]

I. *De Minimis* Doctrine under the 1989 Competition Act[16]

59. Like Article 85 of the *Treaty* establishing the *European Community* (TEC) (now Article 101 of the TFEU), Article 1 of the 1989 Competition Act established no limits to the prohibition of collusion: i.e., it was not confined to conduct appreciably restricting competition. As a result, the provision was interpreted somewhat literally and applied to all collusive agreements, regardless of their effects on competition, whereby even agreements of minor importance were prohibited.

60. According to Article 3.2 d) of the 1989 Competition Act, agreements of minor importance could be exempted if duly authorized.[17] Inasmuch as authorization can only be granted for something otherwise prohibited, the inference drawn was that all collusive agreements of minor importance were prohibited *a priori*.

15. *See* about this debate, Costas, J., 'Prohibición de acuerdos colusorios', in Bello, Mª.P. – Hernández, F. (coord.), *Derecho de la Libre Competencia Comunitario y Español*, Thomson-Aranzadi, Cizur Menor, 2009, pp. 96–102; Ortiz, I., 'La regla *de minimis* en el ámbito de los acuerdos restrictivos de la competencia', *Revist@ e-Mercatoria*, 2009, Volume 8, Number 2, pp. 16–35.
16. *See* Ortiz, I., *Revist@ e-Mercatoria*, pp. 16–19.
17. Section 2 of Art. 3 of the 1989 Competition Act regulated the authorization of collusive agreements in the following terms.

    2. Similarly, agreements, decisions, recommendations and practices as referred to in Article 1 or categories of them, inasmuch as they are justified by the general economic situation and the public interest, may be authorised if they (...) c) are relatively unimportant and unable to exert a significant effect on competition.

61. Subsequent amendments to the 1989 Competition Act generated some confusion around the consequences of deeming agreements to be of minor importance, however.

62. Article 1.3 of the 1989 Competition Act (added under Article 15.One of Royal Decree 7/1996, of 7 June, whose wording was later amended by Article 1 of *Ley 52/1999, de 28 de diciembre, de reforma de la Ley 16/1989, de 17 de julio, de Defensa de la Competencia*) provided as follows:

> 3. The competition authorities may *decide not to initiate or to stay* the proceedings foreseen in this act in the case of conduct whose relative unimportance prevents it from having a significant impact on competition' (emphasis added).

63. In keeping therewith, Article 36*bis* of the 1989 Competition Act (added under Article 23 of aforementioned *Ley 52/1999, de 28 de diciembre*), read as follows:

> Article 36.bis. Cases of inadmissibility and termination by agreement
>
> 1. The Competition Service (*Servicio de Defensa de la* Competencia) may:
>   a) *Agree not to initiate* proceedings derived from presumably committing the acts prohibited by Articles 1 and 6 which, due to their relative unimportance, do not have a significant effect on the competition conditions' (emphasis added).

64. In other words, while Article 3.2 c) of the 1989 Competition Act prohibited agreements of minor importance but envisaged their authorization, Articles 1.3 and 36*bis* 1a) established a sort of administrative immunity where, in the case of agreements of minor importance, the competition authorities could either not institute proceedings or dismiss any already initiated.

65. Consequently, the possible judicial implications of classing agreements as being of minor importance were never clear, given that they could be regarded as: (a) prohibited but subject to authorization; (b) prohibited but not subject to the institution of proceedings or penalties; or even (c) further to some TDC resolution, excluded from application of Article 1 of the 1989 Competition Act, and as exempt therefrom, consequently lawful.[18] A number of authors deemed that Articles 1.3 and 36*bis* 1a) of the 1989 Competition Act, rather than regulating the *de minimis* principle, introduced *Automec* doctrine in Spanish law, which enabled the competition authorities (SDC and TDC) to define their priorities with a view to ensuring that resources would not be wasted on investigating practices (collusive and abusive agreements) with no material effect on competition.

---

18. *See* COSTAS, J., in BELLO, Mª.P. – HERNÁNDEZ, F. (coord.), *Derecho*, p. 97.

66. This uncertainty created other problems.

67. One was the determination of the civil implications of conduct of minor importance. If understood to lie beyond the scope of application of Article 1 of the 1989 Competition Act and therefore lawful, no action against them could be instituted in the civil courts. On the contrary, if such conduct was regarded as prohibited but not subject to investigation and penalization by the competition authorities, action for damages and for nullification of the agreement could be instituted.

68. Second, this uncertainty also obscured the SDC's responsibilities and obligations in connection with such conduct. The debate around the issue was whether it should refrain from initiating an investigation, dismiss any investigation underway or institute authorization proceedings, referring the case to the TDC.

69. A third question that arose was whether the SDC's decisions in this respect would have a bearing on subsequent decisions on matters within the civil courts' jurisdiction. Specifically, the point at issue was whether SDC decisions not to institute penalization proceedings or to dismiss penalization proceedings underway were binding on the courts or, on the contrary, whether judges could nullify agreements or award damages despite such decisions.

70. Whether influenced or otherwise by these uncertainties and controversy, the TDC seldom undertook proceedings involving relatively unimportant conduct.[19]

II. *De Minimis* Doctrine in the LDC

71. Things changed when the new LDC came into force. Although Articles 1–3 (like Articles 1 and 6 and unlike Article 7 of the 1989 Competition Act) failed to make the prohibition of conduct contingent upon the existence of a 'substantial' restriction of competition, Article 5 LDC introduced *de minimis* doctrine in Spanish law for the first time. This provision reads as follows:

> Article 5. Conduct of minor importance
> The prohibitions included in Articles 1 to 3 of this Act shall not apply to conduct which, due to their scant importance, are not capable of significantly affecting competition. The criteria for demarcating conduct of minor importance shall be determined according to regulations, taking into account, among others, the market share.

19. *See* TDC Resolutions of 24 September 1997 (Proceedings 400/97, conduct, *Hüls Española* case); 18 February 1999 (Proceedings 434/98, conduct, *Prensa de Segovia* case); 4 May 1999 (Proceedings 459/99, conduct, *Hoteles Hernani* case); 26 May 1999 (Proceedings 437/98, conduct, *Vileda/TerviK* case); 15 November 1999 (Proceedings A 249/98, conduct, *Cajas Rurales, Jalón y Zaragoza* case); and 12 May 2006 (Proceedings R 517/02, appeal, *Vendedores de Prensa de Barcelona* case).

72. The regulations referred to in the above article were adopted under Articles 1–3 RDC.

73. While Spanish regulation of *de minimis* doctrine draws largely from experience and EU regulations (*see* European Notice 2001/C368/07 on agreements of minor importance which do not appreciably restrict competition under Article 81(1) of the Treaty establishing the European Community (*de minimis* Notice)), it also establishes significant differences with respect to the latter, such as described below.

74. A. Article 1 RDC, like the *de minimis* Notice, defines conduct of minor importance on the grounds of undertakings' market share. Hence, the following are so regarded with no prior decision to that effect being required:

- Conduct between present or potential competitor undertakings whose combined market share is no greater than 10% in any of the relevant markets qualifies for *de minimis* treatment.
- Where the undertakings involved are neither presently or potentially competitors, the threshold is 15% of market share for each undertaking.
- Where it is not possible to determine whether the conduct involves competitors or non-competitors, the 10% threshold is tested in each of the relevant markets.
- When competition in a given market is restricted by the cumulative effects of parallel agreements concluded between different suppliers or distributors for the sale of goods or services, the threshold market share is 5%. However, the latter does not apply if the cumulative effect of such parallel networks of agreements impact no more than 30% of the market in question.

75. B. Article 2 RDC includes a long list of types of conduct that is excluded from the definition of minor importance. Its provisions are practically the same as in paragraph 11 of the *de minimis* Notice (with some differences discussed below). It includes both classic restrictions 'by object' (such as price fixing, limiting sales and production or dividing up markets or customers) and what are known as 'black' clauses. The latter, included in the 1999 EU Regulation on block exemptions for vertical agreements,[20] are essentially the same as contained in the 2010 version of the Regulation presently in effect.[21]

76. C. Along with the similarities, there are also some significant differences between the European and the Spanish regulations.

77. i/ The most prominent relates to the scope of application. In this regard, both Article 5 LDC and Article 3 RDC differ from the European legislation. Unlike the

20. Commission Regulation (EC) No 2790/1999 of 22 December 1999 on the application of Art. 81(3) of the Treaty to categories of vertical agreements and concerted practices.
21. Commission Regulation (EU) No 330/2010 of 20 April 2010 on the application of Art. 101(3) of the Treaty on the Functioning of the European Union to categories of vertical agreements and concerted practices.

latter, Spanish Regulation of *de minimis* conduct applies not only to collusive agreements but also to abuse of a dominant position and distortion of free competition through unfair conducts.[22]

78. ii/ The Spanish Regulation adds to the list of practices not regarded as being of minor importance (Article 2 RDC) some not included in the *de minimis* Notice.

Article 2.2 RDC lists the activities between non-competitors not regarded to be of minor importance, specifically mentioning the following:

> "d) the restriction agreed between a supplier of components and a buyer who incorporates those components which limits the supplier's ability to sell the components as spare parts to end users or to repairers or other service providers not entrusted by the buyer with the repair or servicing of its goods;
> e) the establishment of a non-competition clause of indefinite duration or term of more than five years;"

Article 2.4 RDC provides, in turn, that the following practices are not to be regarded as eligible for minor importance treatment:

> "a) conducts pursued by undertakings that are the holders or beneficiaries of exclusive rights;
> b) conducts pursued by undertakings that are present in relevant markets in which more than 50 per cent is covered by parallel networks of vertical agreements having similar effects."

79. iii/ Article 3.1 RDC introduced a 'release valve' whereby the competition authorities can classify a practice to be of minor importance, even if it does not meet the requirements of Article 1 RDC or appears in the list of exclusions in its Article 2.

The exact wording of the provision is reproduced below:

> Article 3. Other conducts of minor importance
>
> 1. *Without prejudice to what is provided in the preceding articles* and for the purposes provided for in Articles 5 and 53.1.b) of Act 15/2007 of 3 July 2007, the Council of the National Competition Commission *may waive application of Articles 1 to 3 of the said Act* to conducts which, having regard to their legal and economic context, are not capable of having a significant effect on competition (emphasis added).

This affords the Spanish competition authorities a good deal of flexibility when deciding whether or not a practice should be deemed to be of minor importance. The CNC has invoked this clause on a number of occasions. In one instance it was used

22. The exact wording of the provision is reproduced above.

to declare a conduct to be of minor importance even though it fell within the provisions on exclusion laid down in Article 2.4 b) RDC;[23] in another, although the undertaking had a significant market share and the circumstances specified in Article 2.4 b) RDC were in place, the conduct at issue was regarded to be of minor importance because of its minimal impact on the market;[24] in yet another, a undertaking's conduct was regarded to be of minor importance in light of its small market share, even though it could be understood to be subject to the exclusion set out in Article 2.2 a) RDC.[25]

23. *See* CNC Resolutions of 27 November 2007 (Proceedings R 691/06, appeal, *DISA* case); 23 September 2008 (Proceedings 2740/06, conduct, *Total* case); and 29 September 2008 (Proceedings 2739/06, conduct, *Agip España* case).
24. *See* CNC Resolution of 19 February 2010 (Proceedings 2575/04, conduct, *DISA Canarias* case).
25. *See* CNC Resolution of 3 December 2009 (Proceedings S0105/08, conduct, *El Corral de las Flamencas* case).

Chapter 3. Overview of Substantive Provisions

§1. Restrictive Agreements

80. The provision that governs these agreements is Article 1 LDC (Collusive conducts).

81. Section 1 of this article prohibits such conduct, which it first defines in a general clause and then illustrates with a list of examples:

1. All agreements, collective decisions or recommendations, or concerted or consciously parallel practices are prohibited, which have as their object, produce or may produce the effect of prevention, restriction or distortion of competition in all or part of the national market and, in particular, those which consist of:
   a) the direct or indirect fixing of prices or any other trading or service conditions
   b) the limitation or control of production, distribution, technical development or investment
   c) the share-out of the market or sources of supply
   d) the application, in trading or service relationships, of dissimilar conditions to equivalent transactions, thereby placing some competitors at a disadvantage compared with others
   e) the subordination of the conclusion of contracts to acceptance of supplementary obligations which, by their nature or according to commercial usage, have no connection with the subject of these contracts.

82. Section 2 of the article stipulates the judicial implications of that prohibition and its limits:

> 2. Any agreements, decisions and recommendations that, being prohibited by virtue of the provisions in Section 1, are not covered by the exemptions set out in this Act are automatically void.

83. Sections 3, 4 and 5 list the exceptions to this prohibition:

3. The prohibition in section 1 shall not apply to agreements, decisions, recommendations and practices that contribute to improving the production or the commercialisation and distribution of goods and services or to promoting technical or economic progress, without the need for any prior decision for this purpose, providing that:
   a) they allow consumers a fair share of its benefits
   b) they do not impose on the undertakings concerned restrictions which are not indispensable to the attainment of these objectives, and

   c) they do not afford participating undertakings the possibility of eliminating competition in respect of a substantial part of the products or services in question.
4. The prohibition in Section 1 shall not apply to agreements, collective decisions or recommendations, or concerted or consciously parallel practices that comply with the provisions set out in the Community Regulations on the application of Article 81(3) of the EC Treaty for certain categories of agreements, decisions by associations of undertakings and concerted practices, including when the corresponding conduct may not affect trade between EU member states.
5. The Government may also declare through Royal Decree the application of Section 3 of this article to certain categories of conduct, prior report by the Competition Council and the National Competition Commission.

§2. Dominant Undertakings

84. The provision applicable to this question is Article 2 LDC. Section 1 prohibits certain practices that constitute abuse of a dominant position by one or various undertakings, while section 2 lists examples of abusive conduct. Finally, section 3 stipulates that the prohibition applies even where market dominance is the result of legal provisions:

1. Any abuse by one or more undertakings of their dominant position in all or part of the national market is prohibited.
2. The abuse may, in particular, consist in:
   a) the direct or indirect imposition of prices or other unfair trading or services conditions
   b) the limitation of production, distribution or technical development to the unjustified prejudice of undertakings or consumers
   c) the unjustified refusal to satisfy the demands of purchase of products or provision of services
   d) the application, in trading or service relationships, of dissimilar conditions to equivalent transactions, thereby placing some competitors at a disadvantage compared with others
   e) the subordination of the conclusion of contracts to acceptance of supplementary obligations which, by their nature or according to commercial usage, have no connection with the subject of these contracts.
3. The prohibition set out in this article shall apply in cases in which the dominant position in the market of one or more undertakings has been established by legal provisions.

§3. MERGERS[26]

85. Mergers are regulated by two series of provisions. One group, constituting substantive regulation, is laid out in Title I, Chapter II (Articles 7–10) of the LDC. The other comprises provisions governing the procedures to be followed in such operations, which are set out essentially in Title IV, Chapter III (Articles 55–60) of the LDC. In addition to these two series of provisions, the respective implementing regulations are found in Articles 4–6 and 54–71 RDC.

I. Definition of Concentration[27]

86. The first substantive provision, Article 7 LDC, defines an economic concentration. Further to Article 7.1 and 7.2, a concentration exists where a stable change takes place regarding the control of all or part of one or more undertakings, as a consequence of a merger of two or more previously independent undertakings, the acquisition by a undertaking of control of all or part of one or more undertakings, the creation of a joint venture or the acquisition of joint control of one or more undertakings when they perform the functions of an independent economic entity over the long term. Article 7.3 LDC lays down a series of operations that lie outside the definition of concentrations.

II. Scope of Application[28]

87. Article 8 LDC defines the scope of Spanish legislation on control of concentrations. In accordance with its Article 8.1, such legislation is applicable to any inter-company concentration project or operation, which may affect the national market and generates one or more of the following effects.

88. a) The transaction results in acquiring a share of 30% or more of the national or any duly defined regional market for the respective good or service.

89. However, this same section exempts economic concentrations from notifying, even when the aforementioned circumstances are present, when the undertakings or holdings acquired have a turnover in Spain during the previous accounting

26. We follow the exposition of ALONSO, R., in MENÉNDEZ, A. – ROJO, A., *Lecciones*, pp. 322–325.
27. Regarding this definition *see* in detail, FOLGUERA, J. – VIDAL, P., 'Artículo 7 LDC', in MASSAGUER, J. *et altri*, *Comentario a la Ley de Defensa de la Competencia*, Civitas/Thomson Reuters, Cizur Menor, 3rd ed., 2012, pp. 345–366; BARRANTES, B., 'Artículo 7' in ODRIOZOLA, M. (Dir.), *Derecho español de la Competencia*, Tomo I, Bosch, Barcelona, 2008, pp. 252–269.
See also GÓRRIZ, C., 'Control de las concentraciones', in GARCIA-CRUCES, J.A. (dir.), *Tratado de Derecho de la Competencia y de la Publicidad*, Tomo I, Tirant lo Blanch, Valencia, 2014, pp. 347–359; BELLO, Mª.P., 'Control de concentraciones de empresas', in BELLO, Mª.P. – HERNÁNDEZ, F. (coord.), *Derecho de la libre competencia comunitario y español*, Thomson Aranzadi, Cizur Menor, 2009, pp. 390–393.
28. For more details *see infra* Part III Chapter 2 §1.

year of less than EUR 10,000,000 and the participants do not, individually or jointly, have a 50% share in any of the markets impacted, nationally or in a duly defined region.

90. This means that the CNMC does not need to be informed of economically insignificant operations, even where the market share threshold is crossed.

91. b) The combined turnover from all operations in Spain of all participants from the previous accounting year exceeds EUR 240,000,000 and at least two of the participants have an individual domestic turnover of at least EUR 60,000,000.

92. Nevertheless Article 8.2 LDC stipulates that Spanish legislation does not apply to concentrations with a 'Community dimension' (as defined in Council Regulation (EC) No 139/2004 of 20 January 2004 on the control of concentrations between undertakings (the EC Merger Regulation), unless the concentration is referred back to the Spanish authorities by the European Commission.

93. Article 10.4 LDC, in turn, provides that merger control provisions are applicable to the creation or acquisition of cooperative joint ventures, although such operations are assessed with regard to the provisions of Articles 1 and 2 LDC.

III. Substantive Assessment Criteria[29]

94. Article 10.1 LDC provides that economic concentrations are to be assessed on the grounds of their potential to impede the maintenance of effective competition in all or part of the domestic market. The provision stipulates that to this end the following, amongst others, are to be taken into consideration: market structure; market position of the undertakings involved and their economic and financial power; actual or potential competition from undertakings on or beyond the national soil; supplier and consumer ability to choose and their access to the sources of supply or markets; existence of entry barriers in such markets; variations in supply and demand of the products and services in question; supply- and demand-side bargaining power and the ability to offset the market position of the undertakings concerned; and economic efficiencies deriving from the concentration (in particular possible contributions to improving production, marketing and business competition) and how such efficiencies benefit intermediate and end consumers, specifically in the form of more or improved product and lower prices.

---

29. For an in-depth study of these criteria and their application by the Competition Authorities, *see* FOLGUERA, J. – VIDAL, P., 'Artículo 10 LDC', in MASSAGUER, J. *et altri*, *Comentario a la Ley de Defensa de la Competencia*, Civitas/Thomson Reuters, Cizur Menor, 3rd ed., 2012, pp. 394–545; BARRANTES, B., 'Artículo 10', in ODRIOZOLA, M. (Dir.), *Derecho español de la Competencia*, Tomo I, Bosch, Barcelona, 2008, pp. 312–369.
See also BELLO, Mª.P., in BELLO, Mª.P. – HERNÁNDEZ, F. (coord.), *Derecho*, pp. 395–399; VIÑUELAS, M. – GAVELA, A.- HORTALÀ, J., 'Concentraciones de empresas', in LOMA-OSORIO, D., *Tratado de Derecho de la Competencia*, Aranzadi, Madrid, 2013, pp. 369ff.

95. However, unlike the 1989 Competition Act, whose only criterion was the effect of the concentration on competition (Articles 15*bis* and 16, of the 1989 Competition Act), under the LDC concentrations can be assessed using a dual alternative criterion. In addition to the competition criterion discussed in the preceding paragraph, which applies to proceedings brought before the CNMC (Article 10.1 LDC), the Government may also invoke the general interest criterion in concentrations raised to its consideration (Article 10.4 LDC).

IV. Competent Authority[30]

96. The LDC provides a considerable difference from the 1989 Competition Act with respect to this issue. Unlike the former system, where the Government was ultimately responsible for authorizing concentrations (*see* Articles 15*ter*.2 and 17, of the 1989 Competition Act), the LDC vests the CNMC with the power to make such decisions (Articles 10.1, 57.2 and 58.4 LDC). Those provisions aim to reinforce the technical and independent nature of the control exercised in this domain. The CNMC is not attributed full competence, however, to prohibit a merger or to make the authorization contingent upon conditions or commitments. The LDC empowers the Government to intervene, exceptionally, on the grounds of general interest. In such cases the Government may either uphold the CNMC's decision or authorize the concentration, which it may or may not make contingent upon meeting certain conditions (Articles 14 and 60 LDC).

§4. Other Prohibitions. Unfair Competition Conducts as an Antitrust Infringement

97. The treatment of such unlawful conduct is one of the particularities of Spanish antitrust law, which differentiates it from EU and other European country law.[31] The LDC (like the 1989 Competition Act before it) defines three types of anticompetitive practices: collusive conduct, abuse of a dominant position and unfair acts that distort competition and have adverse effects on the public interest.

98. The respective provisions are laid down in Article 3 LDC, which reads as follows:

> Article 3. Distortion of free competition by unfair acts
> The National Competition Commission or the competent bodies of the Autonomous Communities shall hear, under the terms that this act establishes for prohibited conduct, the acts of unfair competition which affect the public interest by the distortion of free competition.

30. *See* Viñuelas, M. – Gavela, A.- Hortalà, J., in Loma-Osorio, D., *Tratado*, pp. 452–456.
31. For a comprehensive analysis of this infringement *see infra* Part II Chapter 3.

§5. TESTS OF ILLEGALITY

I. *Per Se* Prohibitions and Naked Restraints

99. As the LDC is based on the principle of prohibition, all conduct regarded to restrict competition (such as collusive conduct or abuse of dominant position) is ordinarily banned.

100. Such bans are not generally viewed as prohibitions per se, however. Restrictive conducts resulting from the application of an act (Article 4 LDC) or deemed to be of minor importance (Article 5 LDC) are exempt, for instance. Moreover, collusive practices conforming to the conditions laid down in Articles 1.3 and 1.4 LDC are not prosecuted.

101. Nonetheless, exemptions from the rules on certain types of anticompetitive conduct, such as the particularly detrimental behaviours listed in Article 2 RDC, are scantly imaginable.

II. Balancing Tests

102. The LDC, like EU competition law, makes no provision for conducting balancing or rule of reason tests as tools for deciding whether to prohibit or allow collusive practice, abuse of a dominant position or unfair conduct that distorts free competition as per Article 3 LDC.

103. Practically speaking, however, decisions on whether a collusive practice qualifies for the exemptions laid down in section 1.3 LDC call for the de facto performance of a balancing test.

104. Article 1.3 reads as follows:

3. The prohibition in section 1 shall not apply to agreements, decisions, recommendations and practices that contribute to improving the production or the commercialisation and distribution of goods and services or to promoting technical or economic progress, without the need for any prior decision for this purpose, providing that:
   a) they allow consumers a fair share of its benefits
   b) they do not impose on the undertakings concerned restrictions which are not indispensable to the attainment of these objectives, and
   c) they do not afford participating undertakings the possibility of eliminating competition in respect of a substantial part of the products or services in question.

III. Merger Tests

105. The test used in Spanish law to decide whether to prohibit a concentration is the significant impediment to effective competition (SIEC) test, also known as the 'impediment test' (*see* Article 10.1 LDC).

106. It is important to highlight that this test formed part of Spanish law before it was adopted Europe-wide. Until 2004, the Union applied the so-called dominance test, which prohibited concentrations that created or strengthened a dominant position to the point of significantly impeding effective competition (*see* Article 2.2 of Council Regulation (EEC) 4064/89 of 21 December 1989 on the control of concentrations between undertakings). Spanish law, in contrast, applied the 'impediment test' as early as 1989 to determine whether or not to prohibit such operations based on their potential to 'hinder the maintenance of effective competition on the market' (*see* Articles 15*bis*.1 and 16.1 of the 1989 Competition Act). The 1989 act also called for an analysis of the (foreseeable or verified) restrictive effects of such operations. Hence, not only the creation or strengthening of a dominant market position but also the establishment of any commercial concentration that might lead to such a situation, were prohibited by Spanish earlier than by European law.

107. The same criterion is applied in the current LDC, which reads as follows:

Article 10. Criteria of substantive assessment

1. The National Competition Commission shall assess the economic concentrations in light of the possible impediment to the maintenance of effective competition in all or part of the national market.

   Specifically, the National Competition Commission shall adopt its decision taking into account, among others, the following elements:
   a) the structure of all the relevant markets,
   b) the market position of the undertakings affected, their economic and financial power,
   c) the real or potential competition of undertakings located either within or out with the national territory,
   d) the alternatives available to suppliers and consumers, their access to supplies or markets,
   e) any barriers to entry in these markets,
   f) supply and demand trends for the relevant products and services,
   g) the negotiating power of the demand or the supply and their capacity of offset the position in the market of the undertakings affected,
   h) the economic efficiencies derived from the concentration and, in particular, the contribution that the concentration may make to improving the production or commercialisation systems and to business competitiveness, and the extent to which these efficiencies are transferred to the intermediate and ultimate consumers, specifically, in the form of a bigger or better supply and of lower prices.

2. Insofar as the creation of a joint venture subject to concentration control has the object or effect of coordinating the competitive behaviour of undertakings that continue to be independent, this coordination shall be assessed according to the provisions of Articles 1 and 2 of this act.
3. Where appropriate, the assessment of an economic concentration may be understood to comprise certain accessory restrictions to competition, directly linked to the operation and necessary for it to be carried out.

108. That the same test is now applied to concentrations in the EU (*see* Articles 2.2 and 2.3 of the EC Merger Regulation) and Spain does not mean that the wording is identical in their respective legislations.

109. The criterion applied in Article 10.1 LDC is more far-reaching than Article 2.2 of the EC Merger Regulation, for instance. While the latter refers to concentrations 'that could *significantly* impede effective competition' (emphasis added), the former covers concentrations that could give rise to the 'possible impediment to the maintenance of effective competition'. This difference is negligible in practice, however, for the Spanish competition authorities explicitly operate on the understanding that the effect must be significant.[32]

110. The criteria applied to determine whether to allow the creation of a joint venture likewise differ. While Article 10.2 LDC concurs with the provisions of Article 2.4 of the EC Merger Regulation, to the extent that their creation should be assessed in keeping with the rule that prohibits collusive agreements (Article 1 LDC), it adds that the stipulations prohibiting abuse of a dominant position must also be taken into consideration (Article 2 LDC).

32. *See*, for example, CNC Resolutions of 30 October 2007 (Proceedings C/0001/07, concentrations, *Dia/Plus* case, ap. VII.4); and 20 December 2007 (Proceedings C/0025/07, concentrations, *Eiffage/Los Serranos* case, ap. VI).

Chapter 4. Overview of Main Notions

§1. Undertaking

111. There is no legal definition for the term undertaking foreseen in either EU law or the 1989 Competition Act, this concept was gradually formulated on the grounds of European case law and competition authority action. In contrast, the LDC lays down a positive definition in its section 1 of the Fourth Additional Provision as follows:

> any person or entity that carries out an economic activity, irrespective of the legal statute of the organization and its form of financing.

112. This definition ties in perfectly with the term as delimited by ECJ case law and the European competition authorities.

113. The definition was couched in the broadest possible terms, with a view to covering all natural persons or bodies corporate, public or private, and also be bodies without legal personality, as for instance, branches or government bodies. The sole condition is that they must be economic actors conducting business on the marketplace.

§2. Relevant Market[33]

114. In the event of an alleged infringement of competition law, the first element to be taken into consideration is the market concerned. Defining the relevant market essentially entails delimiting the framework within which the competition rules relative to agreements, abuse of dominant position and control of concentrations are applied.

115. Spanish law does not contain any provisions establishing the criteria for the definition of the relevant market. The Spanish competition authorities consequently apply the criteria set out by the European Commission in its 9 December 1997 Notice on the definition of relevant market for the purposes of Community competition law. Further to that document, such delimitation must take into consideration, on the one hand, the products and services concerned ('product market') and on the other, the area where undertakings operate ('geographic market').

116. Product market means 'all those products and/or services which are regarded as interchangeable or substitutable by the consumer, by reason of the products' characteristics, their prices and their intended use' (Notice, paragraph 7). Such

33. *See* García, F., in Bello, Mª.P. – Hernández, F. (coord.), *Derecho*, pp. 46–47.

delimitation calls for ascertaining the effect on supply and demand of a small but significant increase in product price using the SSNIP (Small but Significant Non-transitory Increase in Price) Test.

117. The effects of small price increases in goods or services on supply must also be analysed, because while for consumers some products may not be interchangeable, for producers they may be.

118. Markets must also be defined geographically to determine whether undertakings in different areas constitute alternative sources of supply for consumers. The geographical definition of the marketplace is also based on a supply- and demand-side analysis of interchangeability as a result of changing prices. The question is whether consumers would be willing to resteer their orders to suppliers located elsewhere and whether such suppliers would be attracted to new areas by higher local prices.

119. Lastly, all relevant markets are delimited in time, i.e., undertakings' duration on the market, as well as by product and geography. Since markets, particularly the most dynamic markets, undeniably change over time, any delimitation must bear this dimension in mind as well.[34]

§3. Market Power / Dominant Position

120. Neither EU law, specifically Article 102 of the TFEU, nor the LDC defines dominant position.

121. This was not always the case in Spanish law. In fact, Article 2.2 of the first Competition Act, *Ley 110/63 de 20 de julio, de Represión de las Prácticas Restrictivas de la Competencia*, contained a definition of individual as well as collective dominance. This provision stipulated the following:

> 'Two. For the purposes of this act, it shall be understood:
>
> a) a undertaking holds a dominant positions when is the only supplier or consumer of a given type of product on the domestic market or while not being the sole actor, is simply not subject to any material competition
> b) two or more undertakings hold a dominant position for a given product or service, when no effective competition exists among them or from third parties in all or part of the national market.

34. *See* Signes, J.I. – Fuentes, M., 'Cuestiones horizontales a la aplicación de las disposiciones de competencia', in Signes, J.I. *et altri*, *Derecho de la competencia*, Civitas Thomson Reuters, Cizur Menor, 2013, p. 87.

122. The situation subsequently changed because the 1989 Competition Act failed to include a definition of dominance, following instead the lead of Article 82 of the TEC (now Article 102 of the TFEU).

123. The LDC has continued in this same vein. Its Article 2 prohibits abuse of a dominant position in terms which are practically identical to the wording of Article 102 of the TFEU. For this reason, Spanish competition authorities have always kept in mind the ECJ case law and European Commission decisions when applying Article 2 LDC (and its predecessor, Article 6 of the 1989 Competition Act); key concepts such as 'dominant position' and 'abuse' and the characterization of each conduct covered by the prohibition are practically the same in Spanish and EU law.

124. An example is to be found in the TDC Resolution of 30 September 1999 (Proceedings R362/99, appeal, *Bacardi* case), which first defines a position of dominance as follows:[35]

> 6. A undertaking's dominant position in a given market affords that undertaking the opportunity to alter prices or other product characteristics to its own advantage and to the detriment of its competitors. The existence of such an opportunity depends on a series of circumstances which, in the undertaking at issue, consist essentially of market power and independence of conduct. A undertaking may therefore be said to hold a dominant market position when it has sufficient market power and independence of conduct to be able to act thereon without considering the possible reactions of competitors or consumers and therefore to alter product price or other characteristics to its advantage.

125. Immediately thereafter, the resolution cites the ECJ Judgments of 14 February 1978, *United Brands* case, and 13 February 1979, *Hoffman-La Roche* case, and the European Commission Notice of 9 December 1997 (97/C372/03) on the definition of relevant market for the purposes of Community competition law.

126. Regarding the criteria to take into account to decide if an undertaking has a dominant position or not, the Spanish competition authorities deem that a large market share is not in itself a determinant for the existence of a dominant market position, but just one of the several factors to be taken into consideration when establishing whether a undertaking holds such a position.[36] That may explain why no specific market share threshold has been stipulated as a hard and fast rule for this purpose.

---

35. *See* in the same vein the TDC Resolution of 10 May 1999 (Proceedings r 344/98, appeal, *Aluminios Navarra* case).
36. *See*, for example, TDC Resolution of 30 September 1999 (Proceedings R 362/99, appeal, *Bacardi* case, seventh legal ground).

127. Spanish authorities, then, in line with EU case law, contend that both undertaking structure and its competitive position must be taken into account. The structural factors reviewed in this respect include: resources and production methods; appearance, transport and sales methods; technology; and vertical integration. The factors that must be examined to determine the competitive position include: number and strength of competitors; market share and sales volumes; prices and entry barriers.[37]

§4. Agreements and Concerted Practices

128. Article 1 LDC regulates collusive conduct, defined to include competitors agreements or concerted or consciously parallel practices whose objective or outcome is to prevent, restrict or distort competition in all or part of the national market (Article 1.1 LDC).

129. Collusive conduct covers the following wide range of notions.[38]

130. a) Agreements are written or oral covenants under which undertakings coordinate their behaviour to distort or restrict competition; for these intents and purposes, an agreement exists wherever several persons who may be regarded as independent economic actors harmonize intentions.

131. Cartels constitute one type of agreement. Unlike other legislations, where the term is synonymous with collusive agreement, in Spanish law its meaning is narrower, defined in section 2 of the Fourth Additional Provision LDC, which reads as follows:

> 2. For the purposes of this Act, cartel is taken to be any secret agreement between two or more competitors which has as their object prices fixing, production or sales quotas, market sharing, including bid rigging, or import or export restrictions.

132. Collective decisions or recommendations adopted by associations of undertakings are likened to agreements, for in this case they are regarded as decisions adopted by their members rather than by these entities. This prevents agreements or practices harmonized among various subjects and contrary to free competition from eluding the law under the guise of a decision adopted in the realm of a single association.

133. b) Concerted practice is a uniform practice that because it is not naturally justified by the competitive conditions stemming from the market structure, it infers

37. *See*, for example, TDC Resolution of 30 September 1999 (Proceedings R 362/99, appeal, *Bacardi* case, seventh legal ground).
38. *See* Alonso, R., in Menéndez, A. – Rojo, A., *Lecciones*, p. 300.

the existence of tacit agreements or other manners of coordination among competitors that cannot be proven. In a word, this involves the use of a presumption to prove the existence of agreements that restrict competition.

134. c) Third and last, consciously parallel conduct consists of action by economic operators who, in the absence of any manner of agreement, deliberately mimic the conduct of others with clearly anticompetitive intentions.

135. In contrast, agreements that restrict competition adopted by undertakings (in the legal sense) that form part of one and the same economic group with unified decision-making[39] lie outside the definition of collusion, for such undertakings are regarded as a single entity (for the purposes of competition law) and therefore considered unilateral conducts.

§5. Restriction of Competition

136. Article 1.1 LDC begins with a general clause banning bilateral or multilateral conduct that hinders market access, undertakings' freedom of action or users' freedom of choice or that distorts or disturbs free competition on the market.

137. The LDC draws on this device to establish an objective prohibition, which implies two things. On the one hand, an infringement exists when an agreement is adopted, irrespective of whether it is implemented. And on the other, infringements exist not only in the presence of deliberate action but also where conduct restricts competition unintentionally. Culpability is only taken into consideration for the purposes of imposing fines (Article 63.1 LDC).[40]

138. The general prohibition contained in the first paragraph of Article 1.1 LDC is followed by a list of examples of practice that clearly restricts competition:

- the direct or indirect fixing of prices or any other trading or service conditions;
- the limitation or control of production, distribution, technical development or investment;
- the share-out of the market or sources of supply;
- the application, in trading or service relationships, or dissimilar conditions to equivalent transactions, thereby placing some competitors at a disadvantage compared with others;
- the subordination of the conclusion of contracts to acceptance of supplementary obligations which, by their nature or according to commercial usage, have no connection with the subject of these contracts.

39. *See*, for example, TDC Resolution of 10 May 1999 (Proceedings r344/98, appeal, *Aluminios Navarra* case).
40. *See* Alonso, R., in Menéndez, A. – Rojo, A., *Lecciones*, p. 301.

139. The ban on collusive practice established in Article 1.1 LDC is not unconditional, however. The following are exempt:

- conduct resulting from the application of an act (Article 4, LDC);
- conduct regarded to be of minor importance (Article 5, LDC);
- conduct compliant with the provisions laid down in EU regulations on block exemptions, even where such conduct does not entail trade among EU Member States (Article 1.4, LDC);
- conduct compliant with the provisions laid down in regulations on block exemptions decreed by the Spanish Government;[41]
- and all conduct compliant with the substantive requirements set out in Article 1.3, LDC: first, where they contribute to improving the production or the commercialization and distribution of goods and services or to promoting technical or economic progress; second, where they allow consumers a fair share of its benefits; third, where they do not impose on the undertakings concerned restrictions that are not indispensable to the attainment of the aforementioned objectives; and fourth, where they do not afford participating undertakings the possibility of eliminating competition in respect of a substantial part of the products or services in question.

140. While the requirements are the same for this last group of conducts as laid down in Article 3.1 of the 1989 Competition Act, the LDC amended the exemption system. The system calling for prior authorization envisaged in Article 4 of the 1989 Competition Act (which mirrored the former Community system – *see.* Article 6, Regulation (EEC) 17/62) was replaced by a system of legal exceptions similar to the arrangements laid down in Article 1 of Regulation (EC) 1/2003. Hence, conduct conforming to the conditions listed in Article 1.3 LDC is exempt from the prohibition, no prior decision to that effect being required. The assessment whether these requirements have been met in each specific case is left to the undertakings themselves (self-assessment), although such analysis may be controlled and corrected by the competition authorities *a posteriori*.[42]

§6. Monopolization and Abuse of Dominance

141. Article 2 LDC prohibits any abuse by one or more undertakings of their dominant position in all or part of the national market. This provision attempts to prevent undertakings with market power from using it to the detriment of free competition. The elements comprising this type of prohibition include: existence of a dominant position, abusive conduct and impact on all or part of the national market.

---

41. For instance, Royal Decree 602/2006 of 19 May approving the Regulations on the exemption of certain categories of agreements on exchange of information on credit ratings.
42. *See* Alonso, R., in Menéndez, A. – Rojo, A., *Lecciones*, p. 302.

142. Abusive conduct is unlawful conduct or conduct that distort competition. An undertaking is regarded to abuse its dominant position when it behaves differently than it would if operating on a fully competitive market. To this end, Article 2.2 LDC lists, by way of example, behaviours regarded as abusive: the imposition of prices or unfair trading conditions; the limitation of production, distribution or technical development to the unjustified detriment of other undertakings or consumers; the application of discriminatory conditions; and the subordination of the conclusion of contracts to the acceptance of supplementary obligations which, by their nature or according to commercial usage, are unrelated to the subject of such contracts.[43]

143. Unlike EU law, Spanish legislation specifies that the prohibition of abuse of a dominant position also applies to cases in which the position was acquired under a legal provision (Article 2.3, LDC).[44] This may be, as held by doctrine,[45] because even though the situation has changed substantially over the last ten years, a fairly large number of legal monopolies were in place in Spain when the LDC was enacted. Given Spain's scant tradition in competition law, a need was apparently felt to explicitly provide in the LDC that, despite statutory coverage for the existence of a given monopoly, even where State-owned, the respective undertaking is prohibited from abusing its dominant position.

144. When such an undertaking or any other with a dominant position acts pursuant to a law, however, the situation is reversed. Even though the resulting conduct may be regarded as abusive, the provisions on abusive conduct would not be applicable (Article 4, LDC).

145. Such provisions are not applicable to abusive conducts regarded to be of minor importance (Article 5 LDC).

§7. Concentrations

146. Economic concentration is defined in Article 7 LDC in much the same way as in Article 3 of the EC Merger Regulation. Concentration is therefore understood to mean any operation involving a stable change in the control of all or part of one or several undertakings. Such control, further to sections 1 and 2 of Article 7 LDC, may be obtained by the merger of several formerly independent undertakings, the acquisition by one undertaking of the control of all or part of one or several others, the creation of a joint venture or the acquisition of joint control of one or several undertakings when they perform the functions of an independent economic organization on a permanent basis.

43. *See* Alonso, R., in Menéndez, A. – Rojo, A., *Lecciones*, pp. 302–303
44. *See*, for example, TDC Resolution of 21 January 1999 (Proceedings 412/97, conduct, *BT/Telefónica* case).
45. *See* Hernández, F., 'Prohibición del abuso de posición dominante en el mercado', in Bello, Mª.P. – Hernández, F. (coord.) *Derecho de la libre competencia comunitario y español*, Thomson-Aranzadi, Cizur Menor, 2009, p. 120.

147. The LDC eliminated a contradiction that existed for some time between European Law and Spanish Law. Article 14.2 c) *in fine* of the 1989 Competition Act did not consider as a concentration the joint ventures whose 'object or basic effect (was) to coordinate the competitive conduct of undertakings that continue to be independent'. After amendment of the EC Merger Regulation by Council Regulation 1310/97 of 30 June 1997, however, under EU law such groupings were regarded to constitute concentrations.[46]

148. Certain minor differences persist, however, in connection with acquisition of control.

149. On the one hand, while Article 3.1 of the EC Merger Regulation contains a broad definition of acquisition of control:

> b) the acquisition, *by one or more persons already controlling at least one undertaking, or by one or more undertakings*, whether by purchase of securities or assets, by contract or by any other means, of direct or indirect control of the whole or parts of one or more other undertakings (emphasis added).

150. Article 7.1 b) LDC merely defines the term to mean:

> b) the acquisition *by an undertaking* of the control of the whole or part of one or more undertakings'(emphasis added).

151. On the other hand, when explaining the ways in which control can be acquired, Article 7.2 LDC, in addition to mirroring the criteria laid down in Article 3.2 of the EC Merger Regulation, adds a second paragraph defining control. That definition, taken from the Spanish commercial legislation, namely from Article 4 of *Ley 24/1988, de 28 de julio, del Mercado de Valores*, which in turn cites Article 42.1 of the *Código de Comercio* rests on the notion of unified decision-making and is used in the context of groups of companies.

§8. Joint Ventures

152. Spanish legislation on merger control is applicable to the creation of joint ventures, providing such ventures are capable of conducting the activities characteristic of an independent economic organization on a permanent basis. In other words, so-called full-function joint ventures are regarded as concentrations.[47]

---

46. *See* on the negative consequences of this difference Bello, Mª.P., in Bello, Mª.P. – Hernández, F. (coord.), *Derecho*, p. 391.
47. Folguera, J. – Vidal, P., in Massaguer, J. *et altri*, *Comentario*, pp. 359–360 n. 46, pointed out that, for analogy with the principles applicable to restrictions related to merges, a transitorily period longer than three years could question the concentrative nature of the joint venture.

153. Consequently, joint ventures that are not permanent or which do not conduct their business fully (partial function joint ventures engaging, for instance, in R&D, sales, procurement or non-saleable production) lie outside the definition of concentrations. If such undertakings produce anticompetitive effects, they are analysed in connection with the provisions on prohibited conducts, including the rules that regulate their exemption therefrom.

Chapter 5. Consequences of Violations and Enforcement Institutions

§1. Administrative Enforcement

I. The Antitrust Authorities

A. *Formation, Composition*

154. On 5 June 2013, the Spanish government enacted Act 3/2013, 4 June, establishing the Markets and Competition National Commission (*Comisión Nacional de los Mercados y de la Competencia*, hereinafter CNMC). This Act entered into force on 6 June 2013, replacing the former Spanish Competition Authority (*Comisión Nacional de la Competencia*, hereinafter CNC), starting to operate on 7 October 2013. The new authority merges the Spanish Competition Authority with five Spanish sector regulators[48] creating one single entity. Substantive provisions contained in the LDC (Law 15/2007, of 3 July, hereinafter LDC) were not affected by this act, since it only affected the institutional organization of the competition authority in Spain.

155. The CNMC is an independent authority in charge of applying the competition rules (Spanish and European) in Spain. The CNMC is a public body with legal personality and full public and private capacity, as well as organic and functional autonomy. It is generally admitted as an autonomous authority, organically and functionally independent from the Government but ascribed within the Spanish Ministry for Economy. The CNMC consists of a chairman, the council and four different investigation directorates.

156. The chairman of the CNMC is entrusted with managerial and representation duties. The competition directorate conducts investigations into cases concerning competition rules affecting Spanish territory and prepares files, as well as studies and reports concerning certain sectors. In order to appoint the director of the investigation (competition) directorate, a majority vote of the council is required. This director of the competition directorate is also appointed by the government following a proposal of the Minister of Economy.

157. The Council of the CNMC, which has the final decision-making powers, is composed of the chairman of the CNMC and nine members. The Council comprises of two chambers: a chamber dealing with competition related matters and a

48. These six sector regulators are the National Energy Commission, the National Commission of Telecommunications Market, the National Commission of the Postal Sector, the Airport Economic Regulatory Commission, the Audio-Visual Media Council and the Railway Regulatory Committee. The Spanish Gambling Authority was first also quoted in the Preamble of Act 3/2013, but it was not finally included in the new authority, and it is part of the competences of the Ministry for internal affairs (*Ministerio del Interior*). The website of the new authority is http://www.cnmc.es/ (last time accessed: 7 February 2017).

chamber dealing with regulatory matters.[49] When taking a decision, the chamber for competition matters is chaired by the chairman and composed of another four members. The chamber dealing with regulatory matters is chaired by the Vice-President of the authority. Every member of the CNMC's council is appointed for a non-renewable six-year term by the Spanish government, following a proposal of the Ministry of Economy, and after a hearing which takes place in the relevant committee of the Spanish Parliament.

158. Important technical decisions are taken by the members of the four directorates which make up the new authority (competition directorate, energy directorate, telecommunications and audiovisual directorate and transport and postal services directorate). The members of the four directorates are experts in its field and mainly civil servants, having been also members of the former independent regulators. In addition to these four directorates a fifth one should be mentioned, namely the directorate for advocacy, which depends from the chairman of the authority. The main tasks of this advocacy directorate are to draft reports on regulation proposals, to lead market studies, sectorial reports, guidelines as well as recommendations.[50]

159. It is important to underline that the CNMC is ultimately controlled by the Spanish Parliament. In this sense, the CNMC has to work out an annual report, and its chairman has to appear at the Parliament (Congress of Deputies) on a regular basis, at least once a year. In addition, Act 3/2013 sets out a series of provisions on transparency and orders the publication of all provisions, decisions, agreements and reports, once notified to the parties and once confidential aspects have been deleted.

B. Investigating Powers

160. As mentioned *supra,* the Council of the CNMC is the final decision-making power, whereas the Directorate for Competition is in charge of enquiries, carrying out the investigation of the alleged anticompetitive conducts.

161. Article 27 of Act 3/2013 indicates that career civil servants of the CNMC, when duly authorized by the relevant manager, have the status of an agent of the public authorities and as such they may make the necessary inspections in undertakings and association of undertakings in applying competition law.

In particular, the second paragraph of the mentioned Article 27 of Act 3/2013 provides that personnel authorized for this purpose shall have the following investigating powers:

49. This chamber means that the total number of members of independent regulators has been reduced significantly, because before there were in total fifty members of the councils of the former independent regulation authorities.
50. This directorate is not included in Act 3/2013, but after the creation of the CNMC this directorate, which was part of the former CNC, has been maintained.

- To enter any premises, plant, land and means of transport of undertakings and associations of undertakings, as well as the homes of directors, managers and other members of staff of the undertakings concerned.[51] They may also control the assets assigned to the services or activities that operators or those conducting the activities referred to in this Act realize, the networks installed or operated and those documents they are required to hold or retain.
- To examine the books, records and other documents related to the business, irrespective of the medium in which they are stored, including computer software as well as magnetic, optical or any other kind of files.
- To take or obtain in any form copies of or extracts from such books or records.
- To retain for a maximum period of ten days the books or documents referred to in the second point.
- To seal any business premises and books, documents and other property of the undertaking for the period and to the extent necessary for the inspection.
- To ask any representative or member of staff of the undertaking or association of undertakings for explanations on facts or documents relating to the subject matter and purpose of the inspection and to record the answers.

C. Adjudicating Powers (Ascertaining and Sanctioning)

162. The CNMC has power to impose fines to companies and individuals as a result of having infringed Spanish competition rules. Article 29.2 of Act 3/2013 points out that on this behalf the investigation and the decision-taking step shall be separated. In competition cases, this investigation will be carried out by the personnel of the competent directorate in competition, while the final decision will be taken – as mentioned *ut supra* – by the Council of the CNMC.

163. This decision concludes the administrative proceeding. The procedure related to the sanctioning power of the CNMC shall comply with the specific provisions of the LDC, i.e., with Article 36ff of Act 3/2013. Article 36.1 foresees that the maximum legal period for taking a sanctioning decision and notifying it to the interested parts is eighteen months from the date of the agreement opening the sanctioning procedure.

164. Article 41 LDC enables the CNMC to monitor the fulfilment of obligations, resolutions and decisions adopted by the authority. This way of monitoring has to be carried out under the terms established by the relevant regulations and by the decisions of the CNMC itself. In this sense, Article 42 of Royal Decree 261/2008 mentions the monitoring procedure of decisions of the CNMC foreseeing that

51. So far, there is no news of any inspection carried out in a private home in Spain. In contrast, the 2009 Commission report on the functioning of Regulation 1/2003 stated that the Commission had exercised the power to enter domestic premises in two cases. The first time the Commission exercised its power under Art. 21 was in relation to the Marine Hoses cartel. *See* the *Communication form the Commission to the European Parliament and the Council, report on the functioning of Regulation 1/2003*, COM (2009) 206 final, point 12.

the Council of the CNMC, when adopting a decision, shall mention the period in which the addressee of the decision has to comply with it, mentioning also the amount of the fine or penalty that may be imposed in case of non-compliance with it for each day's delay according to Article 67 LDC.[52]

D. Other Institutional Tasks (Consultancy to Parliament/Government)

165. As mentioned *supra,* there is no mandatory consultancy to the Parliament or Government foreseen in Spanish competition rules. According to Article 19.1 n) of Act 3/2013, the President of the CNMC has to appear before the Spanish Parliament at least once a year in order to expose the basic lines of action of the CNMC, as well as any possible plan and/or any priorities for the future.[53]

II. Government Direct Enforcement Activities

166. The first paragraph of Article 4 LDC foresees that the prohibitions mentioned in the competition rules related to anticompetitive agreements and abuse of a dominant position shall not apply to behaviours which result from the application of a law.[54]

167. Besides, the only field in which the Government could intervene in the field of competition law is regarding merger control. Article 10.4 LDC foresees that the Council of Ministers will have the possibility to assess mergers on the basis of public interest criteria, other than the preservation of free competition in the markets. The law mentions that there are several criteria which can be understood as public interest, namely national defence and security, protection of public health or safety, free movement of goods and services within the national territory, protection of the environment, promotion of research and technological development as well as the ensuring of proper maintenance of the objectives of sectorial regulation. Article 60 LDC specifies that the Minister for Economic and Financial Affairs may raise the merger decision to the Council of Ministers for the mentioned reasons of general interest when, in the second phase of the merger, the Council of the CNMC either has decided to prohibit the merger or has resolved to approve it subject to specific commitments or conditions. The decision of the Minister shall be notified at the same time to the CNMC as well as to the interested parties. The Council of Ministers can either confirm the decision of the Council of the CNMC or authorize the merger, subject or not to the compliance with specific conditions. This agreement of the Council of Ministers has to be duly reasoned taking into account public interest issues, different from the protection of free competition in the markets, as mentioned in Article 10 LDC. Article 60 LDC reminds also that before adopting an

52. Article 67 LDC foresees penalty payments up to EUR 12,000 per day.
53. On this control by the Spanish Parliament, *see also* Art. 39 of Act 3/2013.
54. *See* MARCOS, F. 'State Action Doctrine in Spain: Treatment of State Anticompetitive Restrictions', which is available (in Spanish) in http://bit.ly/1tO5nBX (last time accessed: 7 February 2017).

agreement by the Council of Ministers, the Council may request a report from the CNMC.[55] According to Article 36.3 LDC, the maximum period for issuing and notifying the decision of the Minister for Economic and Financial Affairs regarding the action of the Council of Ministers is fifteen days, which have to be counted starting from the reception of the decision of the Council of the CNMC. Besides, according to Article 36.4 LDC, the Council of Ministers has a period of one month, which has to be counted starting from the decision of the Minister for Economic and Financial Affairs, in order to ask the Council of Ministers about the merger in question. If these time limits expire without having taken neither the Minister nor the Council of Ministers a decision, the decision taken in a second step by the Council of the CNMC has to be considered as effective, immediately enforceable and as a decision which is concluding the administrative proceedings according to Article 60.4 LDC. In this case, the merger will only be authorized if the commitments or conditions foreseen in the decision are fulfilled. Otherwise the merger will be prohibited. In case the concentration should be already implemented and carried out in practice, the Council of the CNMC could even order a 'de-concentration' in order to restore a situation of effective competition in the affected market. Finally, Article 60.5 LDC affirms that the decision of the Council of Ministers will be notified at the same time to the CNMC and to the interested parties.

III. Other Administrative Agencies Applying Antitrust Rules

168. In Spain, there are also some regional competition authorities applying antitrust rules.[56] This possibility was recognized by the Judgment of the Spanish Constitutional Court Number 208/1999, of 11 November. This judgment recognizes that Spanish autonomous regions are empowered to implement national competition rules related to anticompetitive agreements and abuses of a dominant position, except for provisions related to merger control. In order to be able to implement these rules, an anticompetitive conduct shall have effects in a regional territory and may not affect the European market. This constitutional court judgment enabled the enactment of Law 1/2002, of 21 February, which sets out rules on coordination between the Spanish nationwide authority and the regional ones. Thus, Spanish competition law may be applied by regional competition authorities when the anticompetitive conduct in question has a regional scope.

55. According to Art. 70.2 of Royal Decree 261/2008, the CNMC has to issue this report within ten days.

56. Currently there are competition authorities applying antitrust rules in the following autonomous regions: Catalonia, Galicia, Andalucia, Valencia, Aragon, the Basque Country and Castile-Leon. The region of Extremadura has a 'jury' for the protection of competition (with both instruction and resolution powers, as in the rest of the mentioned regions). Murcia, the region of Madrid and the Canary Islands have institutions for instruction purposes, the resolution of the cases falls to the CNMC. Finally, six autonomous regions have no competition authority, which means that antitrust rules are only applied in these regions by the CNMC (Asturias, Castilla-la Mancha, the Baleàric Islands, La Rioja, Navarre and Cantabria). For detailed information about the regional competition authorities see the report on the 'Application of Act 1/2002 on Coordination of National and Regional Powers Regarding Defence of Competition 2008-2013', which is available on the website of the former nationwide authority: www.cncompetencia.es (last time accessed: 7 February 2017).

169. Article 5.4 of Act 1/2002 establishes that the CNMC will request a non-binding report to the competent regional authority (if there is one in the specific region) on a particular case regarding the application of the LDC provisions or Article 101 or 102 TFEU, provided that there is a significant impact of the infringement on the regional territory at issue.

IV. Administrative Fines

170. Competition rules involve the protection of the public interest in maintaining free competition in the markets. In Spain, the CNMC is empowered, according to Article 61 LDC, to impose administrative fines, with regard to both specific and general deterrence. Spanish competition law foresees the possibility to fine both individuals and the legal entity or the undertaking to which they belong.

171. This power of the CNMC of imposing fines is part of the possible legal effects foreseen as consequences after breaching the Spanish competition law rule: the mentioned imposition of an administrative fine, restitution or cessation of the practices or removal of the effects, behavioural conditions, structural constraints and the declaration of an act as null and void and finally the granting of damages by a judge or court in charge with a case. According to Article 53.2 b) LDC, structural measures may only be applied by the administrative authority in the absence of other effective behavioural equivalent measures, or also when any behavioural measures are more burdensome for the undertaking concerned than possible structural conditions. This means in practice that the competition authority in Spain could order the sale of assets or even the fragmentation of the infringing undertaking.[57]

172. The former CNC declared that since its foundation in 1989, one of the main purposes has been to fight against anticompetitive conducts in Spain. This resulted at the same time in a continuous increase of the quantity of the fines imposed. In 2012 for example, the sum of fines imposed was of over EUR 372 million, representing a 48% increase compared with the amount imposed in 2011.[58]

173. Article 62 LDC mentions the infringements which constitute administrative offences whereas Article 63 LDC lists the different administrative sanctions which can arise from these infringements. In addition, the rules contained in Act 39/2015, of 1 October, on the common administrative procedure, are applicable *mutatis mutandis.*

---

57. *See* QUINTANS, R. 'Órganos y procedimiento en el Derecho español de defensa de la Competencia' in BELLO MARTÍN-CRESPO, M. P. and HERNÁNDEZ RODRÍGUEZ, F. (Coords.): *Derecho de la libre competencia comunitario y español,* Aranzadi, Cizur Menor, Navarra, 2009, pp. 267–332, pp. 313 ff.
58. The annual report of the CNC for the biennium 2012–2013 (until April 2013) informed that a total amount of over EUR 454 million were imposed in fines. The annual report of the CNMC for 2014 stated that EUR 56.5 million were imposed as fines.

174. The LDC includes a classification of infringements depending on the seriousness of the conducts, distinguishing between minor, serious and very serious infringements in Article 62 LDC. Thus, the level and the amount of the fine will depend on the seriousness of the infringement. In this sense, Article 63 allocates proportional fines depending on the gravity of the infringement. The maximum fine will amount to up to 10% of the business' total turnover. In case the turnover of a company cannot be calculated, the CNMC can impose a fine of more than EUR 10 million, according to Article 63.3.c) LDC. Article 63.2 LDC foresees that the legal representatives or members of the management body of the company may be subject to a fine of up to EUR 60,000.[59]

175. The LDC sets out in Article 64.1 the different criteria that are taken into account by the competition authority when calculating the exact amount of the fine. It mentions the scope and characteristics of the affected market, the market shares of the responsible undertaking (or, in case several undertakings are responsible, the market shares of all of them), the scope of the infringement, the duration of the anticompetitive conduct, the effects of the breach on consumers or any other undertaking and the unlawful profit obtained through this conduct. The Competition Act under Articles 64.2 and 3 lists a number of aggravating and mitigating factors, which may affect the final amount of the fine.

176. In this sense, the aggravating factors mentioned are recidivism, the position of leader or instigator of the infringement, the assurance by the company in case aiming that the unlawful conduct is carried out in an effective sense, as well as the lack of cooperation or obstruction of the inspection work of the competition authority. The mitigating factors mentioned in the LDC are the implementation of actions carried out by a certain company in order to end an infringement, the lack of effective implementation of the anticompetitive conduct, actions seeking a reparation of the damage caused, as well as the active and effective cooperation with the Spanish Competition Authority (besides the cooperation under the Spanish leniency programme[60]).

177. The former CNC published on 6 February 2009 a guide on the method of setting fines. This communication mentions that first the basic amount of the fine is determined depending on the dimension and characteristics of the affected markets,

59. The former CNC fined in its Decision of 26 September 2012, the Spanish Confederation of Business Organisations (CEOE) EUR 150,000 and the President of the Tourism Council of this confederation EUR 50,000 for a collective price recommendation, after considering that certain statements of the President did amount to a collective recommendation according to Art. 1.1 LDC. In its Judgment of 15 October 2013, the Audiencia Nacional (National High Court) annulled these fines, mentioning that the President of the CEOE, Joan Gaspart, was only expressing his view in an interview which was published in the Spanish economic newspaper 'cinco días' and several affirmations in an International Tourism Fair in Spain, and not recommending prices. Besides, the Audiencia Nacional affirmed in its judgment that Mr Gaspart's affirmations that prices were too low in the sector only generated a debate within companies of this sector and no final conclusion was reached.

60. *See* Arts 65 and 66 LDC and Arts 46–53 of Royal Decree 261/2008.

the infringer's market share and the scope of the infringement, as well as its duration and effects. This basic amount should reach between 10% and the 30% of the infringer's sales volume in the affected markets. Second, the aggravating or mitigating circumstances will be taken into account increasing or decreasing the basic amount by 5% and 15%, depending on the circumstances.

178. Finally, in a third step, the total amount of the fine has to be adjusted so as not to exceed 10% of a undertaking's global turnover, which is the maximum limit and threshold mentioned in Article 61.3 LDC.[61] However, according to the most recent case law of the Spanish Supreme Court from January 2015, this guide should not be applied by the CNMC (*see infra*).

179. It is important to mention that according to Article 61.2 LDC, there is a presumption of joint liability amongst the undertakings that carried out the anticompetitive conduct and the individuals controlling that undertaking. Thus, parent companies can be held liable for the anticompetitive conducts of their subsidiaries. This presumption can be rebutted if a specific company can prove that they did not cause the economic behaviour of the company which carried out the illicit conduct. Additionally, the LDC foresees in Article 61 special rules on the liability of undertakings participating in associations or groups of undertakings. These rules include the following disposals: in case an association, a union or group of undertakings is fined and this company is not a solvent member of the same group belonging to the association, the association has to call for contributions from its members to cover the total amount of the fine imposed.[62]

180. If these contributions are not provided to the association within the deadline set by the Spanish competition authority, it may require the payment of the fine to any of the companies whose representatives are members of the governing bodies of the association in question. Undertakings that demonstrate that they have not implemented the decision or recommendation of the infringing association and either ignored their existence or actively distanced themselves from it before the investigation of the case was initiated are not required to pay the amount of the fine.[63]

181. Bases on the seriousness of the anticompetitive conducts, **minor infringements** are related either to merger control proceedings or to cooperation obligations. In the merger context, minor infringements include submitting a notification of an economic concentration after the established time periods have elapsed (Article 9.3 LDC), as well as failing to notify the CNMC an economic concentration when required. Minor infringements include in connection with the cooperation obligations of undertakings and individuals the failing to supply information required by the CNMC or supplying incomplete, incorrect, misleading, or false

61. *See infra* in connection with the Judgment of the Supreme Court of 29 January 2015.
62. *See* Art. 61.3 LDC.
63. *See* Art. 61.3 LDC.

information, the refusal to submit to an inspection carried out by the CNMC as well as the obstruction of the inspection tasks of the authority by any means.

182. Article 62.2 e) LDC provides that the following conducts, amongst others, will constitute an obstruction of an investigation carried out by the CNMC:

(i) the lack of submission and the incorrect, misleading or incomplete submission of documents requested by the CNMC;
(ii) the refusal to answer or the providing of incomplete, inexact or misleading answers to the questions formulated by the CNMC;
(iii) the breaking of the seals affixed by CNMC personnel.

183. Undertakings liable for minor infringements are fined up to 1% of the undertaking's total global turnover in the business year immediately preceding that of the imposition of the fine (Article 63.1 a) LDC).

184. Infringements that are classified as **serious** include: according to Article 62.3 LDC, collusive conducts among undertakings which are neither current nor potential competitors (e.g., vertically related undertakings), including agreements, decisions, collective recommendations, or concerted or consciously parallel practices; the abuse of dominant position, except when it is committed by a company operating in a newly liberalized market;[64] the distortion of free competition through unfair acts and the execution of an economic concentration subject to control before having notified this conduct to the CNMC or before an express or tacit resolution authorizing it has been issued and made effective, and otherwise without an exemption from the suspension obligation having been granted. Undertakings liable for serious infringements are fined up to 5% of the undertaking's total global turnover in the business year immediately preceding that of the imposition of the fine (Article 63.1 b) LDC).

185. According to Article 62.4 LDC, infringements that are classified as **very serious** include collusive behaviours such as cartels or other agreements, decisions, collective recommendations, as well as concerted or consciously parallel practices between current or potential competitors; the abuse of a dominant position by an undertaking that operates in a recently deregulated market, having a market share near a monopoly, or enjoying special or exclusive rights; and the failure to comply with, or in contravention of a resolution, decision or commitment adopted pursuant to the LDC regarding both restricted conducts and merger control. Given that these infringements are the most serious ones against free competition, fines to be imposed may reach up to 10% of the total global turnover of the infringing undertaking in the business year immediately preceding that of the imposition of the fine (Article 63.1 c) LDC).

64. *See infra*, when it has a market share close to monopoly or when it enjoys special or exclusive rights, then such conduct is classified as a very serious infringement.

186. Fines for undertakings, groups of undertakings and associations are determined in Spanish competition law in accordance with the turnover of their members as described above. However, in cases where the turnover cannot be determined, Article 61.3 LDC provides that fines will be fixed taking into account the following amounts: between EUR 100,000 and EUR 500,000 for minor infringements, between EUR 500,001 and EUR 10 million for serious infringements and more than EUR 10 million for very serious infringements.

187. The former CNC imposed the highest fine so far due to an anticompetitive conduct on 12 November 2009 for a total amount of EUR 120,728,000 in the Spanish decennial property insurance cartel.[65] However, this fine imposed by the former CNC was subsequently annulled by the National High Court in different appeals brought by some of the appellants which had been fined.[66] On a further appeal the Supreme Court has decided that the behaviours of the involved companies could not benefit from EU insurance block exemption Regulation. Two of the insurance companies (Mapfre[67] and Munich RE[68]) do not have to pay any fine due to lack of evidence. In its other decisions from the same cartel, the Supreme Court has ordered the CNMC to recalculate the amount of the fine.[69]

188. In connection with the fining system in Spanish competition law, it is very important to mention the Judgment of the Spanish Supreme Court (Third Chamber) of 29 January 2015, which clarified the procedure for calculating fines under the LDC in Case 2872/2013 *BCN Aduanas.*[70] This landmark judgment decides on how to interpret the 10% limit of the fines mentioned in Article 63.1 c) LDC, as well as the market which has to be taken into account in order to calculate the maximum amount of the fines. The case law of the Spanish National High Court (*Audiencia Nacional*) had established during the last two years that the 10% turnover limit for

65. On the emergence and the evolution of the cartel, *see* MARCOS, F. 'The Spanish Property Insurance Cartel' in *Connecticut Insurance Law Journal*, Vol. 18, nº 2, 2012, pp. 79–101.
66. Two of these judgments of the National High Court were published on 18 December 2012, and another one on 4 January 2013. All of them, after interpreting extensively the facts and assessing the relevant evidence, came to the conclusion that the anticompetitive agreement between the insurance companies had not been sufficiently proven in the Decision of the competition authority. Apparently, there had been a licit cooperation between the insurance companies considering the ten-year warranty, since it was a quite new requirement and the companies involved did not have any consolidated statistical data available. There had been exchanges of information between the different companies involved, including data which served to determine the price of the insurance, and the Competition Authority, considering this homogeneity of the existing insurance premiums in the market, equated them with a price agreement.
67. Judgment of the Supreme Court of 26 May 2015 (number 1304/2013).
68. Judgment of the Supreme Court of 26 May 2015 (number 486/2013).
69. Judgments of the Supreme Court of 26 May 2015 (numbers 483/2013; 583/2013; 481/2013; 2449/2013).
70. *See* Judgment of the Civil Chamber of the Spanish Supreme Court of 29 January 2015 (Number 2872/2013). Other judgments of the same chamber of the Supreme Court have confirmed this approach regarding the method of setting the amount of the fines, e.g., the Judgments of 5 February 2015 (number 1567/2014), 20 February 2015 and 9 March 2015, in which the Supreme Court concludes that the CNMC has to recalculate the import of the fine. In this same sense, the CNMC has already implemented and taken into account the new case law of the Spanish Supreme Court in its decisions of 11 February 2015 and 26 February 2015 in which it was specifically mentioned.

very serious infringements has to be interpreted as a sliding scale for the calculation of the amount of the fines and not, as it had been applied so far, as an *ex post* limit or *cap* on the final fine only once the calculation of the fine has been made.[71] The National High Court further decided that this limit exclusively applies to the turnover of the infringing company in the market affected by the infringement in the year which precedes the decision and not to the global turnover related to all the economic activities in all the markets in which the infringing company is participating. This recent interpretation of the National High Court resulted in drastic reductions of the fines imposed by the Spanish Competition Authority (CNC and later the CNMC), especially in multiproduct companies (since it took into account only the turnover of the affected markets by the infringement).

189. The Supreme Court endorses only partially the National High Court's interpretation considering that the interpretation of the authority regarding the 10% limit as a cap (included also in its Guidelines from 6 February 2009)[72] is contrary to the LDC. The Supreme Court affirms that taking into account the principle of procedural autonomy contained in Article 5 of Regulation 1/2003, the national courts and the Spanish competition authority are not bound by the calculation methods followed by the EU Courts and the European Commission. Thus, the Supreme Court confirms that the criteria set out in Article 63.1 LDC for calculating the fines to be imposed, i.e., 0%–1% for minor offences, 1%–5% for serious offences and 5%–10% for very serious offences should be counted as a scale and not as a maximum cap once the fine has already been calculated. In this respect the Spanish Supreme Court follows – without citing it – the similar conclusions reached by the German Supreme Court in its Judgment of 23 February 2013.[73] The mentioned partial endorsement refers to the fact that the Supreme Court accepted the State Attorney's appeal with respect to the turnover to take into account when calculating the amount of the fine and considered that it has to be based on the global turnover of the infringing company (including all the markets in which the company is carrying out some kind of activities) and not only the turnover in the affected market in the year which precedes the decision of the authority. The Supreme Court orders the competition authority to recalculate the fine in this case (which was a road haulage cartel case) following this new interpretation of the 10% limit and taking into account the total global turnover of the infringers and not its turnover in the affected market. In its judgment, the Supreme Court admits that it can be difficult in practice to find a balance between the principles of effectiveness and deterrent effect, on the one

71. *See*, for example, the Judgments of the Administrative Chamber of the Spanish National High Court of 5 December 2013 (Appeal Number 242/2012), December 23, 2013 (Appeal Number 188/2012), 15 January 2014 (Appeal Number 544/2010), 7 March 2014 (Appeal Number 670/2011), 12 March 2014 (Appeal Number 172/2011), 2 April 2014 (Appeal Number 194/2011), 16 April 2014 (Appeal Number 568/2010), 30 May 2014 (Appeal Number 195/2012), 24 July 2014 (Appeal Number 147/2013) or 29 July 2014 (Appeal Number 172/2013).

72. *See* the Guidelines published by the former CNC on 6 February 2009 ('*Comunicación de la Comisión Nacional de la Competencia sobre la cuantificación de las sanciones derivadas de infracciones de los artículos 1, 2 y 3 de la Ley 15/2007, de 3 de julio, de defensa de la competencia y de los artículos 81 y 82 del Tratado de la Comunidad Europea*').

73. *See* Judgment of the German Supreme Court (*Bundesgerichtshof*) of 23 February 2013, KRB 20/12.

hand, and the principle of proportionality on the other hand. It mentioned also the well-known principle of *nulla poena sine lege* underlining that only the legislator may set out the method for calculating fines by law as the competition authority – the CNMC – is only in charge of the enforcement of competition law in Spain. Currently there is no clear method on how to calculate fines beyond the rules set out by the Supreme Court in this Judgment of 29 January 2015.[74]

190. The German competition authority (*Bundeskartellamt*) changed its guidelines in July 2013 including the case law of the German Supreme Court (*Bundesgerichtshof*) of February 2013.[75] However, it is important to underline that §81.7 of the German Competition Act *(Gesetz gegen Wettbewerbsbeschränkungen)* specifically foresees the possibility that the federal competition authority (*Bundeskartellamt*) sets guidelines on the calculation of the amount of the fine, as well as for the cooperation with foreign competition authorities, whereas in Spain the Third Additional Provision of the Competition Act only considers the possibility of publishing guidelines 'clarifying the principles that guide its performance when applying' the competition act, which does not include procedures related to fines according to the current case law of the Spanish Supreme Court.

V. Experience with Leniency Applications in Spain

191. The leniency programme was introduced in Spain law on 28 February 2008. The leniency programme was introduced in Articles 65 and 66 of the LDC 15/2007 but it was not implemented until the adoption and entry into force of the

---

74. In the decision published on 18 June 2014 (Proceedings S/0469/13, *Fabricantes de papel y cartón ondulado*), the CNMC confirmed that according to the Supreme Court's Judgment of 29 January 2015, the sanctioning scale's upper limit is the 10% of the total turnover of the infringer. Once this scale is determined, an individualization of the amount of the fine has to be carried out, based on the criteria mentioned in Art. 64.1 LDC. The most relevant one for the CNMC seems to be the dimension of the illicit conduct in the affected market (by the anticompetitive conduct). The participation fee of each company in the infringement is determined by the sales of this company during the months the infringement had taken place in connection with the total sales during this period of time. This participation fee apparently reflects the gain and the potential benefits obtained out of the illicit conduct, thus it is implemented in order to comply with the principle of proportionality in fines. The individualization of the fine requires also taking into account the aggravating and mitigating circumstances foreseen in Art. 64.2 and 3 LDC. Besides making sure that the participation fee reflects the gain and the potential benefits obtained out of the illicit conduct, in a third step the CNMC makes sure that the calculated fine is not disproportional with respect to the gain and potential benefits obtained from the anticompetitive infringement. But the CNMC does not specify when exactly this amount has to be considered as disproportionate. In the German Guidelines, the *Bundeskartellamt* specifies that this would be the case if the amount of the fine is between two and six times higher than the illicit benefit obtained by the infringer. The decision was accompanied by two dissenting votes of board members in which they criticized that it was not clear how the factors mentioned in Art. 64 LDC had been taken into account and that the decision is vitiated by a lack of reasoning concerning the calculation of the amount of the fine.

75. *See* the guidelines published by the *Bundeskartellamt* (German competition authority, '*Leitlinien für die Bußgeldzumessung in Kartellordnungswidrigkeiten*'), on 25 June 2013.

Competition Regulation (Royal Decree 261/2008 at the end of February 2008). On 19 June 2013 a procedural notice related to the Spanish leniency programme was adopted.[76]

192. The annual report of the biennium 2011–2012 mentions that during the first four years the leniency programme had been operating, eight fining decisions in cartel cases have been adopted following a leniency application. In two additional cases an application for the fine to be reduced was issued once the investigation had been initiated ex officio. In 2010, the first decision following a leniency application was adopted. During the biennium 2012–2013, eight fining decisions in cartel cases have been adopted following a leniency application. Until September 2013, seventeen cartels were fined on the basis of investigations initiated as a result of a leniency application as of the adoption of the first decision under the leniency programme in January 2010. In 2014, two decisions were adopted as a consequence of a leniency application.[77] In 2015, one decision has been taken as a consequence of an investigation based on the leniency programme.[78]

193. The following table summarizes all these cases in chronological order (including the information which is publicly available):

Decision	*Total Amount of Fines Imposed (EUR)*	*Fine Exemption/ Reduction (EUR)*
S/0085/08 *Dentífricos*: CNC Resolution of 20 December 2009	Lack of anticompetitive conduct due to prescription	
S/0084/08 *Fabricantes de Gel*: CNC Resolution of 21 January 2010 and S/0224/10 *Colomer*: CNC Resolution of 29 June 2011	EUR 15,253,341	Fine exemption: EUR 6,754,229 Fine reduction: EUR 170,300

76. The note is available at https://www.boe.es/boe/dias/2013/08/16/pdfs/BOE-A-2013-9022.pdf (last time accessed: 1 February 2017).
77. *See* Resolution of 26 June 2014, Proceedings S/0445/12, case *Equipos contra incendios*. The total fines imposed amounted to EUR 2,136,975.81 million. The immunity applicant, Todoextintor got exempted from the payment of a fine of EUR 265,411.22. *See also* Resolution of 4 December 2014, Proceedings S/0453/12, case *Rodamientos ferroviarios*. The total fines amounted to EUR 4 million. The immunity applicant, NSK, got exempted from the payment of a fine of EUR 123,815. There were no leniency reductions in this case.
78. *See* Resolution of 23 July 2015, Proceedings S/0482/13, case *Fabricantes de automóviles*. The total fines amounted to EUR 171 million. The immunity applicant, Seat S.A., got exempted from the payment of a fine of EUR 12,674,948. Two other companies got also exempted from the payment of the fine because they are part of the same group: Volkswagen Audi España, S.A. got exempted from the payment of a fine of EUR 26,523,000 and Porsche Ibérica, S.A. got exempted from the payment of a fine of EUR 245,200. There were no leniency reductions in this case.

Decision	*Total Amount of Fines Imposed (EUR)*	*Fine Exemption/ Reduction (EUR)*
S/0091/08 *Vinos Finos de Jérez*: CNC Resolution of 28 July 2010	EUR 6,843,000	Fine exemption: EUR 670,000 No reductions foreseen
S/0120/08 *Transitarios 2*: CNC Resolution of 31 July 2010 and S/0269/10 *Transitarios 2*: CNC Resolution of 1 December 2011	EUR 21,225,000	Fine exemption: EUR 5,194,000 Fine reduction: EUR 1,184,000
S/0086/08 *Peluquería Profesional:* CNC Resolution of 2 March 2011	EUR 60,907,000	Fine exemption: EUR 9,890,000 No reductions foreseen
S/0185/09 *Bombas Fluídos*: CNC Resolution of 24 June 2011	EUR 18,306,081	Fine exemption: EUR 962,500 No reductions foreseen
S/0241/10 *Navieras-Ceuta 2*: CNC Resolution of 10 November 2011	EUR 18,690,947	Fine exemption: EUR 2,351,689 No reductions foreseen
S/0251/10 *Envases hortofrutícolas*: CNC Resolution of 2 December 2011	EUR 12,226,113	Fine exemption: EUR 8,371,740 No reductions foreseen
S/0244/10 *Navieras Baleàres*: CNC Resolution of 23 February 2012	EUR 54,109,768	No fine exemption foreseen No reductions foreseen
S/0298/10 *Postensado y Geotecnia*: CNC Resolution of 31/07/ 2012	EUR 16,860,000	Fine exemption: EUR 5,228,000
S/0318/10 *Exportación de sobres*: CNC Resolution of 15 October 12	EUR 3,361,330	No fine exemption foreseen Fine reduction: EUR 406,630

Decision	*Total Amount of Fines Imposed (EUR)*	*Fine Exemption/ Reduction (EUR)*
S/0331/11 *Navieras Marruecos*: CNC Resolution of 7 November 2012	EUR 88,588,269	No exemption foreseen Fine reduction: EUR 889,335
S/0317/10 *Material de archivo*: CNC Resolution of 21 November 2012	EUR 9,083,780	Fine exemption + fine reduction: EUR 4,733,606
S/0343/11 *Manipulado de papel*: CNC Resolution of 15 February 2013	EUR 9,071,946	Fine exemption + fine reduction: EUR 4,003,179
S/0341/11 *Espuma de Poliuretano*: CNC Resolution of 28 February 2013	EUR 25,304,000	Fine exemption + fine reduction: EUR 12,412,000
S/0316/10 *Sobres de papel*: CNC Resolution of 25/03/2013	EUR 44,581,559	Fine exemption + two fine reductions: EUR 27,975,227
S/0303/10 *Distribuidores Saneamiento*: CNC Resolution of 23 May 2013	EUR 6,459,087	No exemption foreseen No reductions foreseen
S/0380/11 *Coches de Alquiler*: CNC Resolution of 20 July 2013	EUR 35,426,456	No exemption foreseen Fine reduction: EUR 791,958
S/0445/12 *Equipos contra incendios*: CNMC Resolution of 26 June 2014	EUR 2,136,975.81	Fine exemption EUR 265,411.22 No reductions foreseen.
S/0453/12 *Rodamientos ferroviarios*: CNMC Resolution of 4 December 2014	EUR 4,000,000	Fine exemption: EUR 123,815 No reductions foreseen
S/0482/13 *Fabricantes de automóviles:* CNMC Resolution of 23 July 2015	EUR 171,000,000	Fine exemptions: EUR 39,443,148 No reductions foreseen

Source: Annual Report of the CNMC for 2014.

VI. Administrative Injunctions and Other Restrictive Orders

194. Article 28 of Act 3/2013, of 4 June, on the creation of the National Commission of Markets and Competition foresees information requirements of the competition authority, as well as the duty of confidentiality and the access to State Registers.

195. Article 28.1 LDC states that any natural or legal person, bodies and agencies of any Civil Service are subject to the duty of collaboration with the Spanish Competition Authority in the exercise of the protection of free competition. They are also required to provide, upon request of the authority and in time, any kind of data and information available to them which may be necessary for the correct exercise of the work of the authority.

196. Requests for information have to be motivated and proportionate to the aim pursued. The injunction has to detail the specific content of the information which is required, justifying also the adequacy of the required information in connection with the development of the procedure and the use which is pretended to made thereof.

197. The data and information obtained by the CNMC have to be considered as confidential matters and may only be handed to the interested Ministry, to the regional governments, the European Commission or the competition authorities of other Member States of the European Union, as well as to the courts in the framework of judicial proceedings.

198. Article 28.3 of Act 3/2013 foresees that the CNMC shall have access to the public registers related to the sectors included in the scope of the authority.[79] Likewise, the Central Government should have access to the databases held by the CNMC.

VII. Interim Measures

199. In Spain, interim measures can be granted both by the CNMC and by Commercial Judges/Courts. While the CNMC can grant interim measures ex officio or at its own initiative, Commercial Courts can only grant an interim measure upon request of the interested parties.

200. Article 54 LDC foresees that once opened a sanctioning procedure, interim measures can be granted by the CNMC at its own initiative – after a proposal or report of the Competition Directorate of the CNMC – or at the request of a party, in order to ensure the effectiveness of final decision rendered. Article 36.6 LDC sets a maximum period of three months for the CNMC to adopt and notify these interim measures in case of request of interested parties. If the interim measures are

79. *See* footnote number 1.

requested before the opening of the file, then the maximum period of three months starts to run from the day the file is opened. Otherwise, Article 36.6 LDC does not set a maximum period for interim measures adopted ex officio after being proposed by the Competition Directorate of the CNMC or by the Council of the Competition Authority.

201. Article 37.1 k) of Act 3/2013 foresees the mandatory publication of resolutions imposing interim measures. Moreover, Article 38.6 LDC underlines that once the period of three months has elapsed and the CNMC has not taken a decision regarding interim measures upon request of the interested party, they have to be considered as rejected. The infringement of interim measures granted by the CNMC may be sanctioned through penalty payments, according to Article 67 LDC (maximum of EUR 12,000 per day). The LDC does not provide a list of specific interim measures that can be granted. As mentioned, Article 54 LDC merely points out the possibility of granting any measure necessary to ensure the effectiveness of the decision handed down at the time. Article 40 of Royal Decree 261/2008 mentions some of the possible interim measures in an open list, e.g., the cessation of the anticompetitive conduct or a deposit declared by the Council of the CNMC in order to account for a compensation of damages that could be caused. The conditions for the adoption of these interim measures are the existence of *fumus boni iuris* and *periculum in mora.*[80]

202. Besides, Article 41.5 of Royal Decree 261/2008 foresees that interim measures shall be ceased once the decision of the Council of the CNMC has been adopted, clarifying that under no circumstances the proposal, adoption, suspension, modification or revocation of an interim measure shall suspend the course of proceedings. Moreover, Article 41.6 reminds that according to Article 67 LDC, if interim measures granted by the Council of the CNMC are breached, the CNMC may impose fines up to 10% of the turnover of the infringing company, as it is considered a very serious infringement.

203. Behavioural remedies have been often accepted by the competition authority in Spain. For example, in the *SGAE* case, the SGAE was ordered to withdraw a specific clause from its contracts, which was deemed to be unfair and discriminatory.[81]

80. *See* below §2 II. C.
81. *See* the CNMC Resolution of 6 November 2014, in which the CNMC imposed a EUR 3.1 million fine on the Spanish Society of Authors and Publishers (SGAE) for infringing Art. 2 LDC as well as Art. 102 TFEU. The CNMC concluded that the SGAE had abused its dominant position in the market for the management of musical rights when holding concerts in Spain, by charging excessive prices. In this case, the CNMC established that the level of fees charged by the SGAE as consideration for the right to publically play musical content subject to copyright in concerts in Spain was extremely high, especially when comparing them with the rates paid in other European countries, in particular, in Germany, France and Italy. The conditions which were considered as disproportionate and unwarranted towards concert promoters and ticket resellers consisted of the requirement to obtain a licence from the SGAE before initiating the sale of the tickets and the obligation to deposit a guarantee which had to cover the total copyright contribution, or alternatively, the obligation to distribute the tickets through a ticketing operator who has a cooperation agreement with the SGAE.

204. Moreover, structural remedies may be imposed in the absence of equally effective behavioural remedies or when these remedies would be more onerous for the undertaking in question than the imposition of structural remedies.

§2. Civil Enforcement

I. Competent Civil Courts

205. According to the First Additional Provision of the LDC, private actions due to anticompetitive conducts have to be filed before the Spanish commercial courts.[82] These commercial courts are specialized civil courts that have been with applying and interpreting EU and Spanish competition rules, amongst other fields, like for example unfair competition rules or insolvency law. Under Spanish law and after the LDC 15/2007 entered into force on 1 September 2007, the antitrust provisions of both Articles 101 and 102 of the TFEU and/or Articles 1 and 2 LDC are directly enforceable not only by the competition authority (CNMC) but also by the mentioned commercial courts. This was one of the most important changes introduced by the LDC, namely the possibility that provisions concerning the prohibition of anticompetitive agreements and abuses of a dominant position may be directly applied by the commercial courts, once a claim has been filed by the victim, without a previous decision rendered by the competition authority in Spain regarding the unlawfulness of a certain conduct.[83] It goes without saying that the decisions of the CNMC can also be challenged before the competent Spanish administrative Courts, as mentioned *infra* in Chapter 4 §3.

206. The judgments of the commercial courts in first instance (*Juzgados de lo Mercantil*) may be appealed to the Court of Appeal (*Audiencia Provincial*, because there is one in each of the fifty Spanish provinces) on both issues of fact and issues of law. Finally, a further appeal could be made to the First Chamber (on civil matters) of the Spanish Supreme Court (*Sala de lo Civil del Tribunal Supremo*) in order to 'unify the legal doctrine'. This means that the appeal to the Supreme Court is made on the basis that a decision is contrary to the interpretation of the law as stated by the Supreme Court in preceding case law. According to Article 477.2 of the Spanish Code of Civil Procedure, the judgments of the Court of Appeal can be challenged also when the amount of the process exceeds a certain monetary threshold, namely EUR 600,000.[84]

82. *See* Art. 86*ter* 2.f) of the Judicial Power Organization Act (Number 6/1985) of 1 July. Commercial courts were created in Spain by the Insolvency Act 22/2003, of 9 July.
83. Article 13.2 of the former competition of the former Competition Act (16/1989) stated that the action for compensation for damages, based on the unlawfulness of conducts prohibited by the Competition Act, may be exercised by those who consider themselves affected by the damage, once the administrative decision and, if applicable, the judgment of the competent administrative court was issued. The substantive and procedural rules for the action for compensation of damages are the ones provided for in the civil laws.
84. On 1 October 2015, some amendments included in Act 29/1998, from 13 July, governing Administrative Jurisdiction, entered into force. In order to be able to go for a further appeal before the

207. The LDC introduced also in its Second Additional Provision an amicus curiae procedure inspired by Regulation 1/2003, by which the EU Commission, the CNMC and the regional antitrust bodies may submit – at its own initiative or at the request of the competent court – observations regarding the application of Spanish competition rules. According to Article 434.3 of the Code of civil procedure, the commercial courts hearing an antitrust action may also suspend proceedings until an administrative authority, such as the European Commission, the CNMC or a regional authority, has ruled on the competition matter in question, especially when it is known that there is an open case.

208. The amicus curiae mechanism has been used for the first time in Spain in a damages claim proceeding initiated by the consumer advocacy group AUSBANC against Telefónica España in connection with the European Commission Decision of 4 July 2007 fining Telefónica over EUR 15 million for over five years of margin squeezing practices in the Spanish broadband market. Within the framework of this proceeding, the former Spanish Competition authority, the CNC, was called to act as amicus curiae before the commercial court number 4 of Madrid.

II. Sanctions

A. Nullity

209. Both anticompetitive agreements and abuse of dominance conducts may take place within a contractual relationship. Particularly in the case of abuses of a dominant position this illicit behaviour may be carried out through a contract including the conditions which constitute the abuse in question. In this case, the injured party, who is part to the contractual relationship, may invoke the nullity of the whole contract or of a particular contractual clause, if it can be separated from the whole agreement and if this single clause solely constitutes the conduct defined as restrictive of free competition in the affected market(s). Both anticompetitive agreements and abuse of dominance behaviours are expressly prohibited, as mentioned, by Articles 1 and 2 LDC. Thus, those contracts which reflect these anticompetitive conducts or include all or some clauses breaching these provisions have to be considered null and void, according to Article 6.3 of the Spanish Civil Code.[85] In this sense, according to Article 1.2 LDC, those agreements, decisions and

Supreme Court it will not be necessary any more that the amount exceeds EUR 600,000, rather that the matter presents some 'appeal interest' (*interés casacional*), e.g., when the case involves a lot of affected parties, when the public interest has been seriously damages, when the case involves an interpretation of EU law in a different way than the one pre-established by the European Court of Justice or when the appealed decision resolves an appeal against an act or decision of a regulatory or supervisory body or state agency whose decisions have to be challenged at the Spanish High Court (*Audiencia Nacional*). *See* on this behalf Art. 88 of Law 29/1998 after the entering into force. The bill published in the Spanish Official State Bulletin (*Boletín Oficial del Estado*) on 22 July 2015 is available at http://www.boe.es/boe/dias/2015/07/22/pdfs/BOE-A-2015-8167.pdf (last time accessed: 7 February 2017).

85. Article 6.3 of the Spanish Civil Code foresees that acts which are contrary to mandatory rules are null and void, unless a different effect is set for a case of contravention of the rule.

recommendations which are prohibited by the first paragraph of Article 1 are null and void, except when they are covered by an exemption contained in this same act.[86]

210. This declaration of nullity can only be granted by an ordinary court belonging to the civil order, thus, in Spain by commercial courts. Please note the difference with the declaration of existence of an illicit conduct under competition rules, which is carried out by the competition authority.

211. Regarding the active legitimation in nullity actions, the Spanish Supreme Court (First Chamber) declared in its Judgment of 2 June 2000, *DISA*, that not only the contracting parties are legitimated but also anyone interested and affected by the requested nullity of the contract, including the party who induced to the agreement. The Spanish Supreme Court decided regarding to this aspect in the same sense as later the European Court of Justice in *Courage,*[87] mentioning also nullity *ex* Article 6.3 of the Spanish Civil Code can even work ex officio.[88]

212. In Spain, most of the case law related to private enforcement of competition law deals with nullity actions deriving from anticompetitive clauses in contracts.[89] Certainly, claimants have requested damages as compensation in some of the claims reported but most of the remedies awarded by judges have been of a declaratory so far, i.e., of unlawfulness or nullity of the contract which contains an anticompetitive conduct.

B. Damages

1. Types of Actions Available

213. Under Spanish law, damages are available only as means of compensation to the injured party, excluding the possibility of punitive or exemplary damages. As in actions for nullity, commercial courts have jurisdiction in civil actions concerning the request for damages after an anticompetitive conduct which infringes the LDC. The interested party may bring a *stand-alone* (i.e., without being based on a previous decision by a competition authority) or a *follow-on* action before these courts claiming compensatory damages for any losses suffered as a consequence of anticompetitive conduct.[90]

---

86. For example, Art. 4 LDC provides for the possibility that certain behaviours are declared exempt by law.
87. *See* Judgment of the European Court of Justice of 20 September 2001, C-453/99, *Courage Ltd v. Bernhard Crehan.*
88. *See also* the Judgments of the Spanish Supreme Court (First Chamber) of 29 March 1963, and of 30 December 1993.
89. *See* Marcos, F. 'Competition Law Private Litigation in the Spanish Courts (1999-2012)' in *Global Competition Litigation Review*, n° 4, 2013, pp. 167–211, p. 182.
90. Besides the examples which are going to be mentioned in this section, *see* for a complete and monographic study of private enforcement by Spanish courts (based both in Spanish competition rules and

214. In order to obtain damages, it is necessary to prove that there has taken place in practice an unlawful conduct, the harm caused to the victim, and that a causal link exists between the conduct and the harm caused.

215. Regarding the quantification of damages, the judge will prove that the requested sum complies with the rules established in Article 1106 of the Spanish Civil Code, which means that damages will be calculated taking into account the actual damage suffered by the injured party (*damnum emergens*), the loss of profit (*lucrum cessans*) as well as the interests. The *lucrum cessans* refers to the profits that the injured party would have earned if the anticompetitive conduct would not have taken place. It is very important to notice that a causal link must be established between the anticompetitive conduct and the actual damage or loss of profits.

216. The above-mentioned Article 1106 distinguishes between two types of damages:

(1) Damages in respect of what may be called 'actual loss' (*daño emergente*), that is, loss which has actually been suffered and which is identifiable.
(2) Damages in respect of loss of profits (*lucro cesante*), which refers to the profits which the relevant party might have made if the circumstances in question had not arisen. It is generally considered that the potential profits cannot be just mere hopes or expectations. There must be a certain degree of likelihood that they would have been achieved. Besides, there must be a causal link between the act or omission and the loss of profits: the claimant must prove that it was prevented from obtaining the profit in question as a result of the defendant's conduct.

217. As mentioned *supra* with regard to the *stand-alone* actions, since the revision of the LDC in 2007, it is certainly not a precondition anymore that the Competition Authority publishes a decision related to the unlawfulness of a certain conduct in order to be able to bring a civil action before a commercial court in Spain.[91] So far, there is no specific rule within the Spanish law that specially provides for the possibility to sue damages due to an anticompetitive conduct in reliance on the findings of a non-Spanish Competition Authority. This should be possible, according to the progresses carried out by European law in this field, i.e., *Directive 2014/104/EU of the European Parliament and of the Council of 26*

---

in European one), MARCOS, F.: 'Competition Law Private Litigation in the Spanish Courts (1999–2012)' in *Global Competition Litigation Review*, nº 4, 2013, pp. 167–211.

91. This was the case in Spain according to Art. 13.2 of the former LDC 16/1989, of 17 July. This was changed by the First Additional Provision of the current Competition Act 15/2007, foreseeing that commercial courts have jurisdiction over all matters which fall within the competence of the civil courts regarding procedures under Art. 1 (anticompetitive agreements) and Art. 2 (abuse of a dominant position) LDC. On this evolution *see*, for example, VALMAÑA OCHAÍTA, M.: 'Civil Liability for Infringing Competition Rules: Grounds, Standing and Scope of Damages' in VELASCO SAN PEDRO, L. A.; ALONSO LEDESMA, C. and others (editors): *Private Enforcement of Competition Law*, Valladolid, 2011, pp. 565–575, 565 ff.

November 2014 on certain rules governing actions for damages under national law for infringements of the competition law provisions of the Member States and of the European Union.[92]

2. Nature of Antitrust Damages Claims

218. The nature of damages claims is particularly relevant for the purposes of determining the applicable statute of limitations, and in particular, whether the limitation period applicable is that for contractual claims (fifteen years) or that for non-contractual claims (one year).

219. In its Judgments of 8 June 2012 and 7 November 2013, the Spanish Supreme Court analysed the legal nature of the liability of cartel members for the damages caused by their anticompetitive conduct and concluded that the damages caused by the cartel at stake had to be qualified as tort and not as contractual liability. The tortious and illicit conduct was the horizontal price fixing agreement that the claimant had entered into with other sugar producers and which the Spanish competition authority found to have infringed the statutory cartel prohibition *ex* Article 1(a) of the 1989 Competiton Act and, at the time, Article 85(1) EC Treaty. According to the Supreme Court, these illicit agreements resulted in an increase of the sugar prices in the subsequent sales contracts. The illicit behaviour had taken place prior to the conclusion of the sales contracts. The claim could therefore not be considered as a contractual claim but was derived from the infringement of the cartel prohibition by cartel members.

220. Likewise, in the Judgment of 8 June 2012, the Supreme Court specified that the plaintiff's claim was not based on a defective performance of any of the contractual obligations established in the sales contracts (i.e., expressly agreed obligations or accessory obligations based on the duty of good faith). The aim of the action was not seeking a declaration regarding the invalidity of the sales contracts either. Rather, the actions aimed at obtaining compensation for the damages resulting from the illicit agreements restricting competition by determining the price as one of the essential elements of the subsequent sales. On that basis, the Supreme Court concluded, referring to the Anglo-Saxon law principles and using the English terms – that the liability for infringements of competition law falls under '*the law of torts*' and not under '*the law of contracts*'.

92. *See*, regarding to the evolution and all important documents related to the Damages Directive and private enforcement at an EU level, http://bit.ly/1ASkRaT (last time accessed: 7 February 2017). The Directive was published in the Official Journal of the European Union on 5 December 2014 (L 349/1).

3. Start of the Statute of Limitation Period

221. According to Article 1968(2) of the Spanish Civil Code the one-year statute of limitation period for non-contractual claims pursuant to Article 1902 of the Spanish Civil Code starts to run as of the date on which the victim becomes aware of the illicit act. The Spanish Supreme Court has repeatedly confirmed that the statute of limitation period does not start until the potential claimant has access to the complete factual and legal part of a case, having 'full capacity to litigate'. This means in practice being aware of the extent or degree of the harm suffered.[93] To date it remains unclear whether claimants can be deemed to be aware of the extent or degree of the harm suffered at the time a competition procedure is initiated by the competition authority.

222. In the case of continuing or repeated infringements, time shall begin to run on the day on which the infringement ceases.[94] In order to put an end to a continuing infringement an action for injunction is available *ex* Article 32.1.2ª in connection with Article 15.2 of the Spanish Unfair Competition Act 3/1991. According to Article 35 of the Unfair Competition Act 3/1991, the one-year statute of limitation period for this action starts to run as of the date on which the action can be exercised and the victim becomes aware of the identity of the infringer. In any case, this Act also foresees in Article 35 a three-year statute from the day on which the infringement ceases.

223. In its Judgments related to the sugar cartel of 6 June 2012, the Supreme Court[95] rejected the defendant's plea arguing that the claims were time-barred. In the Supreme Court's view, pursuant to Article 1969 of the Spanish Civil Code,[96] the plaintiffs had not been in a position to bring the action for damages foreseen in Article 13 of the LDC 16/1989 prior to the date on which they had become aware of the fact that the decision of the Spanish competition authority establishing the competition law infringement, had become final and binding. The *rationale* of this is that because before the adoption of the Spanish Competition Act 15/2007, it was not possible to file damages claims before the administrative decision had become final and binding, so the parties had to wait until the Decision would be confirmed by the National High Court (*Audiencia Nacional*) and/or the Supreme Court in case

93. *See* Judgment of the Supreme Court of 2 April 2014, citing this *rationale*. This judgment mentions that following a judgment of the Supreme Court of 25 April 2013, the start of the statute of limitation period in actions related to tort liability is determined by the knowledge by the victim of the facts which trigger responsibility ('from the moment the victim learned about it'). The initial day of the statute of limitation period is the day in which the action for damages may be exercised, following the rationale *actio nondum nata non praescribitur* (the action which was not born yet cannot prescribe) (Judgments of the Spanish Supreme Court from 24 May 2010, 12 December 2011 and 9 January 2013). According to these judgments, the statute of limitation period does not start to run while the damaged party does not have 'full capacity to litigate' (i.e., until having a real knowledge of the scope or extent of the damage suffered).

94. *See* Judgments of the Supreme Court of 16 June 2000; 30 May 2005 and 29 December 2006.

95. *See* Judgment of the Supreme Court of 8 June 2012 (number 344/2012).

96. 'In the absence of specific provisions, the limitation period for all actions starts running as of the day on which they can be exercised.'

of appeal and the statute of limitation period of one year only started to run from the date of the notification of the judgment of the National High Court and/or the Supreme Court upholding the administrative prohibition Decision.

224. In the context of the sugar cartel claims, while the Judgment of the Administrative Chamber of the Supreme Court was handed down on 26 April 2005, the notification of the judgment to the plaintiffs' industry associations which had participated as interested third parties in the administrative proceedings, only took place significantly later. On that basis, the Supreme Court concluded the extrajudicial letters which the defendant had received from the plaintiffs on various dates in the end of 2006 validly interrupted the limitation period in accordance with Article 1973 of the Spanish Civil Code[97] and that the damage actions were not time-barred when the plaintiffs started legal proceedings in November 2007.[98]

225. It is noteworthy mentioning that the statute of limitation period can be interrupted by sending a formal notice to the defendant by means of an extrajudicial claim (bureaufax, registered letter, etc.) according to Article 1973 of the Spanish Civil Code.

226. Since the entry into force of the LDC 15/2007 it is no longer necessary to wait until a decision of the competition authority or until this decision has been upheld by the administrative court (in case of being appealed) in order to be entitled to file a damages claim before the relevant civil court. Pursuant to the preamble of the law, this change was introduced on the basis of the direct effect of Articles 101 and 102 of the TFEU.[99]

227. In this context, it can be argued that LDC introduces a certain degree of uncertainty with regard to the starting date of the one-year limitation period and the exact date on which this one-year limit starts to run. With regard to this aspect, some authors have highlighted that the previous regime, based on Article 13.2 of the Competition Act 16/1989, was safer in order to determine when the *dies a quo* started to run, that is, once the judicial decision upholding the Decision under appeal had been notified.[100] In this same sense, other authors have taken the view that it would be more reasonable to consider that the initiation of proceedings by either a

---

97. 'The limitation of actions is interrupted by their exercise before the courts, by extrajudicial reclamation by the creditor and by any act of recognition of the debt by the debtor.'
98. As mentioned *supra*, this judgment is based on the previous Spanish Competition Act of 1989.
99. '(…) the First Additional Provision establishes, under application of the Law of the Judicial Power, the competence of commercial courts in application of Articles 1 and 2 of the Competition Act, as foreseen in a European level with regard to Articles 81 and 82 of the Treaty of the European Community.'
100. *See* Berenger, L. '¿La piedra de sísifo o el tejido de Penélope? Idas y venidas de la norma de la UE para la reclamación de daños en materia de competencia' in Cases, L. *Anuario de Defensa de la competencia* 2011–2012, 2012, pp. 55–84, p. 65.

national or the European competition authority, if related to the same facts, interrupts the statute of limitation period until the conclusion of this administrative procedure or its judicial review.[101]

228. The starting date of the limitation period turned out to be a key point of the damages claim lodged by Céntrica against Iberdrola (in an abuse of dominance case, not a cartel case) before the Commercial Court (*Juzgado de lo Mercantil*) of Bilbao. Iberdrola was accused of having denied access to its customer data information. As the monopolist local distributor, it was legally obliged to deliver this information to third party power supply companies. Céntrica received a fax from Iberdrola on 22 May 2008 about the day and the time both companies should meet in order to deliver the information. Céntrica was finally granted free access to this information on 2 June 2008. Céntrica sent a *bureaufax* to Iberdrola on 28 May 2009 in order to interrupt the statute of limitations period and then filed an action for damages on 26 June 2010. Both the first instance judge and the appellate court considered that the action had become time-barred because on 22 May 2008 Iberdrola informed Céntrica that it had the information and according to both judges since that moment Céntrica could already calculate the amount of the damages. Céntrica had sent the extrajudicial communication in order to interrupt the limitation period one year and six days later, on 28 May 2009. In its Judgment of 4 September 2013, the Spanish Supreme Court decided that Céntrica's action for damages was not time-barred because it considered that the relevant date for the one-year statute of limitation period to start running was 2 June 2008, when Céntrica could effectively have access to the information.

229. Finally, in the context of the Spanish Property Insurance Cartel, the Commercial Court number 12 of Madrid, in its Judgment of 9 May 2014, concluded that the victim could only know the scope and the origin of the anticompetitive agreement as of the date of notification of the decision of the Spanish competition authority and that this date should be the starting date of the statute of limitation period. In the judgment, the judge of first instance of Madrid refers to the case law of the Spanish Supreme Court underlining that the start of the statute of limitation period ought to be interpreted restrictively. The Supreme Court reached this conclusion after mentioning that the statute of limitations is not based on the idea of intrinsic

---

101. *See* SANCHO, I. 'Ejercicio privado de las acciones basadas en el derecho comunitario y nacional de la competencia' in *InDret. Revista para el análisis del Derecho*, nº 1/2009, p. 18, citing Art. 434.3 of the Spanish Code of Civil Procedure: 'The time frame for the delivery of a judgment may be suspended in proceedings related to the application of Articles 81 and 82 of the Treaty of the European Community or Articles 1 and 2 of the Competition Act in case the court becomes aware of the existence of an administrative proceeding before the European Commission, the National Competition Authority or the Regional Competition Authorities, in case it is necessary to know the decision of the administrative authority. Such suspension of the delivery of a judgment shall be carried out by a reasoned decision, after hearing the parties, and it shall be notified to the administrative authority. This, in turn, has to deliver its decision to the court. Against this decision of suspension of the process there is only an internal appeal for reconsideration.' Please note that the Code of Civil Procedure says that it may be interrupted, not that it has to be interrupted.

justice (*justicia intrínseca*) but on the principle of legal certainty (*principio de seguridad jurídica*). This restrictive interpretation of the statute of limitation period has however been tempered by a flexible interpretation of the acts which interrupt this period as mentioned in Article 1973 of the Spanish Civil Code.[102]

230. In cases of contractual liability, the limitation period for bringing a claim challenging the validity of a contract because it has violated competition law rules is five years from the date upon which the contract was entered into, according to Article 1964 *in fine* of the Spanish Civil Code.[103]

4. Burden of Proof and Causal Link

231. According to the Supreme Court's approach (the Civil Chamber) in the judgments related to the sugar cartel (8 June 2012 and 7 November 2013), the facts considered as 'proven' in the administrative procedure, once they have been confirmed by the Administrative Courts, will generally be binding for the Civil Courts, and the margin for a different assessment related to the nature of those facts is, in practice, fairly limited (i.e., a different interpretation of the facts duly motivated would be possible, as long as it would not incur in a contradiction with the conclusions in the earlier judgments).

232. In this context, the claimant has generally to prove a loss as a result of the anticompetitive practice, as well as the causal link between the infringement and the loss. The Supreme Court appears to presume the existence of the loss from the very existence of the cartel in its Judgment of 8 June 2012, but still the claimant needs to prove the *quantum* of the damage suffered.[104]

233. Under Spanish law, in order for liability to arise without the need for fault or neglect misconduct, there must be an express provision to this effect in the relevant Act. Since there is no such express provision thus far, liability is based on the general rules on tort liability *ex* Article 1902 of the Civil Code, which requires the

102. *See* Judgments of the Spanish Supreme Court of 2 February 1984, 6 November 1987, 24 October 1988, 28 December 1989, 18 July 1994 and 26 September 1994.
103. According to the First Additional Provision of Act 42/2015, of 5 October, the statute of limitation period in cases of contractual liability was changed from fifteen years into five years. This provision entered into force on 7 October 2015.
104. *See* Judgment of the Supreme Court of 8 June 2012 (pages 10 and 11) holding that the higher prices paid by the victims due to the anticompetitive agreement were not justified was declared proven by the Appellate court when accepting the report of the expert. This report had quantified the damages caused to the victims arguing that the higher prices did not respond to increasing production costs and that the cartelist could not challenge these proven facts in the further appeal before the Supreme Court. Article 17.2 of the Directive foresees also that '*it shall be presumed that cartel infringements cause harm. The infringer shall have the right to rebut the presumption*'.

existence of fault or neglect on the part of the party causing the damage. It has been argued that in anticompetitive conducts fault is implied except in a case of an excusable error.[105]

234. There is no special provision under Spanish law with regard to the burden of proof in competition-based claims for damages. Therefore, and based on general principles, the burden of proof lies with the party which alleges a fact and wishes to obtain a benefit based on the existence of that fact according to Article 217 of the Code of Civil Procedure. This provision is in accordance with Article 2 of EU Regulation 1/2003, which states that the burden of proving an infringement of Article 101.1 TFEU or 102 TFEU shall rest on the party alleging the infringement. There is no specific legal provision with regard to the standard of proof required in actions for damages based on infringements of competition law. Thus, most forms of evidence will be judged according to the rules of reasonable assessment (*reglas de la sana crítica*)[106] when evaluating documents the law provides for certain *criteria* which have to be followed by the Court. Facts alleged by a party shall only be accepted as true if that party was personally involved in them, if the facts are entirely detrimental to it and if they are not contradicted by other pieces of evidence.[107] Public documents will stand as incontrovertible evidence of any fact or situation documented in them, the date on which they were documented and the identity of the people who took part in the documentation.[108] Private documents will have the same evidencing weight as public documents if they are accepted by the parties as being authentic. If such authenticity is not accepted by the parties or otherwise proved, the Court will assess them according to the rules of reasonable assessment.[109]

235. *Follow-on* actions may be more successful in practice. It is much easier to prove the existence of an infringement, if there is a prior final infringement decision of the European Commission, because the Spanish court has to accept that the infringement as established.[110] According to Article 9 of the Damages Directive, an infringement of competition law found by a final decision of the Spanish Competition Authority has also to be considered as irrefutably established for the purposes of an action for damages brought before a Spanish court. In such cases, the claimant only needs to prove causation and the amount of the loss suffered. Decisions from other national competition authorities may be accepted in Spain as evidence prima facie of the existence of an infringement.

---

105. *See* SANCHO GARGALLO, I.: 'Ejercicio privado de las acciones basadas en el derecho comunitario y nacional de la competencia', page 17.
106. In our case, Art. 348 of the Spanish Code of Civil Procedure is interesting, affirming that expert reports will be judged according to these rules of reasonable assessment.
107. *See* Art. 316 of the Spanish Code of Civil Procedure.
108. *See* Art. 319 of the Spanish Code of Civil Procedure.
109. *See* Art. 326 of the Spanish Code of Civil Procedure in connection with Art. 316 of the same code.
110. *See* Art. 16.1 of Council Regulation (EC) No 1/2003, of 16 December 2002 on the implementation of the rules on competition laid down in Arts 81 and 82 of the Treaty (Official Journal L 1, 04.01.2003, pp. 1–25).

236. In any case, the claimant has to prove a direct causal link between the infringement and any loss suffered. The claimant has to demonstrate that the damage is the direct consequence of the infringement. If the defendant alleges the existence of possible causes of the claimant's loss other than its own conduct, then a reversal of the burden of proof takes place, i.e., in this case the defendant will have the burden of proving those other causes and their effect on the claimant. In competition law cases the alleged non-existence of damages may be important because the exemption mentioned under Article 1.3 LDC (equivalent to Article 101.3 TFEU in Spain) must also be proven by the alleged infringer.

5. Passing-On Defence

237. In its judgments related to the sugar cartel, the Supreme Court considered that while the defendant can rely on the passing-on defence, any defendant raising this argument will have to prove this circumstance in court. Even if the passing-on would be proven, this would not exclude the existence of other losses that can be subject to compensation, as the higher prices passed-on can be just part of the loss suffered, such as fewer sales as a result of the higher prices.

238. In Spain there are neither exemplary nor punitive damages foreseen in the civil code. Only the losses directly suffered by a claimant may generally be compensated. Therefore, if a claimant has *passed-on* all or part of the inflated cost of the products to its clients and has thus minimized the loss incurred, the court will probably take this into account and either reduce the amount of the compensation accordingly or reject the claim for damages on the basis of lack of evidence of the losses suffered. Otherwise, such a situation could cause an unjust enrichment, and only compensatory damages are accepted in Spain, following the European tradition. Under Spanish legislation there is no presumption that higher prices have been 'passed-on' to the next level of the distribution chain or even to the consumers or end users. Therefore, any defendant raising this argument will have to prove it to the court in a sufficient manner, as also included as a rule regarding the burden of proof in this case in Article 13 of the Directive for the European level.

6. Quantification of Damages

239. Damages derived from an anticompetitive conduct are mainly calculated by aggregating the economic damage suffered by the claimant and the economic loss of profit, since claims can be connected to the emerging damage, lost profits and interests. These amounts must be proven by the claimant, either through expert reports or the documentation or evidence that the claimant can provide to the proceedings.

240. In addition, the Supreme Court, in its judgments related to the Spanish sugar cartel, made several considerations regarding damage quantification and the expert reports provided by the claimants quantifying their claims. In this sense, the

Supreme Court argued that when the expert reports have been calculated correctly based on the existence of a cartel and the fact that prices were higher than those resulting from free competition) using a reasonable and economically sound method accepted by courts of other jurisdictions, the defendants cannot refuse or deny the quantification provided by the applicants in their expert report without providing an alternative quantification that is better founded. In these cases, the Supreme Court awarded the full compensation requested by the claimants, as quantified in their expert reports.

241. Expert evidence is certainly one of the forms of evidence recognized in the Spanish Code of Civil Procedure. Each party may provide experts' reports to support its claims and arguments on the case and may request the oral examination of the experts in order to clarify, if necessary, the content of their reports before the Courts. The parties to the procedure are entitled to attach expert reports to their submissions, indicate that such report(s) will be provided as soon as possible or even apply for the appointment of an expert by the Court. Experts' reports may be sought either from an individual or from a legal entity. In the context of claims for damages, experts are usually instructed by the parties in order to prove and quantify the damage(s) and loss of profit allegedly caused by the conducts.

242. Besides, there are no specific guidelines for the calculation of damages resulting from anticompetitive conducts. Therefore, the general rule of '*restitutio in integrum*' contained in Article 1106 of the Spanish Civil Code, which seeks to restore the parties to the positions they would have been in but for the breach or infringement and which is also applicable to liability in tort, should be taken into account.[111]

243. The Spanish Code of Civil Procedure does not establish any specific economic system to be followed by experts when calculating loss for the purpose of civil proceedings. In theory, expert reports may use a variety of accounting and evaluation techniques aimed at identifying and supporting the calculation of the revenues and costs which would otherwise have been received and incurred if the anticompetitive conduct had not taken place. Normally, experts will elect the economic model which is most suited to the case.

244. It is generally considered that the more intelligible, credible and persuasive the evidence submitted by the claimant is, the greater the chance that the judge will be persuaded as to the existence of damage and its exact quantum. It should be objective in nature and supported, where possible, by reports of economics experts and by logical calculations. This is particularly true in the context of the calculation of the loss of profits, in view of the element of uncertainty associated with this type of damage.

111. *See* Art. 1106 of the Spanish Civil Code: '*Damages for loss comprise not only the value of the loss suffered, but also that of the gain that the creditor has been prevented from obtaining* (…).'

245. Please note that there are no established quantity limits in connection with claims for damages based on infringements of competition law in Spain (nor under general liability in tort).

7. Collective Actions

246. The LDC does not contain any specific rule related to the standing of classes, groups or representative bodies in order to bring actions challenging agreements or a claim for damages based on an anticompetitive conduct.

247. The legal framework for collective claims in Spain is contained in Article 11 of the Code of Civil Procedure. As a general rule, consumer and user associations are entitled to bring actions to protect the rights and interests of their members and of the association itself, and those who can be included in these groups. This Article provides that parties are entitled to claim for the protection of 'collective interests' before a court, when those affected by an act causing loss are a group of consumers or end-users whose members are readily ascertained or easily ascertainable. Please note that other types of affected groups (e.g., professional or trade associations) cannot make use of Article 11 to bring a collective action before a civil court. After the hypothetical judgment made within the framework of the collective claim, each applicant has to claim again to the court in order to be recognized as a member of the specific group and in order to quantify the individual damages the applicant has suffered.

8. Cost Rules in *Follow-On* and *Stand-Alone* Claims and Appeals to the Judgments of the Commercial Courts

248. As a general rule, the judge will order the unsuccessful party to pay the successful party's legal costs. This does not apply when the judge considers and explains in the judgment that there were serious doubts in fact or at law.[112] When the judge does not rule entirely in favour of either party, the judge might not expressly determine who has to pay the legal costs, in which case each party will pay its own costs.

249. When the unsuccessful party is ordered to pay legal costs, it will have to pay the lawyers' fees and those of other professionals whose fees are not fixed by official fee scales, which, in any event, cannot exceed one third of the amount of the proceedings in question.[113]

250. Alternative means of dispute resolution are theoretically available, thus, claims can be subject to arbitration procedures.

---

112. *See* Art. 394 of the Code of Civil Procedure.
113. *See* Arts 241–246 and Art. 394 of the Spanish Code of Civil Procedure.

9. Relevant Precedents in Spain: Damages Claims in the Sugar and in the Decennial Insurance Cartel

251. On 8 June 2012 the Spanish Supreme Court issued its first judgment on a *follow-on* action claiming compensation for damages resulting from an infringement of the cartel prohibition in Article 1 of the former 1989 Competition Act and Article 101 TFEU.[114] The judgment concerns the further appeal to the Spanish Supreme Court by Acor, a member of the Spanish sugar cartel, against the judgment of the Court of Appeal of Valladolid, in which the court ordered Acor to pay damages of EUR 1.1 million to nine food and sweets producers. On 10 September 1996, several industry associations in the food sector submitted a complaint to the Spanish competition authority, alleging collusive agreements relating to the sugar price. Following the complaint, the Spanish competition authority conducted an investigation of the Spanish sugar market. On 15 April 2005, the authority issued a fining decision against four producers and traders of sugar.[115] The competition authority fined different members of the sugar cartel because they had been fixing the sales price of sugar for industrial use between February 1995 and September 1996. According to the decision, Acor had participated in the cartel for a shorter period (from 1 September 1995 to September 1996). All cartel members appealed the decision of the CNC, first to the National High Court and subsequently to the Supreme Court. Both courts upheld the decision of the competition authority. The Supreme Court (Administrative Chamber) issued its Judgment on 26 April 2005, rendering the decision ultimately binding effects.

252. In November 2007, six food and sweet producers started legal proceedings against Acor, claiming damages resulting from the sugar cartel. Prior to the action, the plaintiffs had sent extrajudicial letters in accordance with Article 1973 of the Spanish Civil Code to the defendant in which they requested compensation. Article 1973 of the Spanish Civil Code provides the possibility of stopping the statute of limitations period. The plaintiffs made use of Article 13.2 LDC 16/1989 which was in force at the time of the infringement. The provision stated that the action for compensation of damages, based on the unlawfulness of the conducts prohibited by the Competition Act may be exercised by the ones who consider themselves injured, once the administrative decision and, if necessary, the jurisdictional statement, is binding. In consequence, the administrative procedure has to be concluded before starting a damages action procedure. It also affirmed that the substantive and procedural rules for the action for compensation of damages are the ones provided for in the civil laws.

---

114. *See* Schreiber, T. & Pérez Fernández, P. 'Judgment of the Spanish Supreme Court in *Acor* (344/2012) June 8, 2012' in *Global Competition Litigation Review*, nº 1, 2013, pp. 37–41 and Marcos, F. 'Damages Claims in the Spanish Sugar Cartel', in *Journal of Antitrust Enforcement*, Vol. 1, nº 3, 2015, pp. 205–225.

115. Case No. 426/1998 of 15 April 1999, available at http://www.cncompetencia.es/Inicio/Expedientes/tabid/116/Default.aspx (last time accessed: 7 February 2017).

253. Before the Court of First Instance, the plaintiffs argued that their action for an infringement of the cartel prohibition as set forth in the LDC was based on the non-contractual civil liability of cartel members. The legal basis for tort claims was therefore the general tort law liability in Article 1902 of the Spanish Civil Code. In accordance with that, the applicable limitation period was Article 1968.2 of the Spanish Civil Code which provides for a one-year limitation period, starting from the day when the victim knew about the damage he had suffered.

254. The plaintiffs argued that this was the date on which they became aware of the judgment of the Supreme Court which finally upheld the fining decision of the Spanish competition authority. Acor argued that the damages asserted in the action were not true. In particular, the defendant denied the existence of the alleged price overcharges, as well as the validity of the claim regarding the interest. Acor also opposed the statute of limitations for the claim, arguing that since the judgment of the Supreme Court more than one year had passed. Finally, Acor also denied the applicability of the general tort law provision of Article 1902 of the Spanish Civil Code.

255. By Judgment of 20 February 2009, the First Instance Court of Valladolid followed the argumentation of the defendant and dismissed the action. The plaintiffs filed an appeal against the judgment of the Court of First Instance to the Court of Appeal of Valladolid. In its judgment the Court of Appeal concluded that a damage was proven, consisting of '*the difference ... between the sugar price that the applicants had paid to Acor (...) and the price that should have been paid if this amount had been fixed according to the natural market price and not depending on the price fixing agreement*'. The Court of Appeal reached this conclusion after having considered the evidence provided by the parties. In particular, it took into account an economic expert opinion provided by the plaintiffs. In the appeal proceedings both parties had presented economic expert reports on the quantification of the damage caused by the sugar cartel to the plaintiffs. While the plaintiffs' report concluded that the cartel caused damages totalling EUR 1.1 million, the defendant's report concluded that the cartel had not resulted in damages at all. The Court of Appeal followed the argumentation of the plaintiffs' report as it considered that it was more likely that the cartel had resulted in a damage than not. On 9 October 2009, the Court of Appeal of Valladolid therefore revoked the judgment of the first instance court and awarded the plaintiffs damages totalling the mentioned amount of EUR 1.1 million. Acor filed an extraordinary appeal due to procedural infringements and a further appeal to the Supreme Court against the judgment of the Court of Appeal. The Supreme Court decided by Judgment of 8 June 2012.

256. The Supreme Court decided on relevant issues as for example the obligation to state reasons and burden of proof. Acor raised a number of procedural objections against the judgment of the Court of Appeal. Acor argued that the judgment failed to state all relevant factual and legal grounds and thus infringed the duty to state reasons. The facts allegedly omitted by the Court of Appeal mainly concerned the alleged justification of the sugar price in consideration of the production and storage costs as well as the alleged passing-on of the price overcharge by the plaintiffs. The Supreme Court rebutted these objections. It held that the right of litigants to obtain a legal reasoning does not authorize them to require that the argumentation has to be exhaustive in an absolute sense and that a judgment has to cover all aspects and perspectives presented in the matter. The Supreme Court also held that it was inadmissible to make use of the obligation to give reasons as an indirect means of challenging factual aspects of a judgment. The Supreme Court rebutted the objection that the judgment of the Court of Appeal infringed the principles of burden of proof. It held that in the present case, the Court of Appeal, after the decision of the Spanish competition authority had become binding, did not commit an error of law by finding that both the actual damage as well as the scope of the damage had been proven by the economic expert report so that the rules concerning the burden of proof had not been infringed.

257. Acor also argued an infringement of its constitutional right to an effective legal protection (Article 24 of the Spanish Constitution), based on the fact that the Court of Appeal had accepted the conclusions of the claimants' expert opinion while not accepting the conclusions of the expert report submitted by Acor. The Supreme Court did not agree with Acor. It held that the assessment of the evidence by the lower court did certainly fulfil the test of constitutionality as it was not contrary to the elementary rules of logic and experience. The Supreme Court thus implicitly confirmed the reasoning of the Court of Appeal that is was more likely that the cartel had caused damage than that it did not.

258. A main aspect of the dispute concerned the applicable statute of limitation provisions, in particular whether the limitation periods for contractual or non-contractual claims had to be applied. On this regard, the Supreme Court explored the legal nature of the liability of cartel members for damages caused by their anticompetitive conduct in some detail. The Supreme Court confirmed that the damages caused by the sugar cartel for which Acor was held responsible had to be qualified as tort and not as contractual liability. The tortious act was the horizontal price fixing agreement Acor had entered into with other sugar producers and which the Spanish competition authority found to have infringed the statutory cartel prohibition in Article 1(a) LDC 16/1989 and at the time Article 85(1) EC Treaty (nowadays Article 101.1 TFEU). According to the Supreme Court, these anticompetitive agreements resulted in an increase of the sugar prices in subsequent sales contracts of sugar. The tortious act which was the basis of the claim therefore had taken place prior to the conclusion of the sales contracts. Consequently, the claim was not based on a multitude of contractual claims, but on the infringement of the cartel prohibition by the cartel members. The Supreme Court specified that the plaintiffs did not claim a defective performance of any of the contractual obligations established by the sales contracts, related to the expressly agreed obligations or to accessory obligations based on the duties of good faith. Neither was the aim of the action the declaration of the invalidity of the sales contracts. Rather, the action for damages aims at obtaining compensation for the damages resulting from the illicit agreements restricting the free play of competition and autonomy by determining the price as one of the essential elements of the subsequent sales. The Supreme Court therefore concluded – referring to the Anglo-Saxon law principles and using the English terms – that the liability for infringements of competition law fall under '*the law of torts*' and not under '*the law of contracts*'. On the starting of limitation period the Supreme Court decided that it is one year after binding decision confirming the infringement.[116] Consequently, the Supreme Court did not follow the argumentation of Acor that the claims were time-barred. In the view of the Supreme Court, in accordance with Article 1969 of the Spanish Civil Code, the plaintiffs were not in a position to bring the action for damages foreseen in Article 13 of the 1989 Competition Act prior to the date on which they knew that the decision of the Spanish competition authority, which established the competition law infringement, had become binding. The limitation period of one year therefore started to run as of the date of the notification of the final judgment of the Supreme Court upholding the administrative prohibition decision. While the judgment of the Supreme Court dated of 26 April 2005, the notification of the judgment to the industry associations of which the plaintiffs were a member and which had participated as interested third parties in the administrative proceedings, only took place significantly later. The Supreme Court therefore concluded that the extrajudicial letters which the defendant received from the plaintiffs on various dates in 2006 validly interrupted the limitation period in accordance with Article 1973 of the Spanish Civil Code and that the damage action was not time-barred when the plaintiffs started legal proceedings in November 2007.

259. The Supreme Court affirmed also that limited cartel participation does not exclude causality for damage. Acor argued that the condition for the compensation of damages in form of a causal link between the illicit conduct and the damage was not fulfilled as its participation in the price fixing cartel was limited and could only be proven since 1 September 1995, while the other cartel members participated in the collusive agreements since 1 February 1995. The Supreme Court held that this difference regarding the cartel participation was not sufficient in order to exclude the causality of the infringement by the defendant as established by the Spanish competition authority for the damage incurred by the claimants. According to the Supreme Court, the judgment under appeal as well as the expert opinion which formed the basis of the calculation of the damage amount specifically took account of the differences in the periods during which Acor and the other cartel members had participated in the price fixing agreements so that this argument was dismissed.

260. The economic expert opinion of the claimants, which was the basis for the quantification of the damage awarded by the Court of Appeal, relied on a price comparison before, during and after the cartel. The Supreme Court confirmed this approach. In order to '*estimate the overcharge that was paid during the period of the agreement*' the expert correctly stated that it was necessary to establish '*a basis for this comparison, in order to compare the situation before and after the first*

116. According to Art. 1968.2 of the Spanish Civil Code the limitation period for non-contractual claims pursuant to Art. 1902 of the Spanish Civil Code is one year and starts to run as from the date the victim obtains knowledge of the illicit act.

change of the prices in September of 1995' and thus after Acor had joined the cartel. The Supreme Court set out that as a basis for this comparison the expert identified '*the prices received by Acor from its customers at the beginning of the mentioned year (January 1995)*', i.e., a time period prior to the defendant's participation in the illicit arrangements. The Supreme Court concluded that the Court of Appeal had not committed a legal mistake by relying on the expert opinion and that the technical criteria applied by the expert in preparing its opinion could not be reviewed in the context of the further appeal as it was related to the assessment of evidence and facts.

261. In connection with causality and the *passing-on defense*, the Supreme Court rebutted various arguments of Acor which alleged a wrongful application of the legal base of Article 1902 Spanish Civil Code by the Court of Appeal. The defendant alleged that the plaintiffs did not suffer any harm as they had freely agreed on the price and the price was justified in view of the production and distribution costs. Furthermore, the defendant alleged that the plaintiffs had in any event passed-on possible price overcharges to their own customers. The Supreme Court rebutted these arguments and held that the Court of Appeal had not committed an error in law. According to the Supreme Court, the Court of Appeal could rightly base its findings on the economic expert opinion submitted by the plaintiffs which affirmed that the sugar price was increased without a prior increase of the production costs and that the sugar price was not reduced despite a reduction of these costs.

262. With regard to the alleged lack of influence of the cartel agreements on the will of the plaintiffs to buy the product at the price fixed by the sugar manufacturers, the Supreme Court pointed to the decision taken by the Spanish competition authority that concluded that the collusive agreements were anticompetitive and negatively influenced the correct functioning of the laws of supply and demand. Regarding the alleged passing-on of any price overcharge by the defendants to their own customers, the Supreme Court held that the defendant did not support its allegations with any evidence. In the proceedings before the Court of Appeal the plaintiffs had specifically contested having passed-on the price overcharge to their customers and submitted various arguments in this respect. The defendant did not rebut these arguments. The Court of Appeal was therefore right in not declaring the passing-on proven.

263. As a general remark it can be affirmed that the Supreme Court clarified that the determination of the non-contractual liability and of the causal link between the damage and the illicit act is essentially of factual nature and therefore cannot be challenged in the context of a further appeal before the Supreme Court. The Supreme Court thus principally accepted that defendants may rely on the *passing-on defense*. However, they bear the burden of proof and have to provide substantive evidence in this respect and possibly have to rebut counter-arguments submitted by the plaintiffs.

264. The Supreme Court clarified the principles regarding the payment of interest in the context of antitrust damage claims. Acor had argued that the Court of

Appeal wrongly awarded interest on the damage amount as of the time the damage occurred although it was not in default. In addition, the defendant argued that the approach of the Court of Appeal would result in an allegedly illegal compounded interest as the interest had been accumulated on top of the damage amount. The Supreme Court rebutted these arguments and held that the Court of Appeal judgment was right in awarding the interest as of the date the damage occurred and in compounded form. The Supreme Court confirmed the view of the Court of Appeal that the payment of interest was part of the compensation for the damage caused to the plaintiffs as a result of the cartel agreements. Legal interest on the damage amounts was therefore not a way of sanctioning a delay in payment, but a means to adjust the scope of the damages occurred twelve years before. Legal interest thus has to be imposed for compensatory reasons and is directly related to the purchasing power of the currency between the date of the infringement and the date of the judgment. The Supreme Court concluded that this adjustment was necessary in order to ensure the full compensation of the damage in accordance with the principle of real equality. Without specifically mentioning it, the judgment of the Spanish Supreme Court is thus in line with the Manfredi judgment of the CJEU which states that '*interest ... constitutes an essential component of compensation*'.

265. The Judgment of the Spanish Supreme Court of 8 June 2012 is in line with the approach taken also by other Supreme Courts in other Member States, as for example in Austria[117] and Germany.[118] As mentioned, the Spanish Supreme Court confirmed that damage claims resulting from an infringement of a statutory cartel prohibition are of a tortious and thus non-contractual nature. The Spanish Supreme Court clarified that the rather short limitation period of one year foreseen for tort claims in Article 1968.2 of the Spanish Civil Code only starts once the victim has obtained knowledge that the decision establishing the infringement has become final and binding. In the case at hand the one-year limitation period therefore started running once the plaintiffs had received knowledge of the Supreme Court judgment upholding the fining decision of the Spanish competition authority against the sugar cartel. The Spanish Supreme Court in principle admitted that defendants may invoke the *passing-on defense*, bearing the burden of proof in this respect. As the defendant had not substantially rebutted the arguments of the claimants that passing-on was economically not viable, the Supreme Court held that the Court of Appeal was right not to consider the *passing-on defense* in its judgment. The Spanish Supreme Court also upheld the Court of Appeal judgment in as far as it relied on the economic expert opinion submitted by the claimants. In the report the economic expert had estimated the damage caused by the sugar cartel to the plaintiffs, using a before/after comparator method. The Supreme Court confirmed the approach taken by the Court of Appeal that, based on the decision of the Spanish competition authority, had assumed that it was more likely that the cartel had resulted in a damage than not. With regard to the damage amount to be compensated the Spanish Supreme Court held that the principle of full compensation and the principle of

117. *See Oberster Gerichtshof*, Judgment of 2 August 2012, reference 4 Ob 46/12m.
118. *See Bundesgerichtshof*, Judgment of 28 June 2011, reference KZR 75/10 — ORWI.

'effective monetary equality' require compounded interest as of the time the damage occurred. Therefore, the judgment of the Spanish Supreme Court is in line with the Manfredi Judgment of the CJEU which requires interest as an essential component of compensation.[119]

The second judgment of the Spanish Supreme Court dealing with a damages case after a cartel is the one of 7 November 2013. In this judgment the Supreme Court decides a second time about a *follow-on* action for compensation for damages caused by the sugar cartel between 1995 and 1996. This judgment resolves appeals and extraordinary procedural infringements Spain presented by Nestlé SA, SAU Lacasa, Zahor SA and other companies operating in the confectionery industry against the judgment of the Court of Appeal of Madrid. The Court of Appeal of Madrid had dismissed the lawsuit filed against one of the sugar cartel members, Ebro Puleva SA (currently Ebro Foods SA). The Supreme Court sentenced the defendant Ebro Foods SA to pay EUR 4.1 million to the fourteen claimants in compensation for damages, upholding the appeal filed by the victims of the cartel.

266. In the Judgment of 7 November 2013, the Supreme Court gets to deliver on key issues such as the burden of proof, the admissibility of the *passing-on defense* and the importance of expert reports to determine the amount of damage suffered. The Supreme Court also ruled on the importance of the pronouncements of the administrative courts with respect to the civil courts.

267. Regarding the facts proven by the administrative court, according to the Supreme Court in this judgment, the Court of Appeal of Madrid had not followed the anticompetitive facts asserted by the administrative courts, claiming that there was no agreement between several sugar companies, including Ebro Foods SA. The Supreme Court stressed that the successive ascents and descents or even the maintenance of the sugar prices are the materialization of a cartel, which was prohibited according to both Spanish and European legislation on competition. The First Chamber (civil chamber) of the Spanish Supreme Court considered in this judgment that the facts found by the Third Chamber (administrative chamber) were binding regarding this judgment, because '*the factual scenario on which resolutions were passed and one other jurisdiction is, as to the existence of a practice restrictive of competition, the same because what is sought in the civil courts is the compensation for damages caused by the cartel whose work was the subject of the judgment of the administrative court, which prosecuted the anticompetitive behavior from the point of view of sanctioning administrative law*'. According to the principle of legal certainty, '(...) [it] *cannot be accepted that certain facts exist and cease to exist for the organs of the State* (...)'. According to the Supreme Court, the Provincial Court does not take into account as proven the facts established by the administrative courts without adequately explaining the reasoning of this decision. Furthermore, since this is a *follow-on* damages claim, the decision of the administrative court is particularly relevant in terms of its effect with regard to binding and related civil jurisdiction related to the facts. The Supreme Court also held that the

119. Judgment of the Court of Justice of the European Union of 13 July 2006, C-295/04 to C-298/04, *Vicenzo Manfredi v. Lloyd Adriatico Assicurazioni SpA*, paras 95, 97 and 100.

defendant Ebro Foods SA had made use of all the defence mechanisms which were available, both before the competition authority and to the administrative courts (National High Court – *Audiencia Nacional* – and Supreme Court).

268. The Supreme Court confirmed in this judgment the admissibility of the *passing-on defense* by the defendant. This reminds that compensation for damages resulting from illegal anticompetitive has only a compensatory aim, avoiding unjust enrichments. In this case, however, the *passing-on defense* was not accepted because the defendant Ebro Foods SA had failed to prove this extent.

269. In connection with the calculation of damages suffered by the claimants, the Supreme Court highlights the importance of the expert report which was submitted by the victims. The Supreme Court recognizes the difficulty of predicting which would have been the situation in the sugar market in case the cartel had not occurred and appreciates that the report in this case makes a reasonable hypothesis of what would have been the price evolution based on '*verifiable and not misleading data*'.

270. Finally, it is also worth mentioning the Judgment of the Commercial Court (*Juzgado de lo Mercantil*) Number 12 of Madrid, of 9 May 2014. This judgment is delivered after an 'anticipated *follow-on* action'[120] related to the Spanish Property Insurance Cartel.[121] Regarding the start of the statute of limitation period, the judge decided that the victim could only know the scope and the origin of the anticompetitive agreement as of the decision of the Spanish competition authority. This first instance judge of Madrid refers to the above-mentioned case law of the Spanish Supreme Court underlining that the statute of limitations period has to follow a restrictive approach, avoiding any extensive interpretation. The Supreme Court reached this conclusion mentioning that the statute of limitation period is not based on the idea of intrinsic justice (*justicia intrínseca*) but on the principle of legal certainty (*principio de seguridad jurídica*) and that this necessary restrictive interpretation of the statute of limitation period entails a flexible interpretation of the acts which interrupt this period as mentioned in Article 1973 of the Spanish Civil Code.[122]

120. *See* MARCOS, F. 'Indemnización de daños y perjuicios por boicot a raíz del cártel del seguro de daños decenal (SDD): Notas a propósito de la sentencia del juzgado mercantil n° 12 de Madrid de 9 de mayo de 2014 (MUSAAT v. ASEFA, CASER y SCOR)' in *La Ley mercantil*, 29 July 2014, available at http://bit.ly/1klSXiM (last time accessed: 7 February 2017).

121. On the functioning of this cartel, *see* MARCOS, F. 'The Spanish Property Insurance Cartel' in *Connecticut Insurance Law Journal*, n° 18, Spring 2012, pp. 509–529.

122. *See* Judgments of the Spanish Supreme Court of 2 February 1984; 6 November 1987; 24 October 1988; 28 December 1989; 18 July 1994 and 26 September 1994.

C. Interim Measures

271. Interim measures can be granted by commercial courts in Spain, e.g., the suspension of the agreement or contract for which the declaration of nullity has been claimed, or the cessation of the conduct assumed to be anticompetitive.

272. Spanish law allows a wide range of interim measures. Article 727 of the Spanish Code of Civil Procedure includes an open list of measures that can be requested before Spanish courts, e.g., the freezing of property or assets, the judicial administration of goods, the deposit of goods, different orders of cessation like the provisional cessation of the activity being carried out, the order to refrain carrying out particular actions or behaviours or the deposit of benefits obtained by illegal activities. Before adopting an interim measure, the court has to verify that the conditions mentioned in Article 728 of the Spanish Code of Civil Procedure are fulfilled. First, there should exist a certain risk derived from the delay in the adoption of the measure (*periculum in mora*).[123] Second, there should be a presumption of a sufficient legal basis, i.e., the presentation of a prima facie case or 'appearance of good right' (*fumus boni iuris*). In competition cases, the existence of a previous decision by the competition authority is supposed to be very useful in demonstrating the seriousness of a case before the judge, in order to be successful when claiming the interim measure.[124] The assumption regarding the possibility that the right claimed exists in practice has to be examined by the judge in charge of deciding on the claim related to the interim measure. Finally, unless it is otherwise expressly affirmed, the applicant shall provide a deposit or guarantee. The judge has to decide the adequate amount of the deposit, taking always into account the nature and content of the measure claimed and the intensity of *fumus boni iuris* in question.

273. According to Article 725 of the Spanish Code of Civil Procedure, interim measures have to be requested either together with the main claim or before this moment.

274. An example of a request and award of an interim measure is the fine of EUR 400,000 imposed against the Regulating Councils of the Denominations of

123. This means that interim measures directed at modifying a situation that has long been permitted by the claimant are not allowed. This could be the situation when the interim measure consists of the suspension of a contractual clause for which nullity is demanded, in which the validity of an anti-competitive clause is questioned but had been permitted de facto and complied with by the claimant for a long time. This could be very important in competition cases.

124. *See also* Art. 9.1 of the *Directive 2014/104/EU of the European Parliament and of the Council of 26 November 2014 on certain rules governing actions for damages under national law for infringements of the competition law provisions of the Member States and of the European Union*, providing that: 'Member States shall ensure that an infringement of competition law found by a final decision of a national competition authority or by a review court is deemed to be irrefutably established for the purposes of an action for damages brought before their national courts under Article 101 or 102 TFEU or under national competition law.' Article 9.2 foresees the situation when the decision of the competition authority has been taken in another Member State, ensuring that the final decision may be presented before the national courts of a different Member State as 'at least *prima facie* evidence that an infringement of competition law has occurred'.

Origin of 'Jérez-Xérès-Sherry' and 'Manzanilla Sanlúcar de Barrameda' for anticompetitive agreements which were declared to restrict free competition and commercial freedom between wineries. The CNC Council imposed this fine in its Resolution of 4 June 2009.[125] The decision was appealed before the National High Court (*Audiencia Nacional*), and this court lowered the fine to the amount of EUR 100,000 by Judgment of 22 November 2010.[126] Interim measures were requested by the complainant undertakings to both the former CNC (suspension of an agreement of the Council of the Denomination of Origin) and the Commercial court number 1 of Cádiz.[127]

§3. CRIMINAL ENFORCEMENT

I. Criminal Sanctions for Antitrust Violations

275. According to the Spanish competition act, competition infringements are mainly handled as administrative infringements and therefore usually no criminal penalties are imposed. However, the Spanish criminal code provides a few exceptions where cartel conducts are sanctioned with imprisonment penalties. Article 284 of the criminal code refers to price distortion impeding free competition,[128] providing imprisonment penalties from six months up to two years, together with fines from one to two years. This criminal provision is not aimed to protect consumers' interests, rather it is supposed to protect the proper functioning of the market through the protection of free competition.[129] This Article is supposed to criminalize an abstract danger to free competition, without having to prove that a specific case has been in fact dangerous.[130]

276. Article 262 of the criminal code refers to bid rigging in auctions and public tenders and provides imprisonment penalties from one year up to three years, together with daily fines from one to two years and loss of licences from three to five years for public bidding.[131] In this case the crime is supposed to be committed if money is requested in order not to participate in a public tender and no specific result is required. This provision of the criminal code could also be applied in case

125. CNC Resolution of 4 June 2009, Proceedings 2779.07.
126. *See* Judgment of the *Audiencia Nacional* of 22 November 2010, number of appeal 365/2009.
127. The summary of this proceeding is available at http://bit.ly/1MazrCc (last time accessed: 7 February 2017).
128. This danger of price distortion is supposed to happen, according to Art. 284 of the Spanish Criminal Code, through the dissemination of false information, using violence, threat or deception, or privileged information. This Article was amended by the Organic Law 5/2010, of 22 June, amending the Spanish Criminal Code.
129. In this sense, *see*, for example, the Judgment of the Provincial Court of Madrid of 21 February 2001.
130. *See* extensively, ESTRADA, A. 'Presente y futuro del delito de alteración de precios' in *InDret. Revista para el análisis del Derecho,* n° 1, 2014, pp. 1–50, p. 7 ff, available at http://www.indret.com/pdf/1024.pdf (last time accessed: 7 February 2017).
131. This Article was amended by Organic Law 15/2003, of 25 November, amending the Spanish Criminal Code.

the perpetrator tries to avoid that other bidders participate in the tender by means of threats, rewards, promises or any other similar method, as well as if several bidders agree to alter the prices or to leave the tender after having awarded the good.

277. Article 281 of the criminal code may be applied to unlawful competition conducts consisting of withdrawing raw materials or essential goods from the market in order to limit supplies or distort prices, with an imprisonment penalty of one to five years and criminal fines of one to two years.

278. Besides these provisions included in the criminal code, the LDC does not provide for criminal sanctions for antitrust violations, but it foresees in Article 46 LDC the obligation of the CNMC to suspend its proceedings if there are parallel criminal investigations based on the same conduct brought by the Public Prosecution Service or by victims of the infringing conduct. To date we are not aware of any actions against cartels brought under the Spanish criminal code which have been successful.[132]

II. Other Application of Criminal Law to Relevant Conducts

279. See §3.I.

III. Role of Prosecutors

280. None.

IV. Competent Criminal Courts

281. According to Article 14.3 of the Spanish code of criminal procedure, the criminal courts of first instance are the competent ones for the hearing and judgment of the cases derived from criminal offences which do not exceed a penalty of five years of imprisonment or a fine of whatever amount. There is, at least, one criminal Court of First Instance in each of the fifty Spanish provinces.

132. For a brief summary of the evolution in other Member States regarding the criminal sanctions for cartels and its enforcement in practice, *see* Pérez Fernández, P.: 'Repaso de las sanciones penales por ilícitos anticompetitivos en Europa', available at http://bit.ly/1Jj88V1 (last time accessed: 7 February 2017).

Part II. The Application of the Prohibitions

Chapter 1. Restrictive Agreements

§1. Horizontal Agreements

I. Cartels

A. Price Fixing

282. Article 1 LDC foresees a prohibition of anticompetitive agreements in Spain. This provision foresees that any agreement, decision or collective recommendation, as well as any concerted or consciously parallel practice whose object or effect is the prevention, restriction or distortion of competition in all or part of the Spanish market has to be considered as a prohibited conduct by the Spanish competition rules. Article 1 LDC includes an open list of agreements which shall be considered as anticompetitive.

283. In particular, paragraph a) mentions agreements which are aimed to directly or indirectly fix prices or any other commercial or service terms. According to the second paragraph of the Fourth Additional Provision of the LDC a cartel is defined as '*any secret agreement between two or more competitors which has as its object fixing prices, production or sales quotas, sharing markets including bid rigging or restricting imports or exports*'.

284. In line with Regulation 1/2003, the LDC 15/2007 abolished the system of individual exemptions when it entered into force on 1 September 2007. Therefore, the prohibition described above will not automatically apply if the criteria set out in Article 1.3 LDC can be observed in a specific case. It can also be expected that European Commission block exemptions will also apply to agreements even in the absence of a cross-border impact. In addition, the Spanish government is empowered to adopt block exemptions; i.e., Royal Decree 602/2006, of 19 May, implementing the block exemption regulation on late payments information exchange agreements.[133]

285. On 7 November 2012, the CNC fined six shipping companies for participating in a cartel affecting maritime transport of passengers and cargo between the

133. *See Boletín Oficial del Estado* (Official Spanish Gazette) of 31 May 2006.

Spanish Peninsula and Morocco.[134] Total fines were over EUR 88.5 million.[135] The evidence to initiate this investigation was obtained in a dawn raid conducted by the CNC in the headquarters of the shipping companies. Subsequent inspections provided additional evidence of meetings, information exchanges, agreements on prices, commissions, trading conditions and schedules of the different routes. The cartel had been operating between 2002 and 2010. When calculating the amount of the fines, the CNC took into account the seriousness of the infringement, its duration, the scope of the illegal practice and the serious impact on public interest, given that the cartel affected the connection between the Peninsula and Northern Africa. Additionally, several companies received a 5% increase in their fines for recidivism. Baleària received a 40% reduction because of its leniency application.

286. On 10 January 2013, the CNC imposed fines totalling more than EUR 20 million on the trade associations ALTC and Cotransport, as well as on the Port Authority of Barcelona for participating in a cartel affecting the road transport of containers to and from the port of Barcelona.[136] ALTC and Transcont jointly developed the applicable prices, payment terms and discounts applicable to containers transported by road to or from the port of Barcelona. Lorries were counted, increasing this way any fleet required prior authorization from the associations. Also, an individual authorization to enter the port was necessary and monitored to confirm that the agreed conditions were consistently being applied by the members of the cartel. In order to eliminate competition between carriers, a price list had been drafted within the cartel and sent to final customers intermediaries, such as freight forwarders, consignees or customs agents in an attempt to promote those rates as standard port rates. Barcelona's Port Authority was also found liable for this infringement because of its participation in the organization and operation of the cost observatory and the preparation of the relevant documents in order to calculate transport costs.

287. On 28 February 2013, the CNC imposed fines totalling more than EUR 26 million on ten companies and the sector association for being parties to a cartel on the market for the manufacture of flexible polyurethane foam for the comfort industry, which consisted of price fixing and market sharing agreements.[137] These proceedings were initiated by a leniency application of Recticel Ibérica S.L., which was exempted from paying the fine together with its parent company. The CNC stated that the companies had agreed prices and shared out production by reference to quotas that the operators could not exceed. The members of the cartel focused their collusion on agreements regarding price increases taking into account the increase in sales of Portuguese competitors.

134. *See* CNC Resolution of 7 November 2012, Proceedings S/0331/11.
135. A few months before, on 23 February 2012, had already fined four maritime transport companies operating in the Baleàric Islands (*Baleària Eurolíneas, Marítimas, Compañía Trasmediterránea and Isleña Marítima de Contenedores*) for more than EUR 54 million for having participated in a cartel on the maritime passenger transport lines for cargo and passengers that connects the Spanish mainland with the Baleàric islands and the Islands itself with one another.
136. *See* CNC Resolution of 10 January 2013, Proceedings S/0293/10.
137. *See* CNC Resolution of 28 February 2013, Proceedings S/0342/11.

288. On 25 March 2013, the CNC imposed fines to fifteen companies for taking part in a cartel in the paper handling sector.[138] The CNC considered that the companies reached an agreement to share the Spanish market between 1977 and 2010. The CNC affirmed that the companies involved had agreed to share tenders for pre-printed envelopes for elections and political parties, fixing also prices, to share out the manufacture of pre-printed corporate envelopes for large customers, to fix prices for blank envelopes and to limit technological developments in the paper envelope market throughout Spain. The CNC imposed fines amounting EUR 44 million. Unipapel, one of the participants of the cartel, could avoid the fine because of its leniency application. Antalis received a 40% reduction regarding the amount of the fine and the Tompla group received a 30% reduction for having provided valuable information.

289. On 26 June 2014 the CNMC fined six manufactures of fire equipment with fines of more than EUR 2 million because it considered proven that the companies had been participating in price fixing and market sharing agreements between July 2010 and February 2012.[139] The CNMC characterized the conduct as a very serious infringement due to its nationwide geographic scope and the high combined market shares of the participants in the cartel. Todoextintor was exempted from an EUR 265,411 fine due to its leniency application, and for providing evidence that allowed the CNMC to launch an investigation related to the cartel.

B. Market/Client Allocation

290. Article 1 c) LDC mentions as a second example of anticompetitive conducts the share of markets or sources of supply. The horizontal allocation of markets and customers is also prohibited. It is generally acknowledged that market and customer allocation agreements are at least as pernicious as price-fixing agreements. It could even be worse for free competition, since the allocation of markets or customers can be monitored more easily and does not allow for cheating by improving non-price parameters.

291. On 19 October 2011, the CNC sanctioned forty-seven companies that had participated in a cartel related to public tenders for the execution of works on roads, regarding the preservation, improvement, renovation and rehabilitation of road surfaces and platforms with fines over EUR 47 million.[140] The authority concluded that the investigated companies had established a structured system in order to share the market by bid rigging conducts. According to the CNC, the cartel affected at least fourteen public tenders in Spain. The participants would have held secret contacts and attended several meetings, in order to share the content of the offers to be filed by each of them. This system allowed the participants to anticipate the decision of the competent authority. When the information was shared and the potential bidder

138. *See* CNC Resolution of 25 March 2013, Proceedings S/0316/10.
139. *See* CNC Resolution of 26 June 2014, Proceedings S/0445/12.
140. *See* CNC Resolution of 19 October 2011, Proceedings S/0226/10.

and its economical offer identified, the offer would include a discount below the one previously considered. A lower discount meant here a greater profit for the bidder to win the public tender. The participants had agreed on a system by means of which the winner would compensate the rest of the agreement members. The CNC declared that the collusive behaviour of the infringers restricts competition by its object and effects, therefore the Council assessed the conduct as a single infringement under Article 1 of the LDC, taking into account that each agreement was part of a common strategy.

292. On 2 December 2011, the CNC sanctioned a number of manufacturers and retailers of fruit and vegetable containers (INFIA, ILPA and Veripack Embalajes) for having participated in a cartel whose purpose was to fix prices and share the market a total amount of over EUR 11 million.[141] The proceedings were initiated thanks to a leniency application made by INFIA, thus, it was exempted from the payment of the fine. According to the CNC, by the end of each year from 1999 until 2005, the undertakings held annual meetings, usually in Italy, in order to agree on the prices applicable to a series of categories and sizes of certain containers. The infringers agreed on the prices and amounts to be included in their responses to bidding offers issued by large customers, such as cooperatives and associations of cooperatives. The CNC concluded that the conduct qualified as a continuing anti-competitive conduct materially consisting of price fixing and market sharing which were repeated each year at the beginning of the marketing campaign and which together constituted a plan aimed at restricting or distorting competition in the fruit and vegetable containers market.

293. Another example of a market sharing cartel was the fine of more than EUR 54 million imposed by the CNC on 23 February 2012 on different shipping companies.[142] The reason was their participation in a cartel on shipping lines for freight and passengers that connects the Iberian Peninsula and the Baleàric Islands, and the Baleàric Islands with one another. The Council of Ibiza had presented a complaint in April 2010 against Trasmediterránea and Baleària in relation to an alleged conduct prohibited by the LDC. The main argument consisted of the adoption of agreements, the purpose of which would be market sharing and price fixing, in imposing unfair trading conditions in the market for liner passengers and goods between the Iberian Peninsula and the Baleàric Islands. The CNC extended the investigation to other companies after carrying out first inspections. In its Resolution, the CNC declared that between 2001 and 2010, Baleària, Trasmediterránea and Isleña Marítima de Contenedores had taken part in a cartel for market sharing in the shipping lines of goods and passengers between the Iberian Peninsula and the Baleàric Islands. In addition, the CNC concluded that, between 1995 and 2011, Baleària, Sercomisa and Mediterránea Pitusa reached various agreements sharing the shipping market between Ibiza and Formentera.

141. *See* CNC Resolution of 2 December 2011, Proceedings S/0251/10.
142. *See* CNC Resolution of 23 February 2012, Proceedings S/0244/10.

C. Production/Innovation Limitation

294. Article 1 b) LDC mentions the limit or control of the production, distribution, technical development or investments as anticompetitive agreements. Output restrictions very often accompany price-fixing agreements and are also prohibited.

D. Group Boycott

295. Under Spanish law the unilateral recommendation by an undertaking or an association of undertakings to another undertaking or association to boycott a third undertaking may be considered as an anticompetitive conduct according to Article 1 LDC.

296. Also, decisions of associations of undertakings are prohibited when they are aimed to coordinate the behaviour of different undertakings in the market, regardless of any market power of the entity making the recommendation and regardless of whether or not the addressees follow the recommendation. The reasoning is that those associations could be a forum where cartels are organized or where confidential information between the associated undertakings is exchanged. Thus, it is recommended not to discuss in the meetings of the association about prices, the capacity or volume of production, sales strategies, inventory, quota or allocation of the market, expectations about future market developments or advertising rules, just to mention a few aspects.

297. On 24 March 2009 the CNC fined four pharmacist associations between EUR 150,000 and EUR 400,000 for attempting to boycott a producer of generic drugs in an effort to prevent price decreases.[143] The boycott consisted of providing misleading or false information to pharmacists and recommending that they should not sell the producer's products.

298. In its Decision of 26 September 2012, the CNC fined the Spanish Confederation of Business Organizations (CEOE) EUR 150,000 and the President of the Tourism Council of this confederation EUR 50,000 for a collective price recommendation. The CNC considered that certain statements of the President had to be understood as a collective recommendation in breach of Article 1.1 LDC.[144]

299. On 29 November 2012, the CNC imposed fines of more than EUR 1 million on three associations from the grape growing and designation of origin sector

143. *See* CNC Resolution of 24 March 2009, Proceedings 649/08.
144. *See* CNC Resolution of 26 September 2012, Proceedings S/0335/11. On 19 January 2011, Mr Joan Gaspart Solves made statements in the Spanish International Tourism Fair (FITUR) regarding the need to increase hotel prices in Spain. He repeated the same statements in an interview which was published in the newspaper *Cinco Días* on 26 January 2011, mentioning a quantified increase of 6%–7%. In order to determine if this conduct could be defined as a collective recommendation according to Art. 1.1 LDC, the CNC Council analysed the content of this recommendation, the extent to which it had been disseminated and who exactly had made the recommendation.

(*Valdepeñas* wine).[145] The CNC had found out that within several associations exchanges of information had been taken place, which were also related to the reduction of prices in order to avoid that winemakers could decide which price they wanted to pay on their own.[146] The CNC discovered strategic documents containing agreements which had been reached between the different production sector to determine the pricing policy for the purchase of grapes, in order to define the different price bands and the creation of a Committee in order to prove if the different associations were following these agreements.

E. Collusion on Other Objects

300. Exchanges on sensitive information are going to be analysed in *infra* II from a competition law perspective.

301. With regard to collusion on other objects the Resolution of the council of the CNC of 21 January 2010 in *Fabricantes de gel*[147] can be mentioned as an example of the activity of the Spanish authority. In this case, the CNC affirmed that there had been an exchange of information which had collusive effects on the market, due to the relevance of the information exchanged and thus, the information exchanges were 'inherent to the cartel'. The agreement entailed also phased implementation of changes in the formats of the products, besides an exchange of information related to the prices, without raising the product price, as a means of making an increase in the unit price paid by consumers.[148] In this case the exchange of information (of prices, formats, etc.) which took place between this different manufacturers and competitors was the beginning of the cartel.

II. Information Exchange Practices

302. In a competitive market, companies should set its trade and price policy in an independent way. Companies should not exchange any sensitive commercial information that could affect competition in the markets between them.

145. *See* CNC Resolution of 29 November 2012, Proceedings S/0305/10.
146. This case was initiated by the then existing Regional Competition authority of Castilla-la Mancha, describing a possible breach of the competition rules. This competition authority had started an investigation following different Articles which had appeared in the media and which referred to the possible conduct of businesses with respect to the conditions for the purchase of grapes used to produce this wine.
147. CNC Resolution of 21 January 2010, Proceedings S/0084/08.
148. The first meeting held that the companies shared its decision to reduce the format of its gel packs while maintaining price, inviting those present at the meeting to follow that policy and telling them it would be prepared to show the new formats in the following meetings. The price increase was achieved by selling the gel in a smaller container (it was reduced from 750 ml to 650 ml) than the one previously marketed, while maintaining the same price per container. From June 2006 to May 2007 Henkel, Sara Lee and Puig reduced the capacity of the containers for some of their brands (La Toja, Sanex, etc.) by 15%. Colgate did the same from April 2008 onwards. The CNC Resolution is available at http://bit.ly/1nOqkWm (last time accessed: 7 February 2017).

303. Information exchange practices between competitors may either generate efficiencies, benefits or negative effects on competition. Therefore this kind of practices should be analysed on a case-by-case basis rather than to be sanctioned per se as it happens with *hard-core cartels*. Thus, in determining whether an agreement on exchange of information between competing firms has to be considered as an anticompetitive conduct, it is necessary to take into account the economic and legal context in which the exchange takes place, especially the economic conditions in the market, which means carrying out an analysis if the market is highly concentrated or if it has an atomized structure. The characteristics of the system are also important, e.g., the type of data exchanged. An exchange of information which is part of a cartel should always be considered as an illegal conduct. Exchanges of information can help to monitor compliance with the illegal agreement or cartel, enabling the identification of breach of the agreement and coercing participants to enforce the agreement. In these cases exchanges of information are considered as a tool in order to run an anticompetitive agreement itself. When an exchange of information does not complement an anticompetitive agreement or cartel, it can be considered as a lawful conduct, in any case the exchange has to be examined based on the current or potential effects that this specific exchange of information will have on the market.

304. In Spain, two main criteria have been taken into account and analysed cumulatively. These criteria represent the characteristics of the information exchange and the nature of the market in which the exchange of information has taken or is taking place. In general terms it can be said that information exchange practices may be considered anticompetitive when the exchanged information is particularly sensitive, specific and individualized.[149]

305. In the Resolution *Distribuidores Cinematográficos,*[150] the TDC considered that the creation of a database within a federation of movie distributors containing information on planned dates of releases, attendance and revenue figures for types of films, movies as well as cities, was a key element for the competitors in order to determine a joint commercial strategy. Among the strategic data exchanged there were future releases dates for over a year in advance, information related to the revenues by movies, the week of exhibition and other information which produced the effect of restricting competition in the markets according to the authority. The database facilitated the control of a restrictive practice carried out by the distribution companies. Finally the conduct was qualified as an anticompetitive and a single and continuous infringement under LDC 16/1989.

306. The TDC analysed if these exchanges of statistical information between companies, usually carried out within associations, were compatible with the rules

---

149. *See*, for example, the Judgment of the Spanish Supreme Court, Chamber of the Contentious-Administrative (third chamber), of 14 February 2007.

150. TDC Resolution of 10 May 2006, number 588/05, *Distribuidores Cinematográficos*.

of free competition.[151] The TDC affirmed in *Fecavem*[152] that the exchange of information should be based on the rules and principles of statistics. In case these rules are replaced by subjective estimations made by companies involved in the information exchange, this conduct could constitute a violation of Article 1 LDC.

307. The TDC has also clarified a number of features related to the nature of the information exchanged that would make the system compatible with competition law. A system of exchange of information could be accepted if the kind of information exchanged has a historical character, even if the data is collected on a monthly basis.[153] The TDC has also accepted a varied nature of the information exchanged, taking into account elements like for example sales volumes or average prices, as well as the geographical situation. According to this latter aspect, a dispersion of the information between regions is accepted in case this geographical market is not highly concentrated or, in this case, if there is a guarantee that data information is disseminated during at least six months.

308. In *Anuario Videográfico,*[154] the TDC accepted that an exchange of information had not to be considered as an anticompetitive agreement and was, thus, compatible with competition law because a Secretary of an Association, which had absolutely no link with the associated parties and was subject to a confidentiality agreement, had been participating in the collection and processing of the data.

309. It is generally admitted that some characteristics of the information contribute to consider the exchange system as a competition rules complying one. For example, if the access to the information is public or if there are similar publications of information both from public administrations and from private consultancy firms. It has been also considered that an exchange of information system is not anticompetitive if there are many competitors in a certain market, the possibility that any party participating in the exchange of information can disengage from this exchange system, as well as when the information deals with products or services which are not homogeneous, or when the market presents a low degree of brand loyalty.

310. The TDC declared in its Resolution *Información Estadística Fenil*[155] that a decision of the National Federation of Dairy Industries (*Federación Nacional de Industrias Lácteas*) aimed to set up a plan to collect aggregate data on prices and volumes of milk marketed by Spain's Autonomous Regions was not an anticompetitive behaviour. The TDC decided that the production on statistics in accordance with the principles and rules of scientific discipline was a lawful conduct which did

151. *See*, for example, TDC Resolutions of 9 April 2002, *Anuario Videográfico*, Proceedings A 296/01; of 1 March 2003, *Información Estadística Fenil*, Proceedings A 309/01, and of 30 March 2004, *Estadísticas Cerveceros*, Proceedings A 329/02.
152. *See* the TDC Resolution of 29 June 1995, *Fecavem*, Proceedings 358/95.
153. *See* in this sense the TDC Resolution of 1 March 2002, Proceedings A 309/01, *Información estadística FENIL*.
154. TDC Resolution of 9 April 2002, Proceedings A 296/01, *Anuario Videográfico*.
155. TDC Resolution of 1 March 2002, Proceedings A 309/01, *Información Estadística Fenil*.

not need any prior authorization. In this exchange of information system created by this National Federation a notary had also been involved. The notary had been managing the individual information considered as business secrets. This ensured that members of the federation do not have access to individual data, which was positively evaluated by the TDC, confirming the necessity of a case-by-case analysis.

311. In its Resolution *Estadísticas Cerveceros*[156] the TDC decided that the system established by the Spanish Brewers Association for collecting and processing data statistics relating to the manufacture and marketing of beer was anticompetitive because the market was highly concentrated and there was de facto a duopoly situation in many parts of Spain. The exchanged information was very recent, current and specific. Also, in this case the involvement of a notary in order to guarantee the confidentiality was not considered to be effective in such a concentrated market. The TDC took also into account that only part of the exchanged information had a public nature and finally the TDC defined the exchanged information as 'business secrets' (e.g., plans related to investments or advertising spendings).

312. A special category of information exchange agreements is the creation of debtors lists (*Registro de morosos*). The TDC indicated that this kind of lists, when established within business associations and marketed by independent third parties, could constitute a form of consultation between employers to interact and exchange information on the solvency of their clients. This could have a significant impact on a commercial or service conditions which have to be applied to those customers.

313. Thus, it cannot be excluded that the creation of these lists could constitute an agreement of the employers to be subsumed as a conduct prohibited by Article 1 LDC. This is the reason why the TDC has declared in several decisions that some standards and conditions shall be followed in order to avoid an anticompetitive exchange of information with the creation of these lists.

314. In *Prensa Córdoba,*[157] the TDC admitted that these lists of debtors contributed to a clarification and to the transparency of the sector, which also contributed to improve the marketing of goods and services, if certain conditions were observed, such as a voluntary registration, the freedom of the members to organize their own commercial policy regarding the paying debtor, the objective character of the information exchanged with the users or the possibility of the debtors to access to the list and to correct the information in case it is wrong. The TDC has also underlined the importance that the data contained in these lists are not manipulated or used for different purposes than the authorized, the management of these lists should be clearly delimited and the consideration as a debtor cannot contradict the specific regulation in this area. The identity of the creditors should also not be disclosed.

315. Following these requirements, the Royal Decree number 602/2006, of 19 May, approving a block exemption regulation on certain categories of agreements

---

156. TDC Resolution of 30 March 2004, Proceedings A 329/02, *Estadísticas Cerveceros*.
157. TDC Resolution of 22 January 2001, Proceedings 484/00, *Prensa Córdoba*.

of exchange of information about late payment.[158] Article 3 of this Royal Decree foresees the characteristics that have to be observed in order to benefit from the exemption and, in consequence, in order not to be considered as an anticompetitive conduct. These characteristics follow the ones established by the TDC before this Royal Decree was published.[159]

316. More recently, the Spanish Competition Authority has considered in some cases that the exchange of information had to be considered as a way of organizing a cartel between companies and associations.

158. *See* the publication in the Official State Gazette (B.O.E.) number 129, of 31 May 2006, p. 20430.
159. In the Resolution of 3 November 1999, Proceedings A 239/98, *Crédito Asnef-Equifax*, the TDC authorized the creation of a debtor's list for a period of five years (by that time, in Spain the previous Competition Act 16/1989 was still in force and, in consequence, an authorization *ex ante* was still necessary in order not to consider a conduct as anticompetitive) because it understood that the requirements of Art. 3 of Royal Decree 602/2006 were fulfilled, and it underlined that the list had to be accessible to all the financial institutions after paying an appropriate fee under non-discriminatory terms and that the information about creditors should not be disclosed. The National Association of Financial Institutions, which was part of Asnef-Equifax, had presented the application for the authorization. The list contained similar information to that which was included in the Bank of Spain Circular 3/1995, on the Risk Information Centre, which was accessible to financial institutions in Spain. The data in this case were related to the identification and economic activity of the debtors, as well as, were appropriate, special situations such as bankruptcy or insolvency. The Consumer Association Ausbanc filed an appeal and the National High Court granted this appeal in its Judgment of 28 November 2001. According to the National High Court, the list did not respect the requirements of Art. 3 of the Royal Decree 602/2006 and had to be considered, in consequence, anticompetitive according to Art. 1 LDC. Asnef-Equifax filed a cassation appeal in the Spanish Supreme Court and the Supreme Court referred the matter to the European Court of Justice for a preliminary ruling on the interpretation of the creation of such a list in a fragmented market and whether it could be authorized according to Art. 101.3 of the Treaty of Functioning of the European Union (by that time Art. 81.3 EC). The ECJ considered in its Judgment of 23 November 2006, *Asnef-Equifax y Administración del Estado v. AUSBANC*, C-238/05, that a system for the exchange of information on credit like it was the case with this register has not to be considered in principle as anticompetitive if three requirements are met: the affected market should not be highly concentrated, the identity of the creditors or lenders should not be revealed in order to avoid that the register reveals the market position or the commercial strategy of competitors and third, such registers should be accessible in a non-discriminatory manner, in law and in fact, to all operators active in the relevant sphere. The ECJ argues that 'if such accessibility were not guaranteed, some of those operators would be placed at a disadvantage, since they would have less information for the purpose of risk assessment, which would also not facilitate the entry of new operators on to the market' (para. 60) and clarified that 'the applicability of the exemption provided for in Article 81(3) EC is subject to the four cumulative conditions laid down in that provision' (para. 65). Regarding the question whether all consumers derive a benefit from the register, the ECJ states that 'registers such as the one at issue in the main proceedings are capable of helping to prevent situations of over-indebtedness for consumers of credit as well as, in principle, of leading to a greater overall availability of credit. In the event that the register restricted competition within the meaning of Article 81(1) EC, those objective economic advantages might be such as to offset the disadvantages of such a possible restriction. It would be for the national court, if necessary, to verify that' (para. 67). In conclusion, it is the beneficial nature of the effect on all consumers in the relevant markets that must be taken into consideration in order to evaluate if the register or the list is an anticompetitive system of exchange of information, not the effect on each member of that category of consumers.

317. For example, in October 2007 in *Cajas Vascas y Navarra,*[160] the CNC fined the four largest savings banks operating in northern Spain[161] due to their coordination and participation in a cartel against third parties through the Federation of Savings Banks of the Basque Country and Navarre. The savings banks had agreed to exchange information in order to keep their market share and create entry barriers for third parties on elements such as how to compete in the market, the charges or fees for the use of cards, the advertising campaigns on Investment Funds or the required activity related to big accounts.[162]

318. The Spanish Supreme Court confirmed in its Judgment of 24 March 2009 that the fact that a register was created within an association would not automatically mean a violation of European competition law, because the compatibility of a system of information exchange – such as a register – with competition rules '*cannot be assessed in an abstract way*'. In this regard, the economic conditions of the relevant market and the characteristics of the specific system have to be taken into account, such as, for example, the purpose of the register, the conditions of access to the market, the individualized participation in the system of exchange of information, the nature of the exchanged data – public or confidential, global or more detailed, historical or current – the frequency of exchanging data and their importance for fixing prices, volumes or conditions of a specific delivery. In this case the Supreme Court considered that the creation of a register had anticompetitive effects, because it allowed the participants to know the market position and business strategies of competitors.[163]

319. In order to inform within industry associations about the risks of exchanging information, the CNC published in December 2009 a guide for business associations in which the anticompetitive conducts were described.[164]

320. In its Resolution of 2 March 2011, the council of the CNC declared that there was a cartel between different manufacturers of bath and shower gel.[165] This fine was originated by a leniency application in 2008 – even though it was an

160. CNC Resolution of 15 October 2007, Proceedings 617/2006.
161. Caja de Ahorros de Vitoria y Álava (Caja Vital), Bilbao Bizkaia Kutxa (BBK), Caja de Ahorros y Monte de Piedad de Guipuzkoa y San Sebastián (KUTXA) and Caja de Ahorros de Navarra (CAN).
162. This Resolution of the Council of the CNC was appealed to the National High Court. In its Judgment of 23 November 2010, the National High Court affirmed in cases of exchange of information it is necessary to analyse each case separately and taking into account the specific circumstances, such as the economic context, structure and functioning of the market conditions and nature of the goods or services affected. The National High Court partially upheld the appeal and reduced the fine imposed to Caja de Ahorros y Monte de Piedad de Navarra (Caja Navarra).
163. *See* Judgment of the Spanish Supreme Court of 24 March 2009 (Appeal Number 5115/2006), fifth legal ground.
164. The guide is available at http://www.cncompetencia.es/Default.aspx?TabId=177 (last time accessed: 7 February 2017).
165. CNC Resolution of 2 March 2011, Proceedings S/0086/08, *Peluquería Profesional.*

exchange of information a leniency application was accepted. Henkel had submitted a statement to the CNC disclosing the existence of the cartel as well as its participation, mentioning many other firms that were operating in this sector. Consequently, inspections were carried out in the head offices of several companies and also in the Spanish national perfumery and cosmetics association (*Asociación Nacional de Perfumería y Cosmética*, STANPA), after formal proceedings had been opened. The CNC Council stated in this resolution that the eight major companies, which as has been shown and is acknowledged by the parties account for 70% of the professional haircare sector, coordinated their actions from February 1989 to February 2008 through regular, stable and systematic meetings of the most important companies organized on a rotating basis twice a year (February and September). According to the CNC, this did not change when STANPA joined the cartel, although as from that time STANPA's staff requested information before the meetings and organized its presentation at the meetings and subsequent distribution, something which had been a duty of the company who had to organize the meetings. The CNC affirmed that the agreement between the involved companies and the exchange of information involved different companies which had to execute the agreement, regardless of size or importance in the market. During the period of the infringing conduct, the sensitive data that were exchanged included recent price increases and also future increases were planned, together with the exchange of information related to discounts, payment calendars and methods of financing, as well as incentives for sales staff. The CNC concluded that the exchange of information in this case was clearly intended to coordinate marketing strategies, prices and inflows of new competitors, affecting free competition in the market. The CNC considered that the exchanges of information between the competitors in this case constituted an infringement by object and could not be considered as exempted agreements *ex* Article 1.3 of the LDC.[166] In particular, the CNC emphasizes once again the seriousness of sharing pricing or economic conditions offered to customers because it in practice nullifies strategic uncertainty and the independence in determining trade policies between competitors.[167]

166. The CNC clarified that by mere fact of exchanging that strategic information, and all the more over such a lengthy period of time, are knowingly replacing the risks of competition with cooperation, voluntarily relinquishing their independent conduct in the market, thereby reducing the play of competition. This has to be considered as anticompetitive because such exchanges facilitate the price fixing between competitors without the risk of losing market share, with no need to demonstrate that prices have risen. Having been demonstrated the anticompetitive object of the exchange of information, the CNC affirms that it is not necessary to determine whether the practice did or did not have any anticompetitive effects in practice.

167. The highest fine imposed by the CNC in this case was of more than EUR 23 million to L'Oréal España, S.A., STANPA was also fined EUR 900,000. After STANPA joined there was an increase in the quantity of information exchanged, the frequency and disaggregation of data, facilitated by STANPA's organizational resources, thereby heightening the capacity to distort the market. The CNC considered that STANPA had been a co-perpetrator, together with the rest of the accused, for a violation of Art. 1 of the LDC, since it had had an active role in organizing and monitoring the proper implementation of the cartel arrangements, making a considerable contribution to keeping it in effect. The Investigations Division noticed that this case involved the action of this professional association which represents the economic and industrial interests of all member companies,

321. In its Resolution of the CNC from 24 June 2011 in *Bombas de Fluídos,* the CNC investigated the exchange of information on price increases during 2007–2008 in the sector of manufacturing fluid power equipments, as well as the impacts of those increases in wage policy of each of the companies after a leniency application. The CNC affirmed that in this case, the information exchange and harmonization of conditions between the involved companies constitutes an anticompetitive conduct which, by its nature, leads to a partitioning of the domestic market and a potential competitive disadvantage for market entrants. The CNC affirms also that the information exchanged deals with future prices and, thus, as it is not related to an already existing element, it is more likely to result in a reduction of the price competition in this market. According to the CNC, the exchange of this information artificially reduces the uncertainty about the future market behaviour of competitors.[168]

322. In its Resolution of 20 January 2012, the CNC fined two motorbike manufacturers (Honda and Suzuki motors) for having exchanged sensitive commercial information. Staff from the Investigations Division of the CNC had detected the existence of several emails between these companies, containing sensitive commercial information. Each manufacturer had provided the other with detailed information on the wholesale prices (to the dealer) for all motorbike models between 125 cc and 1800 cc, together with the recommended retail prices to the public. The exchange of information affected the prices and margins that were starting to be applied in January 2009 and which in all probability were going to apply throughout 2009. The CNC affirmed that the exchange of this kind of information could affect the free competition in the market. The authority underlined again that it is very important to examine each case separately, as there is no specific definition about what to be understood under commercially sensitive information. Thus, it is an individual and secret concept, related in any case to the specific business (e.g., sales volumes, sales prices, customers, productions costs, commercial strategies). In practice it also has to be distinguished if it is current or future sales prices (in case law there are often related to further agreements) or if it is about other types of commercially sensitive information. In this case the CNC considered that the data on wholesale prices provided important information on the margin that the dealer had to make discounts when marketing the motorbikes, which reduced uncertainty in connection with the current application of the recommended retail prices was going to be. The uncertainty was very low in this case, especially given the timing of the

---

and it contributed actively and deliberately to the prolonged maintenance of this cartel of certain companies in the sector, namely the market leader and the main operators, and served as platform for the cartel's implementation.

168. This Resolution of the CNC was appealed by some of the fined companies but the National High Court dismissed all the appeals in different Judgments of 12, 14, 15 and 20 February 2013 and of 8 March 2013. All the judgments and the decision are available at http://bit.ly/1lS1G7A (last time accessed: 7 February 2017).

exchange of information, which took place after a change to the rates of tax for registering motorbikes against a background of a significant reduction in demand for them. Besides, the information in this case was neither general nor publicly available.[169]

323. The CNMC published on 2 January 2014 a resolution fining the public business entity AENA and eleven car rental companies for having exchanged sensitive commercial information.[170] The CNMC affirmed in this case that the information exchanged affected the uncertain factor of the future behaviour of the car rental companies involved and, thus, it could be considered as a collusive agreement. The aim of the information exchanged was in this case to know the exact market shares of the car rental companies and how their sales evolved monthly (the CNMC underlined that it was a frequent exchange), since they exchanged information related to their billing data and to the number of contracts awarded monthly in almost every Spanish airport. In another Decision from 23 July 2015, the CNMC published a record EUR 171 million fine for twenty car manufacturers and distributors for exchanging commercially sensitive and strategic information in the Spanish vehicle distribution and after-sales market for the brands which were involved in this illicit conduct. The CNMC concluded that these companies had violated Article 1 LDC and Article 101 TFEU because of the 'systematic exchange of sensitive commercially confidential information', covering 'practically all' activities from new and used vehicle sales to workshop and repair services. Also the companies participating in the illicit conducts acted in a way as to 'secretly hide' their exchanges of information, controlling 91% of the Spanish car market.

324. Thus, it can be concluded that according to recent decisions of the competition authorities in Spain, the exchange of information has been, in many cases, the conduct which allowed a cartel to continue. In this regard, the CNMC in its Decision of 3 December 2015, *construcciones modulares,*[171] declared that the exchange of information related to their price offers and the conditions of the prices within the framework of the calls for tenders allowed the functioning and the continuation of the cartel. In a former Decision of 19 February 2015, the CNMC had fined five oil companies, including Repsol, Cepsa and DISA, for price fixing agreements and exchanges of strategic information related to the operating margins and regarding a supply and branding contract between some of the involved companies.[172]

---

169. Therefore the CNC classified the described conduct as a very serious breach of Art. 1 LDC and fined Honda with more the EUR 2 million and Suzuki with almost EUR 2 million.
170. *See* CNMC Resolution of 2 January 2014, Proceedings S/0404/12, *Servicios Comerciales AENA*.
171. *See* CNMC Resolution of 3 December 2015, Proceedings S/0481/13, *Construcciones modulares*.
172. *See* CNMC Resolution of 19 February 2015, Proceedings S/474/13.

III. Cooperation Agreements

A. Research and Development

325. This kind of agreements include the pooling of resources for the research and development of new products and may also include the subsequent exploitation of the results of the research. These agreements can have as positive effects the reduction of unnecessary and/or duplicative costs. They can also facilitate the exchange of ideas and experiences between different companies and enable reaching results more easily and faster. Such agreements could, however, lead to anti-competitive agreements and/or facilitate collusion between companies. These agreements might be problematic from a competition law perspective in case the involved companies have a high market power. In this situation, the same conditions apply in Spain as at a European level. In Spain, in order to verify if these agreements are anticompetitive, they shall be evaluated according to the *Commission Regulation (EU) 1217/2010, of 14 December 2010, on the application of Article 101(3) of the Treaty on the Functioning of the European Union to certain categories of research and development agreements.* Article 4.2 of this Regulation foresees that Article 101(1) TFEU shall not apply to these agreements when the combined market share of the parties to a research and development agreement does not exceed 25% on the relevant product and technology markets.

B. Specialization and Joint Production

326. Specialization agreements are cooperative agreements by which the parties decide to rationalize their joint production. In this context, joint production means manufacturing the product in common, one of them specializing in the production and ceasing to produce or other committing all parties to the agreement to purchase a third party. These agreements may be an improvement in efficiency by exploiting economies of scale or scope, but can also cause coordination of commercial conducts of the companies, as well as foreclosure.

327. As it is the case with research and development agreements, these agreements are usually not considered as anticompetitive when the companies involved are not competitors or when they involve the outsourcing of a production for their own consumption previously made. They could also be justified when they constitute, in practice, the only way of entering companies in a market or launching a new product or service or carrying out a specific product.[173]

173. For example, the formation of temporary joint ventures (*Unión Temporal de Empresas* – UTE) serves this purpose. Sometimes there are big projects tendered by an administration, which would be difficult or risky to deal with by a single company and, thus, several companies could create a joint venture for that specific project. They are regulated in Spain by Law 18/1982, of 26 May 1982, on the tax regime of groupings and joint companies and societies of regional industrial development (National Official Gazette from 9 June 1982).

328. From a competition law perspective it might be problematic if incentives for a coordinated behaviour of the companies appear as a result of the collaboration or if the agreement forces out small businesses of the market. In Spain these agreements have to be analysed according to the *Commission Regulation (EU) 1218/2010, of 14 December 2010, on the application of Article 101(3) of the Treaty on the Functioning of the European Union to certain categories of specialisation agreements*, which foresees in Article 3 an exemption for those agreements in which the combined market share of the companies involved does not exceed 20% on any relevant market.

C. *Standardization*

329. Standardization agreements have as their primary objective the definition of technical or quality requirements thanks to which current or future products, production processes, services or methods may comply. These agreements consist of a definition of common technical specifications. They are not problematic from a competition law perspective if they promote economic interpenetration on the internal market and encourage the entrance of new firms into the market, as well as the development of new and improved products or markets or the supply conditions. Standards may increase competition and lower output and sales costs, benefitting economies as a whole. Standards may also maintain and enhance quality, provide information and ensure interoperability and compatibility. Through this creation of common standards, the size of secondary markets is also increased and this enables also new companies to sell products in secondary markets.

330. Standard-setting agreements can, however, contribute to create restrictive effects on competition by restricting price competition and limiting or controlling production, markets, innovation or technical development. This can in practice occur through reduction in price competition, foreclosure of innovative technologies and exclusion of, or discrimination against companies by hampering the access to the standards. The coordinated effects could close the market to other companies whose products have different technical specifications. It seems probable that the CNMC as well as the Spanish courts would take into account the European Horizontal Guidelines when dealing with standardization cases.[174]

D. *Joint Production*

331. Production agreements may vary in form and scope. Joint production agreements refer to agreements in which the production is carried out by two or more parties. Companies can decide to produce jointly by way of a joint venture, which is a jointly controlled company operating one or several production facilities or by looser forms of cooperation in production, such as subcontracting agreements

174. *See* the *EU Commission Guidelines on the applicability of Art. 101 TFEU to horizontal cooperation agreements*, [2011] OJ C 11/1, paras 257 et seq.

where one party ('contractor') entrusts another party ('subcontractor') the production of a certain good. Subcontracting agreements can be either horizontal, in which case they are concluded between companies operating in the same product market irrespective of whether they are actual or potential competitors, or vertical, in which case they are concluded between companies operating at different levels of the market.

332. The above-mentioned European Horizontal Guidelines apply to all forms of joint production agreements and horizontal subcontracting agreements.[175] In Spain, joint production agreements are examined according to these guidelines.

333. Production agreements could lead the parties to agree directly on output levels and quality, on the price at which the joint venture sells on its products, or on the other competitively important parameters. This could restrict competition if the parties market the products independently and compete in the downstream market, or even lead to anticompetitive foreclosure of third parties in a related market.

334. These agreements are unlikely to raise competition concerns if the parties to the agreement do not have market power (starting point is the market share of the parties) in the market on which a restriction of competition is assessed. The Guidelines clarify that unilateral or reciprocal specialization agreements as well as joint production agreements should be exempted if they are concluded between parties with a combined market share below 20% in the relevant market(s).[176]

E. Joint Purchasing

335. A joint purchasing agreement implies that companies decide to acquire supplies in common. Joint purchasing agreements can adopt different forms in practice: they can be carried out by a jointly controlled company, by a company in which many other companies hold non-controlling stakes, by a contractual arrangement or by 'looser forms of co-operation' (also called 'joint purchasing arrangements'). This kind of agreements usually aim at the creation of buying power which can lead to efficiency improvements by the existence of economies of scale and/or to lower prices or better quality products, as well as services for consumers. These agreements may also cause competition concerns. If the companies which cooperate in a joint purchasing agreement have a very strong negotiation position in the market against the suppliers, they could manage to lower the supplier margins or even pass-on a proportion of excessive risks, which in turn may discourage research and development, innovation or investment in this specific market. This kind of agreements could also lead to a market foreclosure if competitors that are not included in the agreement cannot have similar conditions.

175. *EU Commission Guidelines on the applicability of Art. 101 TFEU to horizontal cooperation agreements*, [2011] OJ C 11/1, paras 146 et seq.
176. *Ibíd.*, para. 163.

336. Joint purchasing arrangements may involve both horizontal and vertical agreements. Therefore, in these cases a two-step analysis is necessary. First, the horizontal agreements between the companies engaging in joint purchasing have to be assessed according to the principles described in the above-mentioned European Horizontal Guidelines.[177] If this assessment leads to the conclusion that the joint purchasing arrangement does not give rise to concerns from a competition law perspective, then a further assessment will be necessary to examine the relevant vertical agreements if there are is also a vertical agreement involved. The latter assessment will follow the rules of the Block Exemption Vertical Restraints and the Guidelines on Vertical Restraints, mentioned in §2 *infra*.

337. In Spain, joint purchasing agreements are examined according to the mentioned European Horizontal Guidelines. These Guidelines clarify that there is no absolute threshold above which it can be presumed that the parties to a joint purchasing arrangement have market power so that the joint purchasing arrangement could result in restrictive effects on competition.[178] If the parties' combined market shares do not exceed 15% on both the purchasing and the selling market or markets, it is likely that they will not cause any competition concerns.

F. Joint Selling

338. Joint selling agreements are part of the commercialization agreements which involve cooperation between competitors in the selling, distribution or promotion of their substitute products. This type of agreements can have widely varying scope, depending on the commercialization functions which are covered by the cooperation. Joint selling agreements may lead to a joint determination of all commercial aspects related to the sale of the product, including also the price. There are also more limited agreements that only address one specific commercialization function, such as distribution, after-sales service, as well as advertising. This kind of agreements could be necessary for competitors that would like to enter new markets and they could generate efficiencies by taking advantage of economies of scale.

339. Commercialization agreements can be problematic from a competition law perspective in several ways, e.g., they could lead to price fixing. They could also facilitate output limitation, because the companies involved may decide on the volume of products to be put on the market, therefore restricting supply. This kind of agreements may become a means for the parties to divide the markets or to allocate orders or customers, for example in cases where the parties' production plants are located in different geographic markets or when the agreements are reciprocal. Finally, they could lead to an exchange of strategic information relating to aspects

177. *Ibíd.*, paras 194 et seq.

178. However, it is mentioned that in most cases it is unlikely that market power exists if the parties to the joint purchasing arrangement have a combined market share not exceeding 15% on the purchasing market or markets, as well as a combined market share not exceeding 15% on the selling market or markets (*see* para. 208 of the Guidelines).

within or outside the scope of the cooperation, as in cases of price fixing conducts which would be considered as collusive agreements.

340. The European Guidelines on Horizontal Cooperation consider agreements limited to joint selling as restrictions by object if they coordinate the pricing policy of competing manufacturers or service providers, even where the agreement is ostensibly non-exclusive.[179] These guidelines are followed in Spain in order to examine these agreements, keeping in mind that these agreements between competitors are only supposed have restrictive effects on competition if the parties have some degree of market power.[180]

§2. Vertical Agreements

341. Article 1.1 LDC prohibits vertical agreements between two or more companies which have the object or effect of restricting competition in Spain.

I. Distribution

A. Exclusive Distributorship

342. The appointment of an exclusive distributor for a specified territory, who in turn is usually restricted to active selling in this allocated territory, is exempted under the Commission Regulation (EU) 330/2010 in those cases in which neither the supplier nor the distributor exceed a market share of 30% and the agreement does not contain any hard-core restrictions.[181] Above the market share threshold of the 30%, the Commission Guidelines indicate a willingness to apply Article 101.3 of the TFEU in individual cases.[182] An 'exclusive distributorship' is an agreement aimed to sell products to only one distributor for resale in a particular territory, and at the same time limitations are placed on the distributor regarding the active selling in other exclusively allocated territories. It is indeed an exclusive customer allocation with the geographic location of the customers as the criterion for this allocation.

179. *See* the *EU Commission Guidelines on the applicability of Art. 101 TFEU to horizontal cooperation agreements*, [2011] OJ C 11/1, para. 234. The Guidelines clarify that: '*such agreements may not only eliminate price competition between the parties on substitute products but may also restrict the total volume of products to be delivered by the parties within the framework of a system for allocating orders. Such agreements are therefore likely to restrict competition by object.*'

180. In most cases, it is unlikely that market power exists if the parties to the agreement have a combined market share not exceeding 15%. *See* para. 240 of the mentioned Guidelines.

181. *See* Arts 2, 3 and 4 of the *Commission Regulation (EU) number 330/2010, of 20 April 2010 on the application of Article 101(3) of the Treaty on the Functioning of the European Union to categories of vertical agreements and concerted practices* as well as the *Guidelines on Vertical Restraints*, [2010] OJ C 130/1, paras 151–167. The Guidelines are available at http://ec.europa.eu/competition/antitrust/legislation/guidelines_vertical_en.pdf (last time accessed: 7 February 2017).

182. In Spain, this rule corresponds to Art. 1.3 LDC.

343. In Spain, exclusive distribution agreements are assessed in accordance with the Vertical Block Exemption Regulation and the Vertical Guidelines published by the Commission. Thus, even if an agreement does not benefit from the Vertical Block Exemption Regulation and contains exclusive distribution clauses, it should not be considered in itself as prohibited according to Article 1 LDC, because exclusive distribution clauses do not have the restriction of competition as its object. An individual assessment of the effects of the agreement should be the way to handle with these clauses.

344. The Spanish Competition Authorities have fined several times manufacturers and their distributors when minimum resale price clauses were included in the distribution agreements.

345. In March 2007, the TDC imposed a fine of EUR 400,000 on a dominant beer producer, Compañía Cervecera de Canarias (Cercasa), for including in its distribution agreements clauses containing minimum purchase requirements and exclusive advertising obligations.

346. In July 2009, a fine of EUR 7.9 million was imposed on three petrol producers (Repsol, Cepsa and BP) for commercial practices which were equivalent to fixing the retail price to be applied by petrol stations towards their customers. The Council of the CNC mentioned its concern about certain elements of the producers' commercial relationships, for example, the manner in which the petrol producers established the price at which petrol stations acquired the petrol, as well as the method of calculating stations' commissions. The CNC found that these practices eliminated de facto the stations' incentives to apply discounts and, therefore, the free competition on prices. Thus, the Council of the CNC concluded that the petrol producers were controlling the resale prices to the end consumer and eliminating competition between similarly situated stations. The Council CNC stated also that the producers had agreed to recommend the same maximum price to their stations in the same geographical area, thereby eliminating any inter-brand competition.

347. On 28 December 2011, the CNC issued a resolution on an infringement proceeding in its *Montesa Honda* case. The CNC affirmed that the manufacturer Montesa Honda SA and nine exclusive distributors located in Madrid, Toledo and Guadalajara had violated Article 1 LDC through agreements setting minimum resale prices of Honda-motorcycles. This case was originated by a complaint filed by a motorcycle dealer of Honda in Madrid, against its supplier and the manufacturer Montesa Honda S.A. and against six of its dealers located in the mentioned provinces. The complainant alleged that the opposition of the complaining dealer to a collusive agreement between the accused for the sale of high cylinder capacity motorcycles of Honda and its subsequent complaint against the Honda parent companies, led to its expulsion from the official network of Honda dealers. The manufacturer Honda and some of the dealers were inspected and the CNC found evidence proving that Honda and its main dealer in Madrid were meeting to discuss sales via agents, with Honda advocating a higher commercial margin for the agents. Honda had also agreed in meetings with brand dealers a list of prices for specific motorcycles as well as the margin to be granted to the agent in Madrid. The CNC assessed the conducts examined in this case as infringements of Article 1 LDC both by object and by its effects. Moreover, the facts on this case proved the existence of a pricing agreement of both an horizontal nature (coordination of competitors-dealers operating at the same level of the market, namely the retailing level) and also a vertical nature (since it was ultimately the manufacturer Honda that wielded the capacity to modify the proposed levels with power to impose them on other dealers that had not been present in the meeting and thus, they had not participated in the discussion of the changes to be made to the price list). The Council of the CNC concluded that the conducts in this case had to be classified as a complex, single and continuing infringement of Article 1 LDC since a fixing of a minimum retail price had taken place, as well as a maximum selling price for the dealers to the agents/subagents in 2008 for certain models of motorcycles, as well as an agreement related to a fixed margin for agents in 2009.

348. In its Resolution of 27 March 2012, the Council of the CNC fined Suzuki and ten of its distributors of motorcycles located in the provinces of Madrid and Granada, after having considered that they all had also violated Article 1 LDC by fixing minimum resale prices of Suzuki motorcycles, besides agreeing profit margins that dealers give their agents or sub-distributors for sales in the mentioned provinces. The CNC underlined in its resolution that Suzuki had held the position as second best-selling brand in Madrid in 2008, also making it the third best-selling brand in Granada. According to the CNC, Suzuki was also one of the most recognized brands of motorcycles by consumers. The CNC considered also that the collusive conduct analysed in its resolution could not benefit from any exemption whatsoever from the prohibition under Spanish competition law neither pursuant to Article 1.4 LDC, since there was a vertical agreement in the area of recommended prices involved, nor to Article 1.3 LDC, since the defendants had not proven that the requirements established in that Article had been met. The Council of the CNC took also the European Guidelines into account, since the importance of the potential harm to intrabrand competition caused by anticompetitive agreements is also very important to keep in mind according to the Council, given that it was driven by the brands' parallel retail distribution networks. In this connection, the Council pointed out that the Guidelines on the application of the EU Regulation on vertical restraints emphasize that the market position of the supplier and its competitors is of central importance in assessing possible anticompetitive effects of the loss of intrabrand competition. In this sense, in certain circumstances where interbrand competition is restricted, a significant loss of intrabrand competition could give rise to an increased risk of collusion between major suppliers.

349. In these agreements, competition risks are potentially the reduced intrabrand competition and market partitioning, which could, in turn, facilitate price discrimination agreements between competitors putting in danger interbrand competition. In cases in which a high number of suppliers apply exclusive distribution, free competition may be softened and this situation may facilitate collusion, both at the suppliers' and distributors' level. The Guidelines on Vertical Restraints of the Commission also warn in paragraph 151 that exclusive distribution may also lead to foreclosure of other distributors and similarly reduce competition at that level.

B. Exclusive Dealing

350. The meaning of the term 'exclusive dealing' is not always easy to determine. The EU Commission uses 'exclusive dealing' only to refer to a specific type of abuse of a dominant position within the framework of the exclusionary conducts.[183] In the Guidelines on Vertical Restraints, the EU Commission refers to 'single branding' when there is an obligation imposed on a distributor to sell only (or almost only) the products of a particular manufacturer.[184] Under 'exclusive supply' the Commission refers to the obligation on a seller to sell exclusively to a particular buyer.[185]

351. Non-competition clauses understood as 'single branding' within the framework of exclusive dealing involve limitations on the distributor, in both cases in which either the distributor may not sell other products, different from the supplier's products or where the distributor may not purchase the contract goods from others different from the supplier. As it also happens at a European level, non-compete clauses related to single branding or exclusive dealing are generally exempted if the supplier's market share is below 30% and either the term of the non-compete clause is limited to five years or less, or the distributor is only obliged to buy 80% or less of its volume from the supplier (Article 1 b) Regulation 330/2010). But even if these non-compete clauses do not benefit from the *safe harbour* provided for by Regulation 330/2010 on Vertical Restraints, they will generally not be found to restrict automatically competition by its object. On a case-by-case analysis it has to be proved that they have the effect of restricting competition in the relevant market in order to be considered as infringing Article 1 LDC. A restriction by effect would be the case if the agreement in itself or in combination with other similar agreements used by the supplier or its competitors contributed to foreclose the market to new entrants.

183. *See* the *Guidance on the Commission's enforcement priorities in applying Article 82 of the EC Treaty to abusive exclusionary conduct by dominant undertakings*, [2009] OJ C45/7 para. 32. This paragraph equates exclusive dealing to singles branding and it defines exclusive dealing as customer foreclosure through exclusive purchasing obligations or rebates.

184. *See* para. 129 of the *Guidelines on Vertical Restraints*, [2010] OJ C 130/1, in which single branding agreements are defined as agreements '*which have as their main element the fact that the buyer is obliged or induced to concentrate its orders for a particular type of product with one supplier*'.

185. *See* para. 192 of the *Guidelines on Vertical Restraints*, [2010] OJ C 130/1, in which exclusive supply agreements are defined as agreements '*which have as their main element that the supplier is obliged or induced to sell the contract products only or mainly to one buyer, in general or for a particular use*'.

352. In Spain, the Competition authority is likely to apply the mentioned Regulation 330/2010 and the Guidelines on Vertical Restraints both to single branding and exclusive supply agreements.[186]

C. Selective Distribution

353. Selective distribution agreements restrict the number of authorized distributors and the possibilities of resale. This also happens within the mentioned exclusive distribution agreements. The difference with the exclusive distribution is that the restriction of the number of dealers does not depend on the number of territories but on selection criteria linked first to the nature of the product. In the selective distribution agreements, the restriction on resale is not linked to the active selling to a territory, in fact it is rather a restriction on any sales to non-authorizes distributors. Only appointed dealers and final customers are left as possible buyers. This method of distribution is usually used to distribute final products. Also in this field of selective distribution agreements in Spain the Commission Regulation 330/2010 and the mentioned Guidelines on Vertical Restraints are followed.

354. Paragraph 175 of the Commission Guidelines on Vertical Restraints deals with the question if and when selective distribution agreements shall be considered as anticompetitive. The Commission mentions that a distinction needs to be made between purely qualitative selective distribution and quantitative selective distribution. The Guidelines provide some criteria in order not to consider purely qualitative selective distribution as anticompetitive. According to these criteria, selective distribution does not restrict competition if the nature of the product requires a selective distribution system according to a principle of necessity (such a system has to constitute a legitimate requirement taking into account the nature of the product concerned in order to preserve its quality and ensure its proper use), when only objective qualitative criteria are used for the selection of the distributors (they have to be laid down in a uniform way for all parties and they need to be available to all potential resellers), when these criteria are applied non-discriminatorily and finally when the criteria do not go beyond what is necessary to pursue the objective that legitimizes selective distribution according to a principle of proportionality.[187] If a selective distribution agreement foresees other selection criteria, different from

186. *See* again Arts 2, 3 and 4 of the mentioned Regulation number 330/2010, which exempt vertical restrictions where neither supplier nor buyer exceeds the market share threshold of 30%, taking always into account the core restraints in Art. 4 and the Guidelines on Vertical Restraints, [2010] OJ C 130/1, paras 129–150 (on single branding) and 192–202 (on exclusive supply).

187. These criteria were mentioned by the European case law. *See*, in that sense, Judgments of the Court of Justice in Case 31/80 *L'Oréal v. PVBA* [1980] ECR 3775, paras 15 and 16; Case 26/76 *Metro I* [1977] ECR 1875, paras 20 and 21; Case 107/82 *AEG* [1983] ECR 3151, para. 35; and of the General Court in Case T-19/91 *Vichy v. Commission* [1992] ECR II-415, para. 65. Besides the judgments of the ECJ, also the former competition authority, the TDC, incorporated these criteria in its resolutions, as for example, in the Resolutions of 19 September 2002, 9 June 2004 or 14 September 2004.

those abovementioned, then it shall be considered as prohibited according to Article 1 LDC and every single agreement has to be analysed case by case in order to determine if it is anticompetitive or not.

355. In case a selective distribution system restricts competition,[188] then Regulation 330/2010 offers an exemption provided the market share thresholds of 30% of both supplier and buyer are not exceeded and no black-listed core restraints are included.[189]

356. The Commission Guidelines on vertical restraints state that possible competition risks of selective distribution are a reduction in intrabrand competition and, especially in case of cumulative effects, the foreclosure of certain types of distributors and softening of competition, as well as the facilitation of collusion between suppliers or buyers. As mentioned, according with Regulation 330/2010 and the Commission Guidelines on vertical restraints, both qualitative and quantitative selective distribution is exempted as long as the buyer and the seller do not exceed 30% of the market share in the relevant market, even if it is combined with other non-hardcore vertical restraints, such as for example non-compete or single branding clauses or exclusive distribution. What is in any case important to stress is that active selling by authorized distributors to each other and to end users may not be restricted. The Guidelines remind in paragraph 176 that the Block Exemption Regulation 330/2010 exempts selective distribution regardless of the nature of the product concerned and regardless of the nature of the selection criteria.

D. *Franchising*

357. Franchise agreements[190] often contain a combination of different vertical clauses concerning the products being distributed, e.g., vertical price fixing or clauses related to the absence of participating during the agreement in any other business which is present in the market. Other clauses could be related to the period

---

188. For example, by employing quantitative criteria or because the above-mentioned criteria are not fulfilled.
189. *See* Arts 2, 3 and 4 of Regulation 330/2010. Paragraph 176 of the Commission Guidelines on Vertical Restraints, [2010] OJ C 130/1, mentions also the 30% as a maximum of common market share threshold of both parts, 'provided active selling by the authorized distributors to each other and to end users is not restricted'. This paragraph reminds that 'the Block Exemption Regulation exempts selective distribution regardless of the nature of the product concerned and regardless of the nature of the selection criteria' but it also notices that 'if appreciable anticompetitive effects occur, the benefit of the Block Exemption Regulation is likely to be withdrawn'. The Guidelines provide also in paras 177–188 guidance for individual cases of selective distribution in which the conditions of Art. 101.3 TFEU / Art. 1.3 LDC may apply and, thus, the agreement is not problematic from a competition law perspective.
190. For example, a licensed practice of using the quite successful business of another company. This business is typically recognizable through the quality and/or uniformity of the products or services offered. The franchisor as a supplier allows an operator, or a franchisee, to obtain and use the benefit of the knowledge, skill, experience of the franchisor including the latter's trademark to distribute the franchisor's goods. The franchisee and operator pays the supplier a fee. Thus, contrary to chain outlets, a franchise system does not have a centralized management system.

after the franchise agreement expires, in which the franchisee agrees not to enter into or start a similar trade in competition against the franchisor for a specified period.

358. In Spain, franchise agreements are assessed according to the mentioned Vertical Block Exemption Regulation 330/2010 and the also mentioned Guidelines on vertical restraints.

359. The Court of Appeal (*Audiencia Provincial*) of Burgos lodged a reference for a preliminary ruling to the Court of Justice of the European Union on 5 March 2012 regarding the scope of application of these clauses, especially in connection with the absence of future competition in the territory in which the franchisee has been operating during the period of the agreement.[191] The question was raised because Article 5 b) of Commission Regulation (EC) 2790/1999 foresees that under certain circumstances a non-compete obligation after the termination of the agreement is exempted from the prohibition of anticompetitive agreements.[192]

360. The European Court of Justice applied a narrow and literal interpretation of the wording contained in Article 5 b) of the Regulation 2790/1999 in its order of 7 February 2013, and considered that this Article should be interpreted as referring to the space in which the franchisee had been operating the business while the franchise agreement was in force and not the entire territory – much wider in this case – assigned in the contract. Thus, the ECJ concluded that non-compete obligations are allowed to benefit from the Block Exemption only if their geographic scope is restricted to the physical space from which the contract goods or services were sold, and not to the territory mentioned in the franchise agreement.[193]

---

191. The questions referred to the European Court of Justice are the following ones:

> *Should the words 'premises and land from which the buyer has operated during the contract period' used in Article 5(b) of [Commission] Regulation [(EC) No] 2790/1999 be understood as meaning that they are limited to the place or physical space from which goods were sold or services provided while the agreement was in effect or can they apply to the entire territory in which the purchaser operated during the contract period?*
>
> *In the event that the Court rules in favour of the first interpretation, in the case of a franchise agreement which allocates a specific territory to the franchisee, can the words 'premises and land' refer to the territory in which the franchisee has operated during the contract period?*

The questions refer to Regulation (EC) number 2790/1999 because this Regulation was in force during the agreement period (it expired on 31 May 2010).

192. These include the condition that the non-compete obligation is limited to the premises and land from which the franchisee has operated during the contract period. The Court of Appeal of Burgos referring the case to the CJEU inquired whether this limitation referred to the physical space in which the franchisee had been operating while the agreement was in force or whether this covered the entire territory assigned in the contract.

193. The court mentions also that the fact that a clause may not be covered by a block exemption does not prejudice the possible application of an individual exemption according to Art. 101.3 TFEU (or Art. 1.3 LDC).

361. In Spain the question whether the franchisor may restrict the customers to which the franchisee may resell the goods subject of the agreement was raised in *Logimail/Unipost.*[194] The CNC affirmed in this case that this conduct could affect intrabrand competition but in this case there were no anticompetitive effects because the franchisor and supplier had a very low market share and only one customer had been restricted.

362. Since Regulation 330/2010 has to be taken into account, the clauses contained in a franchising agreement which restrict competition will be exempted from the prohibition, provided the 30% market share thresholds are not exceeded and the agreement does not contain any hard-core restrictions.[195]

II. Technology Licensing

A. *Patent Licensing and Licensing Agreements for the Transfer of Technology*

363. On 1 May 2014 the *Commission Regulation (EU) 316/2014 of 21 March 2014 on the application of Article 101(3) of the Treaty on the Functioning of the European Union to categories of technology transfer agreements* entered into force. This means that from that date onwards technology transfer agreements have to comply with the conditions foreseen in that Regulation in order to be considered exempt from the prohibition of anticompetitive agreements contained in Article 101 TFEU. This Regulation as well as the guidelines will apply to those agreements by way of which companies authorize the use of patents, know-how or software by another company for the production of goods and services. Where the agreements in question are not capable of affect trade between Member States in an important way, the Spanish competition rules will be applicable. In this sense, the Spanish Patent Act 24/2015, of 24 July, foresees in Article 94 that compulsory licences can be ordered in case of the violation of competition law, e.g., anticompetitive licensing practices.

194. *See* the Decision of the Council of the former competition authority (CNC) of 23 October 2007, Proceedings 618/06, *Logimail/Unipost.*

195. *See* Arts 2, 3 and 4 Regulation (EU) 330/2010, exempting vertical restrictions where neither supplier nor buyer exceeds the market share threshold of 30%, provided none of the hard-core restraints in Art. 4 is present. For franchise agreements, it is worth mentioning that fixing maximum resale prices are not to be considered as anticompetitive according to Art. 4 a) of the mentioned Regulation. *See also* paras 189–191 of the *Commission Guidelines on Vertical Restraints*, [2010] OJ C 130/1. The European framework has been applied in recent decisions of the council of the former competition authority (CNC), as for example, in the Resolution of 12 February 2009, Proceedings S/0073/08, case *Burger King* or the Resolution of the Council of the current CNMC of 10 April 2014, Proceedings S/DC/0508/14, case *DIA, S.A.*, legal ground number one and two. In legal ground number two the CNMC reminds that the establishment of minimum or fix prices is prohibited, contrary to what happens with maximum prices according to Regulation 330/2010, which are not considered as hard-core restrictions.

364. In the pharmaceutical sector, it is likely that the Commission's sector Communication of 10 December 2008[196] will be followed by the Spanish competition authority in this field.

365. The European Commission adopted on 21 March 2014 new competition rules for the assessment of technology transfer agreements (TTBER and Guidelines),[197] through which a licensor permits a licensee to exploit patents, know-how or software for the production of goods and services. The new rules replace the previous TTBER and Guidelines from 1 May 2014 onwards. According to Article 2 of Regulation 316/2014, of 21 March 2014, Article 101(1) TFEU shall not apply to technology transfer agreements. In case the undertakings participating in the agreement are competitors, the exemption provided for in Article 2 shall apply on condition that the combined market share of the parties does not exceed 20% on the relevant market(s) (*see* Article 3.1).

366. TT-BER does not apply to agreements for trademark licences.

B. Trademark Licensing

367. No specific rules apply in Spain.

C. Know-How and Trade Secret Licensing

368. Regulation 316/2014 of 21 March 2014 on the application of Article 101(3) of the TFEU to categories of technology transfer agreements applies also to know-how licensing agreements.

---

196. COM (2008) 666 of 10 December 2008, Safe, Innovative and Accessible Medicines: A Renewed Vision for the Pharmaceutical Sector.

197. *See* the *Commission Regulation (EU) No 316/2014 of 21 March 2014 on the application of Article 101(3) of the Treaty on the Functioning of the European Union to categories of technology transfer agreements (TTBER)*, Official Journal L93, 28.03.2014, pp. 17–23 and *the Communication from the Commission — Guidelines on the application of Article 101 of the Treaty on the Functioning of the European Union to technology transfer agreements (Guidelines)*, Official Journal C89, 28.03.2014, pp. 3–50.

Chapter 2. Dominant Undertakings' Prohibited Practices[198]

369. In order to attempt to prevent undertakings with market power from using it to the detriment of free competition, Article 2 of the LDC prohibits abuse of a dominant position by one or more undertakings in the whole or part of the national market.

370. As abusive conduct, one could understand is an unlawful conduct, as well as a conduct that distorts competition. An undertaking is regarded to abuse its dominant position when it behaves differently than it would if operating on a fully competitive market. In order to ultimately achieve this aim, Article 2.2 of the LDC lists, by way of example, practices regarded as abusive: the imposition of prices or unfair trading conditions; the limitation of production, distribution or technical development to the unjustified detriment of other undertakings or consumers; the application of discriminatory conditions; as well as the subordination of the conclusion of contracts to the acceptance of supplementary obligations which, by their nature or according to commercial usage, are unrelated to the subject of such contracts.

371. That list of abusive practices is more or less the same as the one included in Article 102 of the TFEU, although the provision in Article 2.2 c) of the LDC on the refusal to supply goods or services is not explicitly laid down in the Treaty.

372. Inasmuch as the terms on abuse of a dominant position specified in Article 2 of the LDC are practically identical to the provisions contained in Article 102 of the TFEU (except as regards detriment to the EU market), the doctrine formulated by EU authorities is largely applicable to Spanish legislation.

373. Spanish case law has acknowledged this explicitly: 'given the similarity between Article 82 (former Article 86) of the Treaty establishing the European Economic Community and such Article 6 (Competition Act 1989, precedent of the current Article 2 LDC), which transcribes Community legislation on abuse nearly literally into Spanish competition law, the European doctrine on the abuse of a dominant position may be taken into consideration as an ancillary instrument for interpreting our domestic law.'[199]

---

198. For a general review, *see* DÍEZ, F., 'El abuso de posición dominante en el Derecho Comunitario y Español de Defensa de la Competencia', en GARCIA-CRUCES, J.A. (dir.), *Tratado de Derecho de la Competencia y de la Publicidad*, Tomo I, Tirant lo Blanch, Valencia, 2014, pp. 255–334; GUTIERREZ, A., 'Comentario al 2 LDC', in MASSAGUER, J. *et altri*, *Comentario a la Ley de Defensa de la Competencia*, Civitas/Thomson Reuters, Cizur Menor, 3rd ed., 2012, pp. 174–218; PELLISÉ, J., *La 'explotación abusiva' de una posición dominante (Arts.82 TCE y 6 LEDC)*, Civitas, Madrid, 2002.
199. Supreme Court Judgment of 15 October 2008 (RJ 2008, 5734).

§1. Exploitative Practices

374. Exploitative practice is understood to be conducted in which an undertaking with a dominant position capitalizes on its market power to impose unfair conditions on actors that depend on them for their supply of goods or services.[200]

375. This type of conducts is regarded to directly reduce consumer well-being. Nonetheless, Article 2 of the LDC (like its predecessor, Article 6 of the 1989 Competition Act) is more a tool to protect the marketplace than to directly protect a dominant undertaking's trading partners (suppliers and/or consumers). Hence, injury to private interests does not suffice for competition authorities to judge that exploitative practice exists. Rather, the general interest must be impaired in the form of severe market inefficiency that disrupts economic order.

I. Excessive/Unfair Pricing[201]

376. The paradigmatic example of exploitation of a dominant position, overpricing, is addressed in Article 2.2 a) of the LDC insofar as it is regarded to inherently constitute unfair trading conditions. However, distinguishing between high prices, which are lawful and generally believed to encourage innovation and the entry of new competitors, and the abusive prices referred to in this provision is no easy matter.

377. As a rule, goods or services are regarded as overpriced when no reasonable relationship exists between price and economic value.

378. That notwithstanding, determination of the economic value of goods and services and their reasonable relationship to price is not always possible and the competition authorities have no list of specified methods for ascertaining when price fails to match economic value.

A. Iberdrola *Case*[202]

379. This case addressed whether Iberdrola, a major player in the electric power market, had abused its dominant position by overpricing its products.

380. In order to solve this issue, the CNC conducted a three-phase analysis.

200. *See* Rodríguez, V. – Aranda, B. – Pastor, F., 'Abuso de posición de dominio', in Loma-Osorio, D., *Tratado de Derecho de la Competencia*, Aranzadi, Madrid, 2013, p. 199.
201. *See* Rodríguez, V. – Aranda, B. – Pastor, F., in Loma-Osorio, D., *Tratado*, pp. 200–201; Gutiérrez, A., in Massaguer, J. *et altri*, *Comentario*, pp. 174–180; Allendesalazar, R. – Vallina, R., 'Artículo 2 de la LDC: El abuso de posición dominante', in Baches, S. (coord.), *La ley 15/2007, de Defensa de la Competencia. Balance de su aplicación*, La Ley, Madrid, 2010, pp. 182–186.
202. CNC Resolution of 14 February 2008 (Proceedings 624/07, conduct, *Iberdrola* case).

381. In such analyses, the first phase entails studying the existence or otherwise of certain structural circumstances, such as the existence of a monopoly or quasi-monopoly, high entry barriers and relatively inelastic demand. These circumstances raise the likelihood of high prices constituting abusive pricing.

382. In the second phase, the allegedly abusive prices are compared to the undertaking's costs or to the prices applied in a competitive environment.

383. These two phases, whose purpose is to identify problematic cases and lower the risk of false positives, are followed by the third, which is more directly geared to analysing whether a price is abusive. That calls for determining whether the price is objectively justified or not.

384. Such objective justification might include, for instance, remuneration for making substantial investments in product innovation or development, assuming higher business risk, incurring sizeable sunk costs or absorbing a competitive disadvantage or significant externalities.

B. Iberia Líneas Aéreas de España S.A. *Case*[203]

385. In these proceedings the prices analysed were the fares charged by Iberia in its Madrid-Oviedo route, in which it was the sole operator. The CNC deemed that the existence of a dominant position was indisputable, inasmuch as Iberia was the only operator on the route at issue. The Commission therefore proceeded to compare the price applied to Iberia's own fares in other routes where it was the sole operator, and in routes where it competed with other carriers.

386. The outcome was that in the CNC's opinion, the fares for the Madrid-Oviedo route did not initially appear to be abusive.

C. Funerarias de Madrid 2 *Case*[204]

387. This case addressed a price hike implemented by the company *Empresa Mixta de Servicios Funerarios de Madrid, S.A.* The TDC deemed a mean rise in prices of 15.92%, the withdrawal of two types of high demand services and their inclusion in other packages at double the price, and the establishment of a 300% surcharge (which although never applied, was envisaged for certain users) to be abusive. The TDC found the rise in prices to be abusive especially because it was not substantiated by higher costs and was much greater than the 5.5% inflation rate and the increases applied by other undertakings.

---

203. CNC Resolution of 10 July 2009 (Proceedings S/0138/09, conduct, *Iberia Líneas Aéreas de España, S.A.* case).
204. TDC Resolution of 30 December 1997 (Proceedings 361/1995, conduct, *Funerarias de Madrid 2* case).

D. Canarias de Explosivos *Case*[205]

388. Here the question studied was the pricing policy implemented by Canarias de Explosivos, the only company commercializing explosives for blasting on the Canary Islands.

389. The CNC determined that differentiating between high and abusive prices called for analysing a number of structural criteria (existence of monopoly, high entry barriers, inelastic demand) and drawing comparisons (to costs and to prices in other more competitive environments).

390. After analysing the circumstances, the CNC deemed that the company was overpricing its products, for its conduct concurred with the aforementioned structural and comparative criteria. It further found that it had exploited its market power abusively, particularly respecting customers with lower bargaining power, applying inordinately price increases compared to the rates in place in more competitive situations. It also ruled that the company had maintained the entry barriers to reinforce its dominant position.

E. SGAE *Case*[206]

391. These proceedings referred to the royalties charged by the Sociedad General de Autores y Escritores (SGAE) to hotel establishments for playing dance music on the occasion of private celebrations such as weddings, christenings and first communions. The SGAE is a collectively managed intellectual property rights association and the only such organization in Spain handling this type of authorizations and royalties.

392. The CNC deemed that the SGAE's conduct constituted a complex infringement consisting of two practices based on its dominant market position. On the one hand, it applied discriminatory, non-transparent discounts; and on the other, beginning in 2009 it instituted a so-called substitutional rate schedule, which the CNC found to be disproportionate and unjustified by the costs of handling royalties (and discriminatory, for it envisaged differential rates for different users with no objectively substantiated justification).

F. Caso SGAE/Conciertos[207]

393. In these proceedings the prices analysed were the royalties charged by the Sociedad General de Autores y Escritores (SGAE) to promoters of public concerts.

205. CNC Resolution of 12 February 2008 (Proceedings 626/08, conduct, *Canarias de Explosivos* case).
206. CNC Resolution of 3 July 2012 (Proceedings S/0220/10, conduct, *SGAE* case).
207. Resolución de la CNMC de 6 noviembre de 2014, Expediente S/0460/13, Caso *SGAE Conciertos*.

394. The CNMC deemed that the SGAE had abused its dominant position in the market for the management of the rights when holding concerts in Spain. In particular, the CNMC established that the level of fees charged by the SGAE as consideration for the right to publically play musical content subject to copyright in concerts in Spain (i.e., 10% of the play or 9% when the capacity is less than one thousand seats) is extremely high and in breach of Articles 2 LDC and 102 TFEU, because the promoters in Spain are obliged to pay much higher rates than those applicable in other European countries (e.g., Germany, France or Italy). The CNMC noted that promoters are forced to pay rates which are significantly higher than those that would be applicable in a context of free competition.

395. In addition, the CNMC reminded that the potential abusive character of a fee has to be evaluated taking into account the possible equity ratio existing between the specific fee and the value of the remunerated good or service. The CNMC mentioned that certain practices carried out by the SGAE reinforced the mentioned abusive conduct, namely the imposition of disproportionate and unwarranted conditions to promoters and indirectly also to ticket resellers. These conditions consisted of the requirement to obtain a licence from the SGAE before starting the selling of the tickets, the obligation to deposit a guarantee which had to cover the total contribution of copyright or, alternatively, the obligation of the developer to distribute the tickets through a ticketing operator which should have a previous agreement of collaboration with the SGAE, in order to avoid the mentioned the deposit. The CNMC affirmed that the requirement to obtain a licence before even starting the selling of the tickets is an abusive conduct because apparently the SGAE had less burdensome alternatives for the promoters in order to avoid the non-compliance of the licence-requirement.

396. In fixing the amount of the fine, the CNMC took into account the size of the relevant geographic market, which covered the whole Spanish territory in this case, plus the very significant market share of the SGAE, i.e., it is the single entity authorized in the Spanish territory for the management of the rights related to public performances. The authority took also into account the scope and the duration of the infringement (from 2002 until 2013, both inclusive), the effects on the consumers and other operators in the same market, as well as the illegal benefits made by the SGAE due to this infringement. The CNMC confirmed that it had taken into account the total turnover of the SGAE in 2013. The decision also obliges SGAE to reduce the level of such fees within a three-month period and to avoid future anti-competitive practices as the ones already fined or similar conducts. Within the CNMC the Competition Directorate is responsible for following up the implementation of this resolution.

G. AIE *Case*[208]

397. The question addressed in these proceedings was essentially whether the prices charged by Artistas, Intérpretes o Ejecutantes, Sociedad de Gestión de España (AIE) (also a collectively managed intellectual property rights association, primarily for musicians and musical works) were disproportionate, abusive and unfair and whether the conditions applied to SOGECABLE, a media company, constituted discriminatory abuse of a dominant position.

398. The CNC ruling concluded that AIE used its dominant position to directly or indirectly impose unfair prices or other conditions on SOGECABLE, essentially by setting unilateral, a priori general rates lacking of objective elements on which to base negotiations and bearing no relation whatsoever to the economic value of the service rendered. AIE also abused its dominant position by discriminating against SOGECABLE, placing it at a competitive disadvantage by establishing conditions less favourable than offered other companies.

II. Discrimination[209]

399. Article 2.2 d) of the LDC defines abusive discrimination as 'the application, in trading or service relationships, of dissimilar conditions to equivalent transactions, thereby placing some competitors at a disadvantage compared with others'. This rule primarily attempts to prevent a dominant company's discriminatory treatment of customers from distorting competition among them, benefitting some to the detriment of others.

A. Televisiones *Case*[210]

400. These proceedings challenged the pricing established by the Asociación Fonográfica y Videográfica Española (AFYVE) and its successor, the Asociación de Gestión de Derechos Intelectuales (AGEDI), collective royalty management agencies for phonographic producers, for their dealings with television broadcasters.

401. The TDC deemed that the associations' practices entailed abuse of a dominant position, insofar as they applied, for no objective reason, dissimilar conditions for equivalent use of their repertory, favouring Spanish public television over its competitors Antena 3 de Televisión S.A. and Gestevisión Telecinco S.A.

208. CNC Resolution of 23 February 2011 (Proceedings 2785/07, conduct, *AIE* case).
209. For an in-depth study, *see* Díez, F., *La discriminación de precios en el derecho de competencia*, Thomson-Civitas, Madrid, 2003.
210. TDC Resolution of 13 July 2006 (Proceedings 593/05, conduct, *Televisiones* case).

B. Vale Music/SGAE *Case*[211]

402. Here the proceedings analysed the rates applied to phonogram producers by the Sociedad General de Autores (SGAE), a collective royalty management agency, for use of its repertory of protected works, which were lower for AFYVE (Asociación de Productores de Fonogramas y Videogramas de España) members compared to non-members.

403. The TDC deemed that the SGAE was entitled to entertain special agreements with associations, but that it had to justify the objective reasons for applying more favourable prices and conditions to their members. The competition authorities decided that in this case discrimination was not backed by any objective reason and entailed an advantage for both the SGAE, which capitalized on its monopolistic position, and the AFYVE member producers because it afforded them a competitive edge over non-members. It consequently ruled that the practice constituted an abuse of a dominant position.

404. In addition to this first group of cases in which the affected customers were competitors, at times the Spanish competition authority has extended the bounds of both discriminatory prices and excessive prices, deeming abusive practice to exist when a dominant company applies discriminatory prices to customers that do not compete with one another.

C. Prensa/Correos *Case*[212]

405. These proceedings revolved around ascertaining whether Correos (Spanish national postal service) had abusively discriminated between two categories of customers (professional press compared to other publishers) by applying dissimilar conditions for equivalent services (distribution by post of periodicals). Correos contended that it had committed no infringement because the customers affected by the presumed discrimination were not competitors.

406. The TDC, however, interpreted the LDC provisions to constitute a ban on 'unfair' (here likened to 'discriminatory') prices. In other words, the customers charged higher rates were subject to 'unfair' prices, considered not objectively but in comparison to others, not necessarily competitors, who were charged lower rates. The ruling established the existence of abuse, consisting of 'discriminating against professional press publishers by charging prices that are unfair compared to the prices charged to AEDE [Asociación de Editores de Diarios Españoles] member publishers'.[213]

211. TDC Resolution of 25 January 2002 (Proceedings 511/01, conduct, *Vale Music/SGAE* case).
212. TDC Resolution of 16 June 2005 (Proceedings 584/04, conduct, *Prensa/Correos* case).
213. Section one of the Judgment.

III. Unfair Trading Conditions[214]

407. Article 2.2 a) of the LDC defines this type of exploitative abuse as 'the direct or indirect imposition of [...] unfair trading or service conditions'.

A. Telefónica-Ibertex *Case*[215]

408. In these proceedings an Internet service company challenged practices implemented by Telefónica, at the time the sole provider of Internet access.

409. The TDC found that Telefónica's unilateral discharge of a contract of adhesion which it had itself proposed and which governed its relations with the Internet service company and its replacement with a new adhesion contract, likewise drafted unilaterally by Telefónica, constituted abuse of a dominant position, as it imposed particularly onerous conditions that would hardly have been accepted by companies not clearly dependent upon the dominant concern.

IV. The Limitation of Production, Distribution or Technical Development to the Unjustified Prejudice of Companies or Consumers[216]

410. Although this type of abuse is defined in Article 2.2 b) of the LDC, it has been applied only rarely in Spanish law, more than likely because of its exceedingly general terms.

A. Gas Natural Castilla y León *Case*[217]

411. This may be the most specific example of application of this rule. The proceedings analysed a series of practices that included the geographic distribution of markets among a dominant natural gas utility's installers and collaborators.

412. The TDC deemed that the agreement constituted collusion and fined the participating companies. In addition, it found that the dominant company, which was not a party to the restrictive agreement, had encouraged and endorsed the market slice-up by its collaborators by assigning each a single area. That sufficed for the competition authorities to hold that the company had abused its dominant position and committed a separate infringement distinguishable outside the agreement concluded by its collaborators.

---

214. *See* Pellisé, J., *La 'explotación abusiva' de una posición dominante (Arts.82 TCE y 6 LEDC)*, Civitas, Madrid, 2002, pp. 540–542; Gutiérrez, A., in Massaguer, J. *et altri*, *Comentario*, pp. 189–195.
215. TDC Resolution of 27 July 1999 (Proceedings 394/97, *Telefónica-Ibertex* case).
216. *See* Gutiérrez, A., in Massaguer, J. *et altri*, *Comentario*, pp. 180–181.
217. TDC Resolution of 5 January 2001 (Proceedings 482/00, conduct, *Gas Natural Castilla y León* case).

§2. EXCLUSIONARY PRACTICES

413. Exclusionary practices exist where a dominant company attempts to limit competition to maintain or raise its market power.

I. Predation[218]

414. Spanish competition authorities have followed the direction of the EU Commission in their rulings on predatory prices.

A. Tabacos de Canarias *Case*[219]

415. The object of these proceedings was the pricing policy implemented by Tabacalera, a tobacco company, for cigars in the Canary Islands. In applying EU case law, the TDC deemed that the company had abused its dominant position by applying predatory prices to eliminate existing competitors and discourage new entrants. Although this decision was confirmed by the National High Court (*Audiencia Nacional)*, it was subsequently overturned by the Supreme Court which, while deeming the principles set out in EU case law to be applicable, found that Tabacalera's production costs had not been substantiated.

II. Tying[220]

416. Article 2.2 e) classifies the 'subordination of the conclusion of contracts to the acceptance of supplementary obligations which by their nature or according to commercial usage have no connection with the subject of these contracts' to constitute abusive practice.

417. While this paragraph uses the term 'subordination', the principle refers not only to strictly subjecting the conclusion of one contract to concluding another (i.e., the joint conclusion of both, whereby the former service cannot be obtained without acquiring the latter as well), but also covers cases in which the first contract is economically more advantageous if the second is also concluded. Competition authorities have even interpreted this rule more broadly on occasion, including cases in which the dominant company does not require its customers to acquire two distinct goods or services, but rather to meet a certain condition in connection with the acquisition of one, such as not dealing with competitors.

---

218. *See* in detail HERNÁNDEZ, F., *Precios predatorios y derecho 'antitrust': Estudio comparado de los ordenamientos estadounidense, comunitario y español*, Marcial Pons, Madrid, 1997; NÚÑEZ, M., *El abuso anticompetitivo en precios. Rebajas y precios predatorios*, La Ley, 2012. *See also* GUTIERREZ, A., in MASSAGUER, J. *et altri*, *Comentario*, pp. 213–214.

219. TDC Resolution of 16 February 1999 (Proceedings 375/96, conduct, *Tabacos de Canarias* case).

220. *See* DÍEZ, F., In GARCIA-CRUCES, J.A. (dir.), *Tratado*, pp. 318–324; GUTIERREZ, A., in MASSAGUER, J. *et altri*, *Comentario*, pp. 195–198.

418. In such cases, the dominant company tends to use its command over a specific market to obtain a competitive edge in an associated market, expelling competitors that commercialise only the associated product under conditions more favourable for the consumer than for the dominant company.

A. Arquitectos de Madrid *Case*[221]

419. These proceedings analysed the Madrid Offical College of Architects' practice of making validation of professional assignments contingent upon substantiation of deposit of the design architect's fees and upon adjusting the project budget to the institute's own modules.

420. The TDC deemed that abuse existed in the form of denial of validation of a professional assignment until the aforementioned deposit was substantiated and of making such validation subject to acceptance of the institute's own criteria.

B. Gas Natural *Case*[222]

421. These proceedings challenged Gas Natural de Castilla y León, S.A.'s practice of offering gas pipe installation and distribution for commonhold facilities (service connections co-owned by all holders, running from the street to the meter in each home) jointly with the installation and maintenance of individual facilities (within each home).

422. The TDC deemed that such behaviour constituted abuse, given that Gas Natural de Castilla y León, S.A. held a dominant position in the former market (commonhold gas pipe installation and distribution), its offers effectively expelled possible competitors from the latter.

423. In this case, the competition authorities ignored the fact that the dominant company did not itself operate on the second market: rather, the actors were third companies it had authorized to do so. That fact was taken into consideration in subsequent decisions. In these decisions, however, the anticompetitive nature of a certain conduct was rejected.[223]

221. TDC Resolution of 19 November 1999 (Proceedings 446/98, conduct, *Arquitectos de Madrid* case).
222. TDC Resolution of 14 November 2003 (Proceedings 540/02, conduct, *Gas Natural* case).
223. *See*, for instance, TDC Resolution of 12 April 2007 (Proceedings R 713/07, appeals, *Special Prices/ Binter Canarias* case).

C. BT/Telefónica *Case*[224]

424. These proceedings were brought in connection with certain practices implemented by Telefónica when the telecoms market was first liberalized. More specifically, they analysed its treatment of companies highly dependent upon international voice communications, such as the members of the Asociación de Mediadores del Mercado Monetario Internacional (AMMI, association of international money market mediators) and the consequences of such treatment for other operators such as BT Telecomunicaciones S.A., which also sought to provide such companies with international voice services.

425. Claims were filed against two such practices:

(1) Telefónica applied different rates for telephone line rentals depending on whether the customer was also a competitor for a rental-related service or not. If it was, as in the case of BT, Telefónica only offered (and applied) its official rates; if the customer was not a Telefónica competitor or the incumbent used the lines itself to offer the related service and the customer had received a competitor's offer, it applied sizeable discounts to land the contract°.
(2) In international voice service, in which Telefónica applied predatory prices (lower than the cost of line rentals), it made conclusion of the contracts contingent upon accepting exclusive service conditions and linked services rendered on the competitive international voice communications market to others such as national voice communications provided under monopoly arrangements, and sold both at very inexpensive rates.

426. The TDC did not confirm the existence of predatory pricing, although it did detect practices prohibited under Article 6 of the 1989 Competition Act (presently Art. 2 of the LDC). On the one hand, it identified abuse of a dominant position consisting of applying dissimilar conditions for equivalent services (prohibited by Article 6.2 d) of the 1989 Competition Act, equivalent to the present Article 2.2 d) of the LDC).[225] On the other, it ruled that Article 6.2 e) of the 1989 Competition Act (equivalent to the present Article 2.2 e) of the LDC) had been violated, for Telefónica made applicability of its agreement with the AMMI contingent upon the acceptance of exclusive service conditions and linked the provision of services subject to a competitive market (international voice) to others where it had barely any competition (national voice communications).

427. Here, then, the competition authorities interpreted Article 2.2 e) of the LDC broadly, applying it to circumstances in which the dominant company did not require the customer to acquire two goods or services, but rather to comply with a given condition in connection with a single good or service, such as the acceptance of exclusive arrangements.

224. TDC Resolution of 21 January 1999 (Proceedings 412/97, conduct, *BT/Telefónica* case).
225. *See* item V.A below for more on this abusive practice.

III. Rebates[226]

A. Asempre/Correos *Case*[227]

428. The conduct examined in this case was a practice implemented by Correos, the monopoly provider of postal services by law, consisting of offering huge discounts to large postal service accounts, a market that had been recently liberalized, in exchange for the exclusive provision of joint postal services, covering both its legally monopolized activity as well as the liberalized business.

429. The TDC ruled that this practice constituted abuse of a dominant position because it was implemented by Correos as the monopoly provider of reserved services to keep new entrants out of the associated liberalized market.

B. Iberia *Case*[228]

430. These proceedings dealt with the air carrier's decision to change the system for remunerating travel agencies for their ticket sales and establish loyalty discounts for which the agencies were eligible when they reached certain sales figures.

431. The TDC deemed this to constitute abuse of a dominant position because such loyalty pricing altered market competition. The competition authority noted that while EU doctrine allows dominant companies to offer their customers discounts based on quantitative criteria (essentially, economies of scale), it bans bonuses that aim to enhance customer loyalty. The discontinuous nature of Iberia's bonuses and their weight relative to the agents' total commission made them a strong incentive to steer customers toward Iberia flights. The TDC therefore deemed that it constituted a loyalty practice that tended to ensure that passengers would continue to travel with the dominant company.

IV. Refusal to Deal[229]

432. Although refusal to supply goods or services is not explicitly listed in Article 102 of the TFEU as an example of abusive practice, it is included in Article 2.2 of the LDC.

433. The supply goods or services may be refused directly or made contingent upon consent to unacceptable or unfair conditions.

---

226. *See* Gutiérrez, A., in Massaguer, J. *et altri*, *Comentario*, pp. 209–213; Ruiz, J., 'Los descuentos y su problemática', in Martínez S. – Petibò, A. (dirs.), *El abuso de la posición de dominio*, Marcial Pons, Madrid, 2006, pp. 322–325.
227. TDC Resolution of 15 September 2002 (Proceedings S 568/03, conduct, *Asempre/Correos* case).
228. TDC Resolution of 1 April 2002 (Proceedings 514/01, conduct, *Iberia* case).
229. *See* Rodríguez, V. – Aranda, B. – Pastor, F., in Loma-Osorio, D., *Tratado*, pp. 210–211; Gutiérrez, A., in Massaguer, J. *et altri*, *Comentario*, pp. 181–188.

434. Not all such refusals necessarily restrict competition, however. Refusal to deal with regular customers or to supply a good or service required to operate on another market is presumed to restrict competition unless that refusal is objectively justified. Nonetheless, the actual or potential existence of an economically viable alternative supply must be taken into consideration, for if one is in place, abuse of a dominant position is difficult to uphold.

435. The central consideration in the analysis of refusal to supply goods or services is that any company, dominant or otherwise, is entitled to choose with whom it deals and freely dispose of its property.

A. Olympus Medical Systems Europa GmbH *Case*[230]

436. Here the CNC reviewed a medical and hospital product manufacturer's refusal to supply spare parts to a dealer. The Commission deemed that further to the definition given in Article 2 of the LDC, refusal could not be said to exist, for the dealer could have opted to honour the brand's quality standards, which were not discriminatory. The CNC also noted that alternatives were in place, for the dealer could have chosen to market other manufacturers' products and services. Lastly, further to the criteria applied in recent years with respect to the core of the prohibition, the CNC regarded the practice to be non-prosecutable because it was not detrimental to consumers.

B. McLane/Tabacalera *Case*[231]

437. These proceedings were brought to determine whether Tabacalera S.A.'s refusal to supply its tobacco to McLane was lawful or constituted abuse of a dominant position.

438. The TDC found that Tabacalera held a dominant position in two associated markets on which it operated: both the manufacture and the wholesale distribution of tobacco products. In the former it was the monopoly manufacturer in Spain and in the latter, despite recent market liberalization, it continued to be the sole operator, de facto. In light of those circumstances, the competition authorities deemed that Tabacalera's refusal was wholly unjustified and constituted abuse of a dominant position, inasmuch as it was designed to shield its distribution market position by barring McLane, a duly authorized EU tobacco distributor, from entry. In other words, Tabacalera intended to use its dominant position on the manufacturing market to defend its strength on the distribution market, which would have otherwise been challenged by McLane.

230. CNC Resolution of 14 June 2009 (Proceedings S/0034/08, conduct, *Olympus Medical Systems Europa GmbH* case).
231. TDC Resolution of 24 April 2002 (Proceedings 486/00, conduct, *McLane/Tabacalera* case).

C. Correos *Case*[232]

439. This case analysed the postal company's refusal to allow competitors in downstream markets wholesale access to the public postal network. The specific service refused was the delivery of official notices under the conditions of veracity and verifiability required by the existing legislation, Correos being the sole operator authorized by law to provide such authentication.

440. The CNC deemed such refusal to constitute abuse of a dominant position in the absence of any objective or legitimate commercial justification therefor, other than to exclude competitors from the retail official notices market. Moreover, such a practice could adversely affect competition in the traditional postal service market, given governments' significant weight in the demand for these services and the prominent role played by economies of scale and scope.

D. Caso Istobal[233]

441. This case addressed the conduct of Istobal, a Spanish manufacturer of machines for car washing, consisting in its refusal to supply spare parts to the independent technical assistance services (the so-called independent SATs) that did not form part of its authorized network. In addition, Istobal refused to provide independent repairers with the technical information needed to repair car washing machines.

442. The CNMC established that these refusals were an abuse of a dominant position, because it had the aim to exclude the independent SATs from the market of technical assistance services.

V. Price Squeeze[234]

443. The term 'price squeeze' is used to mean a pricing strategy implemented by a vertically integrated company with a dominant position in an upstream market designed to obstruct or even prevent its competitors from operating on a downstream market. It consists of selling the upstream market (intermediate or input) product to its competitors at a price so high that the margin between it and the price they can command for their downstream market product is too thin.

444. Nonetheless, such terminology has not always been used by Spanish competition authorities to refer to such practices, which they initially likened to discrimination.

232. CNC Resolution of 22 April 2013 (Proceedings S/0341/11, conduct, *Correos* case).
233. CNC Resolution of 30 June 2016 (Proceedings S/DC/0540/14, *Istobal* case).
234. *See* DÍEZ, F., In GARCIA-CRUCES, J.A. (dir.), *Tratado*, p. 329; GUTIERREZ, A., in MASSAGUER, J. *et altri*, *Comentario*, pp. 214–215.

A. Iasist/3M *Case*[235]

445. These proceedings analysed a practice implemented by 3M España S.A. The company was present on two associated markets, one for classification and grouping software designed to perform financial calculations relating to hospital admissions and lengths-of-stay, and the other for analysis software, used to make the predictions required for hospital management based on the codes delivered by grouping software. The company presented the two types of products as complementary software that had to be used jointly.

446. 3M España held a dominant position in the classification and grouping software market. The proceedings attempted to ascertain whether its sales conditions for this product distorted competition on the analysis software market.

447. The TDC deemed that 3M España had abused its dominant position in the former market by imposing, with no objective justification whatsoever, limitations and disadvantages on its sole competitor in the latter (Iasist, S.A.). Specifically, 3M España raised the price of its grouping software, unjustifiably making the combined product offered by Iasist, S.A. more expensive than its own and thereby practically nullifying the latter's ability to compete on that market.

B. Correos 2 *Case*[236]

448. These proceedings aimed to evaluate a pricing policy implemented by Correos, specifically the relationship between the wholesale prices charged to alternative postal operators for services associated with its postal network and the retail prices applied to bulk mail senders for the provision of traditional postal services.

449. The CNMC deemed that this pricing policy constituted abuse of a dominant position on the wholesale postal service market, for the price squeezing involved prevented alternative operators from competing in the large postal account segment of the market.

VI. Exclusive Distribution Agreements

A. Airtel/Telefónica *Case*[237]

450. This case analysed, among others, whether the exclusive distribution contracts concluded by Telefónica with a number of mobile telephony distributors constituted abuse of a dominant position, for they could restrict new entrants on the mobile telephone market.

---

235. TDC Resolution of 5 April 2002 (Proceedings 517/01, conduct, *Iasist/3M* case).
236. CNMC Resolution of 21 January 2014 (Proceedings S/0373/11, conduct, *Correos 2* case).
237. TDC Resolution of 26 February 1999 (Proceedings 413/97, conduct, *Airtel/Telefónica* case).

451. The competition authorities, drawing from ECJ case law, ruled that obliging distributors (even when at the latter's request) to obtain all or most of the supplies needed from the seller constitutes abusive exploitation of a dominant position, regardless of whether it is established as a requisite or incentivised by discounts. This ruling is justified by the fact that, when an operator has a strong market position, demanding exclusive purchase arrangements for a sizeable proportion of the market constitutes an unacceptable obstacle to entry. The behaviour challenged aimed or could have aimed to affect a market structure in which competition was already weakened by the presence of a dominant company.

B. Polvorines *Case*[238]

452. The practice challenged here, implemented by Unión Española de Explosivos, consisted of concluding agreements with its dealers whereby the seller purchased the buyers' warehouses and then leased them back subject to exclusive supply arrangements.

453. The TDC deemed that this practice constituted abuse of a dominant position, for by acquiring and controlling the distribution of industrial explosives it aimed to close the market to competitors just as it was being liberalized.

238. TDC Resolution of 26 January 2000 (Proceedings 450/99, conduct, *Polvorines* case).

Chapter 3. Unfair Practices as an Antitrust Infringement[239]

§1. Introduction

454. Article 3 LDC reads as follows:

> Article 3. Distortion of free competition by unfair acts
> The National Competition Commission or the competent bodies of the Autonomous Communities shall hear under the terms that this Act establishes for prohibited conducts the acts of unfair competition which affect public interest by the distortion of free competition.

455. EU Competition Law does foresee neither this antitrust provision nor any general legislation on unfair competition. Consequently, the restraints on or distortion of competition stemming from unfair practices is only prohibited EU-wide if such conduct involves prosecutable collusion *ex* Article 101 of the TFEU or the unilateral behaviour of an undertaking with a dominant market position that can be regarded as abuse under the provisions of Article 102 of the TFEU.

456. Although this issue is not regulated in EU law, Member States are not prevented from establishing national prohibitions on unilateral[240] market behaviour that are stricter than the Union's provisions on the abuse of a dominant market position (*see* Article 3.2 and Recitals 8 and 9 Regulation 1/2003).[241]

§2. Legislative Precedents for Spanish Competition Law

457. While in Article 3 d) of the first Spanish Competition Act of 1963 (*Ley 110/ 1963, de 20 de julio, de Represión de Prácticas Restrictivas de la Competencia*), unfair competition was regarded as possibly constituting a violation of antitrust law, that provision cannot be viewed as a precedent to Article 3 LDC because it was confined to conducts resulting from collusion or abusive conduct.

239. *See* Costas, J., 'Prohibición de falseamiento de la libre competencia por actos de competencia desleal', in Bello, Mª.P. – Hernández, F. (coord.), *Derecho de la libre competencia comunitario y español*, Thomson Aranzadi, Cizur Menor, 2009, pp. 213–231; Massaguer, J., 'Comentario al art. 3 LDC', in Massaguer, J *et altri*, *Comentario a la Ley de Defensa de la Competencia*, 3ª ed., 2012, Civitas/Thomson Reuters, Cizur Menor, pp. 218–243; Díez, F., 'El artículo 3 LDC: Falseamiento de la libre competencia por actos desleales', *Noticias de la Unión Europea*, 2012, No. 330, pp. 83–94.

240. The fact that these behaviours can be carried out by different companies at the same time does not change their unilateral character (*see*, in this regard, CNC Resolution of 17 September 2013 (Proceedings S/410/12, *ASCENSORES-2* case).

241. Costas, J., in Bello, Mª.P. – Hernández, F. (coord.), *Derecho*, p. 214.

458. The precedent of the current Article 3 LDC is Article 7 of the 1989 Competition Act,[242] the first provision which classified certain unfair practices[243] (those that significantly distort competition and then affect public interest) as a violation of antitrust law (and hence punishable by competition authorities), even where such conducts are not the outcome of collusion or abuse by an undertaking with a dominant market position.

§3. ANALYSIS OF THE PROVISION

459. The wording of Article 3 LDC implies that three circumstances must be present for the provision to be applicable: an unfair practice, a distortion of free competition and a detriment to public interest.[244]

I. Existence of an Unfair Practice[245]

460. The first circumstance that must be present is a conduct that can be regarded as unfair practice.

461. Antitrust legislation does not, however, establish its own distinct definition of such behaviour. The applicable definition therefore lies in *Ley 3/1991 de Competencia Desleal* (LCD) (Act against Unfair Competition). This Act lists a series of behaviours classified as unfair and includes a general clause that defines as unfair

---

242. The original wording of this provision was as follows.

> Article 7. Distortion of free competition by unfair acts
> All cases on unfair practices resulting in an appreciable distortion of free competition that affects the public interest in all or part of the national market shall be tried by the Competition Court under the terms on prohibited conduct stipulated in this act.

Under Art. 5 of Act 52/1999 of 28 December, the article was amended to read as follows.

> Article 7. Distortion of free competition by unfair acts
>
> 1. The Competition Court shall be informed, according to the terms established in the present Act for prohibited conduct, about the acts of unfair competition as long as the following circumstances are present:
>   a) that this act of unfair competition seriously distorts the competitive conditions in the market
>   b) that this serious distortion affects the public interest.
> 2. When the Competition Service deems that the above circumstances are not present, it shall shelve the proceedings.

243. *See* about this provision TRONCOSO, M., 'El marco normativo de los ilícitos desleales de relevancia antitrust (Reflexiones en torno al art. 7 LDC)', in *Estudios jurídicos en homenaje al Profesor Aurelio Menéndez*, Tomo I, Civitas, Madrid, 1996, pp. 1034–1079.

244. *See*, by way of examples, CNC Resolution of 28 May 2010 (Proceedings S/0227/10, *ATR ENDESA* case).

245. We follow in this section the opinions of MASSAGUER, J., in MASSAGUER, J. *et altri*, *Comentario*, pp. 232–234.

any behaviour objectively contrary to good faith (Article 4 LCD), in turn understood as taking into account the principles that inform constitutional economic order in Spain.

462. In order to be classified as unfair no prior court judgment declaring a conduct is required for Article 3 LDC to be applicable. Competition authorities have themselves the power to issue a preliminary decision in order to apply this provision.

463. Further to other requirements of this provision and in particular of the affection of public interest in the context of economic public order, they would normally be regarded to exist as the result of the commission of infringements such as 'unfair market practices', especially any practice that may somehow affect other undertakings' ability to compete. Examples of this aspect would be obstructive imitation (Article 11.3 LCD), alienation of employees (Article 14.2 *in fine* LCD), abuse of economic dependence (Articles 16.2 and 3 LCD)[246] and obstruction[247] as well as other similar conducts contrary to the general clause of Article 4 of the LCD.

464. Unfair practices may also be detrimental to the maintenance of a plural market structure (such as predatory practices as described in Article 17.2 c) LCD) or affecting the playing ground more in general (such as the infringement of the provisions included in Article 15 LCD).

465. Nevertheless, Article 3 LDC can be also applied with regard to unfair behaviour affecting consumers or other unfair conducts expressly forbidden by the LCD,[248] or even or that are against the general clause of Article 4 LCD.

---

246. *See* CNC Resolution of 17 February 2010 (Proceedings S/0038/08, conduct, *FEVE v. Laboratorios y almacenistas farmacéuticos* case).

247. *See*, for example, CNC Resolution of 17 September 2013 (Proceedings S/410/12, *ASCENSORES-2* case) and CNMC Resolution fo 12 January 2016 (Proceedings S/DC/0522/14, *THYSSENKRUPP* case).

248. In this sense, the CNMC Resolution of 12 January 2016 (Proceedings S/DC/0522/14, *THYSSENKRUPP*) considers the possibility of applying Art. 3 LDC as a consequence of affecting Art. 5 LCD (deception) or of Art. 9 LCD (denigration). This was also considered by the CNC Resolution of 17 September 2013 (Proceedings S/410/12, *ASCENSORES-2*), but without mentioning Art. 5 LCD regarding deception cases.

In this sense the TDC Resolution of 31 March 1997 (Proceedings R 189/96, appeals, *Resopal*) is also interesting, where the possibility of applying Art. 7 of the Competition Act of 1989 was considered (precedent of the current Art. 3 LCD), due to an infringement of Arts 13 (violation of company secrets) and 14 LCD (induction to a breach of contract). This case was initiated following a claim by the undertaking bearing the same name against an alleged anticompetitive conduct carried out by several competitors with the purpose of excluding it from the market place. The TDC affirmed that Art. 13 LDC, related to the breach of trade secrets, was not applicable since the one of the companies involved in the case (MACTAC) did not have access to Resopal's client list, which was in this case the trade secret referred to by the claimant, nor had MACTAC exploited such list to their advantage in the event it ever came in their possession. Moreover, the TDC argued that MACTAC and Resopal had different clients, since the clients of MACTAC were distributors or wholesalers – including Resopal –, which adapt the product for its final sale to consumers, while Resopal's clients were final customers. The TDC added that Art. 14 related to an inducement to a breach of the contract was not applicable either, 'as there was no evidence that

II. Distortion of Free Competition[249]

466. The second condition set out in Article 3 LDC for unfair practice to be an antitrust infringement is that it must distort free competition.

467. The need for this condition would seem obvious, insofar as what is at issue is the existence of a type of antitrust infringements that are prosecutable because, like collusion and abusive practices, they alter free market competition. What should be understood as distortion of competition is laid down in Articles 1 and 3 LDC. These rules are similar to the definition included in Articles 101 and 102 TFEU.

468. Unlike its predecessor, Article 3 LDC does not stipulate the extent of the distortion that would be required for the provision to be applicable. Article 7 of the 1989 Competition Act restricted applicability to significant distortion,[250] i.e., conducts of a certain dimension in order to alter the normal functioning of the markets. The absence of that restriction should not, however, be interpreted in order to understand that any distortion is subject to application of Article 3 LDC, because in that case the provision would be aimless, since any anticompetitive conduct and consequently any unfair behaviour would by definition lead to a distortion of free competition. The removal of the mention has to do with the need to coordinate this condition, distortion of competition, with the last one: affection of public interest. Distortion is only taken into consideration, then, when it is significant. Only in these cases it can be regarded to affect public interest.

469. In other words, all the legal doctrine in connection with this condition implemented by the competition authorities in light of the terms of Article 7 of the 1989 Competition Act continues to be applicable. In that Act, distortion was understood both structurally and functionally. Structurally, possible instances of distortion included the risk of eliminating competition via the exclusion of competitors, the obstruction of their presence and the prevention of new entrants on the market. Functionally, distortion was regarded as the inducement of a significant change in demand-side behaviour, in which particular stress was placed on the capacity of the unfair conduct at issue in order to influence consumer choice, ultimately seeking demand-side disregard for a given offer or customer switch. From that perspective, a change in consumer conduct in this context would be characterized by the initiation of a slide in demand whose end result may be a competitor's exclusion from or inability to consolidate a position on the market. The importance (not always explicit) attached by competition authorities to this functional factor would derive,

---

MACTAC had led to the regular or irregular termination of any agreement –business or franchise–, undertaken between Resopal and others, nor has been an agreement to eliminate Resopal from the market (...)'.

249. This section is based on the positions of MASSAGUER, J., in MASSAGUER, J *et altri*, *Comentario*, pp. 234–239.

250. The original wording of this article provided that unfair practice was to constitute an '*appreciable* distortion of free competition' (emphasis added), whereas after the 1999 amendment it stated that such conduct must '*seriously* distort competitive market conditions' (emphasis added).

then, from a given actor's power to eliminate competitors from the marketplace, or stated more generally to limit competition on markets where this practice may be implemented.

470. By way of summary, under Article 3 LDC, distortion only constitutes an antitrust infringement when it has or may have an adverse effect on the assumptions on which free competition stands as an institution and a principle of economic order that guarantees satisfactory market operation,[251]

471. The inference is, on the one hand, that distortion of free competition is a real or potential assault on the competitive structure of the market or the conditions that determine that structure or ensure the normal roll-out of competition as a market process. Of particular importance in this context are unfair conducts that prevent or may prevent competitor's entry to the market, consolidation or continuance, either as a direct consequence of unfair competition for competitors positions or conduct or its effect thereon as a result of its impact on demand.

472. That also means that in order for unfair conduct to be justifiably regarded as an antitrust infringement subject to the remedies and fines set out in the LDC, the distortion of free competition, which is a common effect of all unfair conducts, involved the necessity of having a sufficient dimension not only to establish market trends but also to prove detrimental to public interest. That circumstance obviously depends on the extent of the distortion. This element of the infringement consequently combines the structural component discussed above and a qualitative component or requirement for applicability. Distortion of free competition according to Article 3 LDC does not consist of just any adverse effect that unfair competition may have on the competitive structure of or the conditions prevailing on the market, but only the effects that involve appreciable, severe or significant distortion or obstruction That must be determined on the grounds of market characteristics, the possible implications for competitors and the number of consumers affected.[252]

III. Detriment to Public Interest

473. This last of the conditions laid down in Article 3 LDC is the most problematic one.

474. It is indisputably related to the first two, inasmuch as the existence of detriment to the public interest would stem from unfair conduct in which free competition is distorted. The main problem is to determine whether the distortion of free competition and detriment to public interest are related but distinct conceits, or whether the two constitute a single condition and then it is not possible to distinguish between them.

251. CNC Resolution of 30 June 2010 (Proceedings S/0137/09, *Telefónica* case).
252. CNC Resolution of 29 July 2011 (Proceedings S/0184/09, conduct, *Gas Natural* case).

475. This issue, which was also discussed concerning the precedent of Article 3 LDC, i.e., Article 7 of the 1989 Competition Act, has given rise both to divergent opinions among authors and to inconsistencies in decisions of the competition authorities in Spain, which have not been overly clear in this regard.

476. Some authors have stated that any significant distortion of free competition necessarily involves some detriment to public interest protected under the LDC. Further to this premise, these two conditions are in fact inseparable.[253]

477. Nonetheless, other authors, while not denying that material distortion of free competition is always affecting public interest,[254] have affirmed that this condition is not a mere formal expression of the interest protected by antitrust legislation, because in that case it would be superfluous, but rather one of the elements that structures this antitrust infringement. Under that premise, this third condition is narrowly and inter-dependently related to the first two and in particular to the distortion of free competition, which it characterises and from which it stems. Unfair practices also constitute an antitrust infringement because they affect public interest and that detrimental effect stems from the fact that such conducts entail the risk of distorting free competition. Further to this opinion, as an element of the infringement in itself, detriment to public interest would be characterized by two factors: first, by its *raison d'être*, i.e., it would be the outcome of distorting competition; and second, by implicitly meeting the significance condition in light of the definition of distortion of competition. According to that notion, competition is only distorted if the effect is significant, i.e., if the real or potential consequences of the conduct, judged from the perspective of maintenance or promotion on the marketplace, is of qualitative importance.[255]

478. Competition authorities, in turn, while formally deeming that detriment to public interest is a condition distinct from distortion of free competition,[256] in fact have often failed to distinguish clearly between the two requirements.[257] Nor has their definition of the content of this condition been consistent.

---

253. Costas, J., in Bello, Mª.P. – Hernández, F. (coord.), *Derecho*, p. 225; Montañá, M., 'Artículo 3' in Odriozola, M. (Dir.), *Derecho español de la Competencia*, Tomo I, Bosch, Barcelona, 2008, p. 213.

254. In other words, for antitrust infringement to exist, according to Art. 3 LDC, the unfair conduct must affect the public interest as a result of the inherent risk of distorting free competition.

255. Massaguer, J., in Massaguer, J. *et altri*, *Comentario*, pp. 241–242.

256. *See*, by way of example, TDC Resolution of 28 June 2006 (Proceedings r663/05, appeals, *Transporte de viajeros Lugo* case).

257. *See*, for instance, TDC Resolutions of 31 May 1995 (Proceedings r114/95, appeals, *Enoquisa* case); 3 November 1995 (Proceedings r120/95, appeals, *Manuart* case); and 31 March 1997 (Proceedings R 189/96, appeals, *Resopal* case), an extract from which reads: 'Article 7 LDC is not intended to inhibit all manners of unfair conduct or directly protect the interests of aggrieved competitors. That is incumbent on the *Ley de Competencia Desleal*. The *Ley de Defensa de la Competencia* [LDC] is an element of public law that *pursues the public interest*, with a view to ensuring that unfair conduct does not *distort the competitive operation of markets*' (emphasis added).

479. In most of its resolutions, the TDC interpreted the public interest to be equivalent to economic public order governed by the principle of free competition, which would be altered by an unfair conduct.[258]

480. The CNC did not follow this line of reasoning, however, but rather defined detriment to the public interest to involve other conceits or specific situations regarded as covered by the LDC, including:

– the ability to restrict effective market competition;[259]
– the obstruction of liberalization of a public service;[260]
– status as a basic input for undertakings and consumers;[261]
– the alteration of widespread demand;[262]
– significant distortion of competition.[263]

See also TDC Resolution of 30 May 2002 (Proceedings 521/01, *Agentes Propiedad Inmobiliaria* case) in which the public interest was deemed to be affected because the unfair conduct involved was detrimental to market competition.

258. *See*, for example, TDC Resolution of 30 December 1991, *Electromedicina* Case.
259. CNC Resolution of 15 December 2011 (Proceedings S/0350/11, *Asistencia en carretera* case).
260. CNC Resolution of 24 February 2012 (Proceedings S/0213/10, *Iberdrola Sur* case).
261. CNC Resolution of 24 February 2012 (Proceedings S/0213/10, *Iberdrola Sur* case).
262. CNC Resolution of 29 July 2011 (Proceedings S/0184/09, conduct, *Gas Natural* case).
263. CNC Resolution of 11 March 2008 (Proceedings S/0041/08, *Tu billete* case).

Chapter 4. Concentrations

§1. Horizontal Mergers

481. Mergers that eliminate a direct competitor may obstruct effective market competition if they significantly reduce competitive pressure to the detriment of customers and clients.[264]

I. Bolton/Garavilla[265]

482. This operation consisted in the acquisition of full control of Grupo Conservas Garavilla S.L. (GCG) by Bolton Group S.R.L. (Bolton). Bolton is an Italian holding company that manufactures and markets goods for mass consumption. It engages in a number of industries, including seafood (primarily tuna fish) conserves as a vertically integrated business, from fishing and processing to distribution and sale of the end product. GCG is a vertically integrated Spanish company with a worldwide value chain, likewise engaging in seafood conserves. In Spain it operates on the retail seafood conserves market, while also marketing salads and other types of ready-to-eat food in tins.

483. The competition authority analysed the merger, differentiating between the fish conserves and other prepared food markets. It deemed that the operation entailed horizontal overlaps in many of the fish products, although the joint market share was below 10%–20% in all retail seafood conserves with the exception of mussels, where the two actors had a joint share of 20%–30%. Those percentages were higher in the 'manufacturer brands' market, i.e., excluding 'white label' goods (in tuna fish they would have a joint share of 40%–50% (that means an increase of 10%–20%) and in mussels a joint share of 50%–60% (an increase of 20%–30%) more).

484. Despite such high market shares, the operation was not deemed to be a threat to effective competition for a number of reasons. First, seafood conserves (tuna fish in particular) were perceived as a commodity product targeting price-sensitive more than brand-sensitive consumers, with demand shifting in accordance with price variations and promotional sales, irrespective of brand. Besides, competitive pressure was particularly high at the retail level, because the competition exerted by other manufacturer brand competitors was reinforced by white label brands, which had gained considerable market power (with a share of 50%–60% to 70%–80%, depending on the type of seafood conserve). Second, no significant advantage was perceived to stem from having a wide product range, inasmuch as many medium-sized manufacturers with narrower ranges had ready access to distributors. Third, the market was characterized by excess capacity and operators could quickly raise their output in response to higher demand. In the fourth place,

264. Folguera, J. – Vidal, P., in Massaguer, J. *et altri*, *Comentariok*, p. 431.
265. CNMC Resolution of 30 June 2015, Case C-0667/15, *Bolton/Garavilla*.

no significant entry barriers were in place in these markets, for the technology and know-how required to offer competitive products were not determinants for market access. Finally, demand for these products consisted primarily in large distributors with substantial bargaining power, reinforced by the fact that their white label seafood conserves accounted for close to 70% of the retail market.

485. The operation would also entail vertical overlapping, for both actors were present in all the links of the seafood conserve production chain. Such vertical integration was found to afford no competitive edge, however, given that fish suppliers can be readily accessed.

486. The two companies had a joint retail share of the market for ambient temperature, fish-based prepared food of 40%–50% (a 30%–40% gain). Even though the operation led to such a significant rise in market share, however, it was not expected to restrict competition for several reasons. On the one hand the IAN Group constituted a strong competitor with a market share (20%–30%) that had grown substantially in the run-up to the merger. On the other hand, fish-based and other prepared foods were regarded as highly exchangeable, with the ingredient not constituting a meaningful factor in consumer choice between them. Furthermore, 'white labels' exerted strong competitive pressure. Finally, demand consisted primarily in large distribution chains with considerable bargaining power vis-á-vis manufacturers.

487. In light of the foregoing, the merger was not deemed to have an adverse effect on competition and was consequently authorized.

*II. **Repsol/Petrocat***[266]

488. This case involved a merger in the oil derivatives distribution industry essentially affecting the region of Catalonia. It consisted in the acquisition by Repsol Comercial de Productos Petrolíferos, S.A. (Repsol) of full control of Societat de Petrolis, S.A. (Petrocat) via the purchase of 45% of the latter's share capital from Cepsa Comercial Petróleo, S.A. (Cepsa). Prior to that operation, Repsol and Cepsa each held 45% of Petrocat's share capital, while the remaining 10% was in the hands of the Institut Catala d'Energia (ICE), a public body under the aegis of the regional government (Generalitat de Catalunya).

489. In its report and proposed resolution raised to the CNMC's *Dirección de Competencia* deemed that, unless sufficient remedial action were adopted, the operation would reinforce Repsol's horizontal and vertical position on the oil derivatives distribution market, for it entailed the disappearance of Petrocat as a significant competitor in Catalonia. This market, already highly concentrated and headed by Repsol, was characterized by parallel exclusive supply network arrangements that limited inter- and intra-brand competition.

266. CNMC Resolution of 3 April 2014, Case C-0550/14, *Repsol/Petrocat*.

490. The Dirección de Competencia therefore proposed authorizing the merger subject to compliance by Repsol of the final commitments the company itself had proposed. In essence, Repsol committed to refrain from growing its petrol station network and to ensure that third parties would supply a minimum volume of the product distributed by the stations acquired. The proposal was adopted by the CNMC Council, which authorized the merger subject to compliance with the aforementioned commitments.

III. Air Liquide/Gasmedi[267]

491. In this case the operation consisted in the acquisition by Air Liquide of full control of Gasmedi. Air Liquide is the French parent company of an international group comprising many firms engaging in the production and supply of gases for industrial, medicinal and environmental use. In Spain it operates through several industrial gas producers and distributors, while also providing home health care and hospital services and supplying medicinal gas. Gasmedi, a Spanish business group, provides home health care and supplies hospitals with medical gas and other services.

492. When analysing this transaction, the competition authorities differentiated between hospital medicinal gas supply and the home health respiratory services markets. Although Air Liquide led the former, as Gasmedi's share was scantly significant (no greater than 0%–10%), the joint post-operation share would amount to just 30%–40%. The main effects of the operation would be felt in the latter market, for as the third largest supplier in Spain with a market share of 20%–30%, Gasmedi's disappearance as an independent operator would mean that Air Liquide, until then the fourth ranked firm, would take the lead with a share of 30%–40%.

493. The competition authorities did not deem that the merger would entail a risk of a loss of competition on the markets involved, however. Their reasoning was based on the volatility of operators' market shares in such markets, the fact that after the operation there would still be a sufficient number of actors and, above all, the considerable countervailing power wielded by both the public hospitals that tender such services and private hospitals and insurer-owned health centres.

IV. Mapfre Automóviles/Mutua Valenciana Automovilista[268]

494. In this case the transaction entailed the absorption of Mutua Valenciana Automovilista by Mapfre Automóviles, a Mapfre Group company. Mapfre Group is

267. CNC Resolution of 5 September 2012, Case C-0458/12, *Air Liquide/Gasmedi*.
268. CNC Resolution of 22 November 2007, Case C-0013/07, *Mapfre Automóviles/Mutua Valenciana Automovilista*.

a Spanish multinational insurer present in a host of countries. It provides automobile insurance through its Mapfre Automóviles subsidiary. Mutua Valenciana Automovilista was an insurer providing cover essentially for automobiles.

495. In 2006 Mapfre Automóviles led the Spanish automobile insurance industry with a single market share of 10%–20% and a joint share, counting other group companies, of 20%–30%. Mutua Valenciana Automovilista, in turn, had a market share of 0–10%. The merger consequently reinforced Mapfre Automóviles' position in this market segment, affording it a share of 20%–30%.

496. That notwithstanding, in its report and proposed resolution raised to the CNC, the *Dirección de Investigación* deemed that the operation entailed no significant change in automobile insurance supply-side structure. That was due, on the one hand, to Mutua Valenciana Automovilista's small market share (which, in the absence of significant growth, was not anticipated to become a key player) and on the other, to the existence of a large number of competitors, including national and international insurance majors such as AXA Aurora-Winterthur-Direct Seguros (10%–20%), Allianz-Fénix Directo (10%–20%), Mutua Madrileña (0%–10%) and Zurich (0–10%). The relatively small rise in market share, together with the presence of a flurry of competitors and the absence of unsurmountable entry barriers justified the authorization of the operation on the grounds that it posed no threat to effective competition.

*V. **Dow Deutschland Anlagengesellschaft/UPPC AG**[269]*

497. Here the merger consisted in the acquisition by Dow Deutschland Anlagengesellschaft, subsidiary of Dow Chemical Co., of full control of UPPC AG and its subsidiaries. As a result of the operation Dow, which already engaged in the manufacture of basic raw materials for epoxy-based products and certain specialized components, would acquire UPPC's business: the manufacture of specialized amine adduct-cured epoxy polymerising agents and certain mixes of liquid epoxy resins.

498. In the epoxy polymerisation market, Dow would add UPPC's market share to its own 0%–10%, scaling its portion of the domestic market up to the same percentage as on the European Union market 0%–10%.

499. Dow's pre-merger 20–30% share of the European liquid epoxy resin and liquid epoxy resin blends market would grow very little with the operation, by less than 0%–10%. The strengthening of its Spanish domestic market position, where its initial share amounted to 30%–40%, would also be confined to 0%–10%.

---

269. CNC Resolution of 9 October 2007, Case C-0002/07, *Dow Deutschland Anlagengesellschaft/ UPPC AG.*

500. In light of these figures, the operation was deemed to entail no significant change in the supply-side structure in any of the product markets concerned. That, in addition to the absence of significant or unsurmountable entry barriers for the products at hand and the presence of strong actors, led to the authorization of the merger.

§2. Vertical Mergers

I. Domtar/Indas[270]

501. The operation at issue here consisted in the purchase of full control by Domtar Corporation of Laboratorios Indas. Domtar is a US manufacturer and distributor of paper, paper pulp and, on a smaller scale, absorbent hygiene products. Its presence was limited in Spain, where it did not sell adult incontinence products, but rather small amounts of absorbent composites used as a raw material by other companies to produce them. Indas, a Spanish company, manufactures cellulose, gauze and cotton products primarily intended for the production and sale of incontinence products for adults.

502. When assessing the merger, the *Dirección de Competencia* deemed that no risk of market foreclosure existed for Indas' competitors, despite Domtar's vertical integration, given its very small share of the absorbent fibre market (from 0% to 10%) and the existence of other sizeable suppliers of absorbent fibre in Spain. Nor would there be any risk for the operators that had been supplying Indas prior to the merger, for a number of large clients also operated on the domestic market. Another factor considered was that SCA, one of Indas' main competitors, is also vertically integrated in the absorbent fibre market.

503. In light of these circumstances, the *Dirección de Competencia* deemed that the operation should not be regarded as a threat to competition on the market analysed. It consequently raised a commitment-free authorization proposal in the first phase, which was approved by the CNMC Council (with the exception of one of the terms of a non-competition clause of the sale contract).

II. Carefusion/ARX[271]

504. This merger consisted in Carefusion's acquisition of the entire share capital of the ARX Group companies. Carefusion is a US market leader in the manufacture and sale of automated storage systems with a 40%–50% market share in the EEE and 70%–80% in Spain. ARX is the distributor of new and semi-new 'Rowa' automated storage systems of Carefusion for pharmacies in Spain, Belgium, France, Ireland, Norway, Switzerland and United Kingdom. In Spain, Carefusion was present

270. CNMC Resolution of 19 December 2013, Case C-0542/13, *Domtar/Indas*.
271. CNMC Resolution of 29 April 2015, Case C-645/15, *Carefusion/ARX*.

only in manufacture and sales, whereas ARX distributed wholly automated storage systems. After the acquisition, Carefusion would gain control of the sole distributor of its products in Spain.

505. The competition authorities approved the operation on the grounds that it entailed no horizontal business overlapping in Spain, but merely the vertical manufacturer-distributor integration. Furthermore, as ARX distributed CAREFUSION products nearly exclusively, the risk of market foreclosure for other distributors was ruled out.

III. San Miguel/Montycarrera[272]

506. This case resembled the Carefusion/ARX operation. The merger consisted in the Mahou San Miguel Group's acquisition of full control of Comercial Montycarrera, S.A. Mahou San Miguel engages mainly in beer manufacture and marketing. Montycarrera, in turn, distributes and markets food and beverages and provides logistics services, primarily for the Mahou San Miguel group, on the Baleàric Isles. Consequently, the merger would enable Mahou San Miguel to control its main distributor on the islands.

507. The competition authorities waved the operation through because it was deemed to pose no threat to competition. In other words, it was not expected to distort the markets affected or entail a risk of market foreclosure for other brands.

§3. Market/Product Extension (Conglomerate) Mergers

508. The term conglomerate merger covers operations in which the participant companies do not compete on any market and which involve no vertical integration. There are three types of conglomerate mergers: market extension mergers, product extension mergers and pure conglomerate mergers. In market extension mergers the companies concerned share a product but operate on different geographic markets. In product extension mergers, the participants operate on the same geographic market but with different albeit related products. Pure conglomerate mergers are operations in which the companies involved share no product or geographic market.

I. Bagoeta/Tubos Reunidos[273]

509. This case entailed the review of a merger whereby Bagoeta, S.L. attained control of Tubos Reunidos, S.A. Bagoeta is a holding company with subsidiaries

272. CNC Resolution of 24 April 2014, Case C-0565/14, *San Miguel/Montycarrera*.
273. TDC Resolution of 25 October 2007, Case C-0007/07, *Bagoeta/Tubos Reunidos*.

engaging, among others, in small-scale welded steel pipe manufacture. Tubos Reunidos, in turn, was a seamless pipe and tubular product manufacturer, distributer and marketer.

510. Since Bagoeta only made welded pipes and Tubos Reunidos only seamless pipes, the operation constituted a product extension merger. It was authorized because it was not expected to have an adverse effect on competition, inasmuch as other competitors could produce small-scale, welded and seamless carbon steel pipes, which tend to be the objects of separate demand.

II. Cardinal/Cordis[274]

511. Here the merger consisted in Cardinal Health Inc.'s acquisition of Cordis Corporation and its subsidiary Flexible Stenting Solutions Inc., as well as related Johnson & Johnson's Cordis business assets. Cardinal is a multinational firm providing health industry goods and services. Globally, it is present in two market segments, the pharmaceutical and the medical. Cardinal operated primarily in the US with no sales in Spain. Cordis develops, manufactures and sells minimally invasive devices used to treat vascular disease. It has two business units: (i) Cordis Cardiology, which sells devices for heart surgery; and (ii) Cordis Endovascular, which sells endovascular devices. Unlike Cardinal, Cordis was present on the Spanish market, with a turnover in 2014 of under EUR 60 million.

512. The operation was authorized on the grounds that it would not obstruct effective competition, given the absence of any horizontal or vertical overlapping.

III. Cunext/ECN[275]

513. This case involved a merger in which Cunext Copper Industries, S.L. acquired 100% of ECN Cable Group S.L.'s share capital. Cunext engages in copper transformation, with facilities in Cordoba, Madrid, Barcelona and Oviedo, all in Spain. ECN manufactures and commercializes bare as well as insulated low-voltage aluminium electric wires and cables.

514. The operation was likewise authorized in the understanding that it would not obstruct effective competition, given the absence of any horizontal or vertical overlapping.

---

274. CNMC Resolution of 7 May 2015, Case C-0649/15, *Cardinal/Cordis*.
275. CNMC Resolution of 29 April 2015, Case C-0646/15, *Cunext/ECN*.

IV. *Enaex/HBE*[276]

515. This merger consisted in Enaex S.A.'s acquisition of 100% of Harle Bickford Expansion, S.A.'s (HBE) share capital. Enaex, a Chilean company forming part of the Sigdo Koppers Group, engages primarily in the production and commercialization of ammonium nitrate (input used to manufacture explosives), the production and commercialization of civil explosives and the provision of comprehensive consultant services for rock fragmentation. HBE Group, in turn, focuses on producing and commercialising electric, non-electric and electronic detonators and detonating fuzes.

516. The operation was approved by the authorities, who deemed that it would not obstruct effective competition, given the absence of any horizontal or vertical overlapping.

§4. Pure Conglomerate Mergers

517. As noted above, pure conglomerate mergers are operations in which there are no product or geographic connections between the markets of the companies involved, which sell unrelated products and lack any customer-supplier relationship. Such mergers do not normally pose competition problems and hence are generally authorized.[277]

518. The *Watling/Mirion* case[278] affords a recent example. In this merger, Watling Street Capital Partners LLP acquired full control of Mirion Technologies, Inc. Watling Street Capital is the parent firm that ultimately controls the Charterhouse investment fund, headquartered in the United Kingdom. Charterhouse provides private fund and capital management services, including investment management and consultant services for a number of investment funds. It indirectly controls a number of companies in a wide spectrum of industries, none related to Mirion's business.

519. The operation was approved because the authorities deemed that it would not obstruct effective competition, given the absence of any horizontal or vertical overlapping between the parties.

---

276. CNMC Resolution of 14 May 2015, Case C-0650/15, *Enaex/HBE*.
277. *See*, for instance, CNMC Resolution of 11 February 2015, Case C-0632/15, *Hearst/Fitch*.
278. CNMC Resolution of 15 January 2015, Case C-0631/14, *Watling/Mirion*.
A similar pure conglomerate merger was analysed in CNC Resolution of 2 November 2011, Case C-0391/11, *Bridgepoint/Activos Eólicos de ACS*.

§5. JOINT VENTURES

520. Spanish competition authorities have been notified of a substantial number of joint ventures in recent years. Most were authorized unconditionally in the first phase. Many consisted in the entry of a new controlling partner in a company formerly controlled by one[279] or several others.[280] In some cases the operation entailed a change in the joint venture's control[281] or the joint acquisition of control of one company by two others.[282]

521. The DISA/Shell operation was the most complex of the recent ventures.[283] DISA is the holding company of an oil industry group in Spain. It operates primarily in the Canary Islands, although it also has a network of petrol stations on the Iberian Peninsula. Shell is a multinational engaging in the exploration, production and sale of oil and natural gas, the production and sale of petrochemical products and electric power generation. The merger consisted in the acquisition by DISA of joint control over Shell Aviation España, S.L., formerly fully owned by Shell, through the purchase of 50% of the company shares. As a result, Shell Aviation España would be a Spanish aviation fuel company jointly controlled by DISA and Shell.

522. When analysing the operation, the CNC observed that it could obstruct effective competition on the Canary Islands. DISA was the sole available entry point on certain islands for aviation fuel storage and logistics, as it was the sole logistics operator with a fleet of vessels for inter-island shipments. In addition, on some islands DISA's were the sole airport access infrastructures, with no alternative options for the remaining operators.

523. Such problems necessitated second phase analysis of the operation. It was ultimately authorized, subject to compliance with a series of commitments submitted by the participants.

524. Two involved third party access to DISA's infrastructures (one to stationary fuel shipping and storage on the islands and the other to inter-island maritime shipping of aviation fuel). These agreements were carried out by publishing on DISA's website the necessary information in order to keep them alive, as well as

---

279. *See*, among others, CNC Resolutions of 7 January 2009 (Case C-0122/08, *Iberia/Gestair/Corjet*), 14 December 2011 (Case C-0411/11, *FERRER/ROVI*), 12 December 2012 (Case C-0484/12, *Mitchell/EINSA/GT Motive*) and 6 February 2014 (Case C-0549/14, *Plenium Partners/FCC/FM Green Powers Investments*).

280. CNC Resolution of 17 March 2010, Case C-0214/10, *ENAGAS/BBG/JV*.

281. For instance, CNC Resolution of 8 February 2012 (Case C-0417/11, *ENAGAS/GASCAN*) and CNMC Resolution of 2 June 2015 (Case C-0652/15, *ENAGAS/OSAKA/UFG/SAGGAS*).

282. *See*, for example, CNMC Resolutions of 14 May 2015 (Case C-0654/15, *Ontario/ONEX/North American Tillage*) and 11 June 2015 (Case C-0657/15, *LFPI/Montefiore/Grupo Interflora*).

283. CNC Resolution of 25 March 2013, Case C-0468/12, *Disa/Shell/SAE/JV*.

the contracts related to the transport of these infrastructures. In this way, the access to the information in an objective, transparent and non-discriminatory way is ensured.

525. The third commitment revolved around the possible reinforcement of structural links among competitors on the aviation fuel supply market. DISA and Shell committed to refrain from including in the joint venture their respective holdings in CMD Aeropuertos Canarios S.L. and Spanish Intoplane Services S.L., companies providing aircraft fuelling services.

Part III. Administrative Procedure

Chapter 1. Administrative Investigations Before the Antitrust Authority

§1. INITIATIVE

I. General Sectors Inquiries

526. Article 5 h of Act 3/2013, from 4 June 2013, provides the CNMC with the power to promote and conduct studies and research on competition, as well as comprehensive reports on economic sectors. Not enough time has passed in order to evaluate the attitude of the CNMC in this matter,[284] but the former CNC considered sector inquiries as an important measure within its advocacy functions,[285] and in recent years many sectors have been looked at, e.g., the transport market of goods by rail, the automotive fuel distribution market, the postal or the agricultural sector.

II. Ex Officio Investigations

527. According to Article 49 LDC, proceedings related to anticompetitive conducts are initiated ex officio by the Competition Directorate of the CNMC, which is the branch of the CNMC entrusted with investigative powers,[286] either on its own initiative or where competition law infringements are brought to their attention. This could be by the Council of the CNMC or after receiving a complaint from individuals or undertakings, which do not need to be affected by the alleged infringement,

284. It should be noted that there is a specific subdirectorate of studies and reports within the Department of competition advocacy of the CNMC.

285. On the website of the former CNC it is mentioned that: '*market studies and sectorial reports test the situation in terms of competition of a sector or an industry or, also, the effect of an anticompetitive situation which is common to different sectors. These reports take into account in the analysis the legal and economic framework of the sector involved as well as the undertakings' economic behaviour. They have as their object the formulation of recommendations to public bodies or to undertakings in order to enhance competition and efficiency to the benefit of consumers, including proposals to improve regulation or clarifications and even warnings addressed to undertakings and Public bodies in order to remove obstacles to competition.*'

286. The Law mentions the Research Directorate of the former CNC but the second additional disposition of Act 3/2013 clarifies that all the references made to this Research Directorate of the CNC should be understood as now turned into the Competition Directorate of the CNMC.

i.e., they might be considered as an interested party in a specific proceeding or not. This final decision to initiate proceedings will depend on the existing evidence of the alleged breach of the LDC.

528. Ex officio investigations may also be triggered by leniency applications, sector enquiries, news appeared in the media or even by the just mentioned complaints from customers, suppliers, competitors, employees or anyone else. According to Article 25.3 of Royal Decree 261/2008, from 22 February, these complaints have to necessarily include the name of the complainant, thus, they cannot be anonymous.[287]

529. The annual report published by the CNMC for 2014 mentions that during that year fifteen ex officio investigations were initiated.[288]

III. Complaints

530. Complaints are usually merely an informal way of bringing an infringement to the authority's attention, and the Competition Directorate of the CNMC will then decide if the procedure shall be initiated. An informal complaint will, in itself, not confer any special status in the proceedings that may be initiated by the CNMC to the complainant.

531. If the complainant wishes to participate in the proceedings with special procedural rights, he/she needs to make an application to be joined as a party in the proceedings under Article 25.2 b) of Royal Decree 261/2008. But it is within the CNMC's discretion both to initiate the proceeding (Article 25.5 of the same Royal Decree) and to decide if the applicant can be considered as joined as a party to a specific proceeding.

287. If the Competition Directorate finds that there is sufficient evidence of an infringement of competition law, it will send a statement of objections to the companies involved, including all the facts which support the apparent competition infringement. The affected companies have then fifteen days to reply to the statement and also to offer counter-evidence (Art. 33 of the mentioned Royal Decree 261/2008). The Competition Directorate will then end the investigation phase and prepare a proposal for a decision. This proposal will include a description of the background, i.e., the proven facts, the addressees, the legal charges and, if applicable, a statement of the evidence of the effects caused in the specific market, the liability of each of the addressees, any aggravating and mitigating circumstances, and a proposal concerning any exemption or reduction of fines pursuant to the leniency programme. The proposal will be sent to the parties, who will then be given another fifteen days to submit any arguments in response, as well as to make suggestions for any further evidence gathering and, in case they are interested, to request a hearing. The Competition Chamber of the CNMC Council may, on its own initiative or at the request of any of the interested parties or companies, gather further evidence or carry out a complementary investigation to the one already carried out by the Competition Directorate. For more details, please *see* Arts 25–39 of the Royal Decree 261/2008.

288. *See* Annual Report of the CNMC for 2014, p. 17.

532. The annual report published by the CNMC for 2014 mentions that during that year 19 complaints were filed before the Spanish competition authority.[289]

§2. POWERS

I. Requests for Information

533. Article 39 LDC provides a general obligation of cooperation and information with the competition authority, stating that any natural or legal person, as well as the offices and public administration agencies are subject to the duty of cooperating with the CNMC. They are moreover obliged to provide all types of data and information available to them, which might be necessary for the CNMC for the application LDC, in order to promote effective competition in the markets. The time limit to provide this information is set by Article 39.1 LDC in ten days, except when the nature of the information requested or the circumstances of the specific case justify a different time limit.[290] Article 39.2 clarifies that this cooperation, on its own initiative or at the request of the CNMC, shall not imply or result in the condition of interested party in the underlying proceedings. It is important to remember that the lack of cooperation, or the provision of incomplete, inexact or misleading information, constitutes a minor infringement according to Article 62.2. c) LDC and can thus be subject to fines which could reach the amount of 1% of the total sales of the infringing company in the fiscal year immediately preceding that in which the fine is imposed or, in case the total sales cannot be determined, a fine of EUR 100,000 to EUR 500,000.

II. Investigating and Search Powers

534. Article 27 of Act 3/2013 grants broad investigative powers to the Spanish competition authority.[291] This provision states that the statutory officers and civil servants '*duly authorized by the corresponding director shall be considered as an agent of the authority*'. They may conduct all necessary inspections of undertakings and associations of undertakings in order to ensure the application of the competition rules in Spain. To this end, according to section 2 of this Article, the CNMC agents may:

- Enter any premises, plant, land, or means of transport of the undertaking(s) and/or associations, as well as the private homes of the entrepreneurs, managers and other staff members of the companies. They may also control the assets assigned

289. *See* Annual Report of the CNMC for 2014, p. 17.
290. Article 28 of Act 3/2013, from 4 June, also foresees the obligation of cooperation with the competition authority in Spain, reminding that the requests for information have to be motivated, in proportion to the relevant purpose.
291. The sole repeal provision of the mentioned Act 3/2013 abolished Art. 40 LDC, which was the former norm foreseeing the investigating and search powers of the competition authority in Spain. The content of both Art. 40 LDC and Art. 40 of Act 3/2013 is essentially the same.

to the services, activities or operators they carry out and which could be affected by carrying out activities mentioned in this act, as well as the networks installed or operated and the documents they are required to own or keep.
- Access and checking of books and other documents relating to their business activities, regardless of the medium on which they are stored, including also software and magnetic, optical or other kind of files.
- Take or obtain in any form copies of, or extracts from, such books, documents or records.
- Retain for a period of ten days the books documents or files mentioned above.
- Seal all premises of the companies, books, records, or other business assets during the period of the inspection and to the extent required for the inspection.
- Ask any representative or staff member of the undertaking(s) or associations being inspected for explanations on facts or documents related to the object and purpose of the inspection and to record these answers.

535. Article 27 foresees also that the entrance to the premises of the company or the private homes, as well as the sealing of premises or assets of the company require the prior agreement of the affected party or, if this consent is not granted, a judicial authorization in order to maintain the right to privacy and the protection of personal communications. Paragraph four of the same Article mentions that if the undertaking or association of undertakings opposes an inspection ordered by the Director of the respective investigation, or if there is a risk of such opposition, a judicial authorization must be requested and is certainly necessary in this specific case. The competent Administrative Court has to deal with the request within forty-eight hours. The judicial authorization is necessary due to the inviolability of the home, which is guaranteed by Article 18.2 of the Spanish Constitution.[292]

536. In refusing authorization, individuals risk violating the LDC by impeding the investigation because the LDC requires that undertakings and associations of undertakings submit to inspections duly authorized by the Director of Investigation. For example, *Caja De Seguros Reunidos, Compañía De Seguros Y Reaseguros, S.A.* ('CASER') was fined on 24 July 2008[293] a total amount of EUR 133,500 for the obstruction of an investigation at its registered office in October 2007. In this case, one of the undertaking's executives had initially denied the CNC access to the premises, after calling their lawyers, they decided to authorize the access to their office three hours later.

537. The company *Extraco* was also fined EUR 300,000 on 6 May 2010 by the Council of the CNC[294] for impeding an investigation in their office by withholding an envelope and pictures and avoiding thus the inspection of these documents by the CNC, denying permission to inspect an office without the presence of an external lawyer, and denying permission to inspect a safe-deposit box. The CNC

292. This Article provides that '*the home is inviolable. No entry or search may be made without the consent of the owner or a judicial resolution, except in flagrant cases of offence.*'
293. CNC Resolution of 24 July 2008, Proceedings SNC/02/08, *CASER-2*.
294. CNC Resolution of 6 May 2010, Proceedings SNC/0007/10, *EXTRACO*.

reminded the investigation has not to be necessarily impeded in order to be able to fine these conducts, it is enough that the company renders it more difficult, prevents access to or delays the inspection.

538. On 21 September 2011 the former CNC imposed a fine of more than EUR 2 million upon *Trasmediterránea* and its subsidiary *Europa Ferries* for hindering the initiation and development of the inspection, providing incomplete information, preventing contacts with the board of the companies and making access to information difficult.

539. It is also important to mention that the exercise of the powers related to the entrance and the seal of the premises requires the prior express consent of the affected party, or, alternatively, the prior authorization of the competent Spanish judicial authority. It is also worth mentioning that even though Article 27.2 of Act 3/2013 provides a list of the investigative powers of the CNMC, this is not an exhaustive list. The Directorate for Competition is entitled to use other means of investigation in order to carry out its searches, having to respect always the Spanish constitutional and jurisdictional rules.

540. The undertakings and associations of undertakings are required to submit to inspections authorized by the competent authority. If the undertaking or association of undertakings does not agree to submit to the inspection or if there is certainly a risk of such opposition in practice, the CNMC has to apply for a judicial authorization from the competent administrative court (if a fundamental right can be affected). The judge asked to authorize the inspection has to take a decision within a maximum period of forty-eight hours. Public authorities are supposed to provide, if necessary, protection and assistance to the staff of the CNMC for the exercise of these investigating powers, including also regional competition authorities.[295] As mentioned above, inspections of private domiciles will only take place in cases in which there are well-founded indications that books or other documents may be found which can be used to prove the existence of a serious or very serious infringement.[296] CNMC inspectors or personnel do not have to wait for the arrival of legal advisors before starting to search for evidence but they usually inform the investigated companies that they may be accompanied by external or in-house legal advisors if they wish to and usually they wait a reasonable period of time for their arrival before starting their searches.[297]

541. Civil servants shall draw up a record of the inspection proceedings.[298] The extended nature of records will become public documents and has to be considered as evidence of the facts on which they were made, unless the contrary is proved.

295. Mentioned later in B.III.
296. So-called fishing expeditions shall be avoided.
297. Article 15 of Royal Decree 261/2008 foresees, in line with Regulation 1/2003, that the CNMC is the competent authority to collaborate on inspections and share powers of investigation with the European Commission and with the Competition Authorities of other Member States.
298. The annual report of the CNMC for 2014 mentions that 198 civil services are in charge of inspections.

542. The sixth paragraph of Article 27 provides as an important limit that data and information obtained in the context of an inspection may only be used by the CNMC for the purposes provided for in Act 3/2013 and in the LDC. That is why the investigating powers of the CNMC may not violate the rights of the person being investigated related to the possibility of not testifying against him- or herself or not to confess guilty. In practice, the CNMC usually requests a judicial authorization before carrying out investigations in order to avoid delays and/or denials of the members of the investigated company. These investigations of the CNMC are restricted to the matter at hand in this authorization and the information found cannot be used for other purposes different than those include in the scope of the investigation.

543. Spanish competition law foresees that the fact of providing incomplete, incorrect, misleading or false information, as well as the submission to an inspection or obstructing monitoring purposes, are minor infractions according to Article 62.2 LDC. This rule tries to avoid that someone hinders research activities which have to be carried out by the CNMC.

544. Article 13 of the Royal Decree 261/2008 provides that the personnel of the CNMC may, while carrying out an investigation, be accompanied by experts or specialists duly authorized by the Director for Competition (e.g., experts in IT). The CNMC officials may also call the police in case of obstruction. On 15 October 2009, during the inspection of the construction company *Extraco*, in the context of a suspected bid rigging cartel for road constructions, the officials of the former CNC called the police in order to have access to a safe box because *Extraco* refused to open this box.[299]

545. Finally, it is worth mentioning that the Spanish competition rules and specific case law do not explicitly explain whether in-house lawyers are protected by the *legal privilege* principle. According to the Judgment of the Spanish Supreme Court of 27 April 2012 in the *Stanpa* case,[300] one can conclude that, in line with the EU case law resulting from *Akzo Nobel,*[301] in Spain in-house legal advice is not protected by *legal privilege*. In accordance with this, documents written by external lawyers are protected by *legal privilege.*

III. Cooperation with Other State Institutions

546. The Competition Act empowers the Spanish antitrust authorities to gather evidence throughout Spain. In addition, the Act empowers the Spanish antitrust

299. *See* the Decision of the former CNC of 19 October 2011, Case Number S/0226/10.
300. *See* Judgment of the Spanish Supreme Court (Third Chamber) of 27 April 2012 (Appeal Number 2829/2011).
301. *See* extensively in Pérez Fernández, P. 'The Difficult Relationship Between Restraints to the Attorney-Client Privilege and Compliance with the Law by Companies – Commentary on *Akzo Nobel Chemicals and others vs. Commission* (Case C-550/07)' in *European Criminal Law Review*, Vol. 1, nº 3, 2011, pp. 274–285.

authorities to collaborate with the national authorities of other EU Member States and the EC in line with the provisions of the TFEU and EC Regulation 1/2003. These Articles, as well as Article 18 LDC allow the Spanish competition authority to exchange evidence, including confidential information, with the European Commission and national authorities of other Member States, and use such obtained evidence in their own Spanish investigations.

547. With respect to cooperation with other jurisdictions, Spain is not party to any formal legal assistance treaty or cooperation agreement concerning competition jurisdiction issues. However, in recent years, there has been increased contact with competition authorities from other countries, for example, through the International Competition Network or by virtue of multi- or bilateral contacts with Latin American competition authorities.

§3. Right of Defence

I. Content and Notification of Opening Decisions

548. The content and notification of opening decisions is foreseen in Article 28 of Royal Decree 261/2008. This Article provides that the opening of the file shall be formalized with the following minimum content:

(a) Identification of the alleged perpetrators and complainants, if any.
(b) The facts giving rise to the initiation.
(c) The instructor(s) and, where appropriate, the Secretary of instruction, indicating disqualification regime.
(d) If applicable, persons who have the status of interested.

549. The initiation of the procedure or the opening decision shall be notified to the interested parties and the accused parties have to be given a copy of the report of the complaint. The initiation of the proceedings will be announced on the website of the competition authority. Article 37.1 m) of Act 3/2013 underlines that the CNMC will announce the opening of a sanctioning procedure. Article 28 of Royal Decree 261/2008 also determines that the period of investigation of a case is of twelve months from the date of opening of the proceedings. If the maximum period of eighteen months passes from the date of the decision opening a procedure and the proceeding has not been resolved in this period, than the procedure has to be considered as expired according to Article 38.1 LDC.

II. The Proceedings: Hearings, Access to File, Briefs

550. Article 31 of Royal Decree 261/2008 foresees that once the file has been opened, interested parties may have access to it and they may also get individualized copies of all the documents which form part of the file of the competition authority, except for business secrets of other stakeholders or other third parties, as well as other confidential information.[302] This access will be carried out by appearing at the authorities' offices, in order not to disturb its effectiveness and in order to avoid a generic request. According to Article 32 of Royal Decree 261/2008, the instructor will carry out the necessary actions in order to clarify all the facts and determine liabilities. In order to achieve this purpose, all the relevant information and data will be collected, as well as relevant evidence in order to determine if there is a violation taking place and allowing the participation of stakeholders when appropriate. Stakeholders/interested parties may, at any time during the investigation within the sanctioning proceeding answer the arguments and propose taking evidence which they consider relevant to the defence of their interests. The authority has to decide on the taking of evidence specifying the reasons for its decision. There shall be no appeal against any rejection on the taking of evidence.

551. Protection is granted – with regard to the client-attorney communication or *legal privilege* when the purpose of the communication is to provide legal advice to the client (according to Article 542.3 of the Judiciary Law and Article 32 of the General Regulation of the Legal Profession). In order to grant protection two combining elements must be shown:

- The data or documents must refer to the activities of the undertaking or make reference to the need of the undertaking's legal advisers to obtain the data or documents in order to prepare the defence of the undertaking in a legal proceeding.
- The undertaking's legal advisers must have participated in the request and the preparation of the data, together with the undertaking, for the purpose of the legal defence of the undertaking's interests.

552. Only advice concerning defence on legal proceedings will be privileged, including any spoken or written communications, documents or correspondence exchanged between an external lawyer and the client, i.e., documents prepared by the lawyers for their clients in order to analyse a potential acquisition of assets may not be privileged. Only evidence that is exchanged with external lawyers is subject of being protected by the legal privilege is the one related to communications/documents. Advices from in-house lawyers are not privileged.[303]

553. Any internal documents that merely reproduce a piece of advice provided for an external lawyer should be also covered by the legal privilege. In the context of dawn raids, the inspected company should explain the reasons why a certain type of information has to be considered as protected by the attorney-client privilege.

302. In Spanish administrative law, Art. 4 of Act 39/2015 defines the notion of interested party or stakeholder as follows: (a) those who promote the administrative procedure it as holders of rights or legitimate – individual or collective – interests; (b) those who, without having started the procedure, hold rights that may be affected by the decision which will be adopted in the procedure at stake; (c) those whose legitimate – individual or collective – interests may be affected by the decision and appeared during the proceedings as long as no final decision has been taken.

303. *See* Resolution of the CNC of 4 May 2009, case *Colgate Palmolive*, Proceedings 0011/09.

III. Statement of Objections

554. Once the authority has initiated proceedings, the investigation phase will start. Article 33 of Regulation 261/2008 notes regarding to the statement of objections that in accordance with the provisions of Article 50.3 LDC the facts that may constitute infringement be collected in a statement of objections made to be notified to the interested parties, who in within fifteen days may answer it and, where appropriate, propose evidence which they consider relevant. Allegations received and practiced the evidence or, where appropriate, within the period of fifteen days, the Research proceed to close the preliminary investigation, notifying stakeholders in order to draft the proposed resolution referred to in Article 50.4 LDC.

555. When facts that may constitute infringement can affect the territory of an Autonomous Region, the Competition Directorate may notify the respective regional authority a copy of the statement of realization of facts and, where appropriate, of the complaint and the documents and practiced evidence on the record, to submit a report within twenty days, which is non-binding for the nationwide authority. This application required report shall be notified to the interested parties for the purposes of Article 37.1 LDC.

556. When the Competition Directorate considers that it has not shown the existence of prohibited practices it shall notify the interested parties, who shall have fifteen days to make claims or propose the use of evidence they deem relevant. Allegations received and practiced the evidence or, where appropriate, within the period of fifteen days, the Research proceed to close the preliminary investigation, notifying stakeholders in order to draft the proposed resolution referred to in Article 50.4 LDC.

IV. Final Hearing and Decision

557. Article 34 of Regulation 261/2008 foresees that the proposed resolution must contain the history of the case, the facts established, the authors, the legal qualification of the facts in case, the proposed declaration of infringement and, where appropriate, the impact on the market, his liability to the authors, the aggravating and mitigating circumstances and concurrent proposal of the Competition Directorate on the exemption or reduction of the fine to which Articles 65 and 66 LDC. In case the Competition Directorate deems not to consider as proven the existence of prohibited practices, they will inform about this in its draft resolution.

558. The proposed resolution, including the arguments raised by stakeholders throughout the investigation and the evidence offered by them, indicating whether practiced or not, shall be notified to the parties concerned, within fifteen days, who can subsequently formulate claims as they consider appropriate. The allegations in the proposed resolution of the Competition Directorate shall include, where appropriate, proposals to the parties with regard to the taking of evidence and complementary actions to the Council of the CNMC, as well as the request for a hearing.

559. The Competition Directorate will not consider the allegations in the report submitted by interested parties outside the time period of fifteen days since they received the statement of objections under paragraphs 1 and 3 of Article 33 of Regulation 261/2008 to answer the statement of objections made or, if applicable, the notification of the Competition Directorate has confirmed that no anticompetitive conducts exist. Furthermore, the Competition Directorate may deny the practice of additional evidence after this deadline. These documents will be added to the file, explicitly indicating that they have been presented by the parties out of time.

560. Once received the file, the Council of the CNMC may order, according to Article 36 of Regulation 261/2008, the examination of evidence, ex officio or at the request of stakeholders. The Council of the CNMC may also reject the practice of evidence proposed by stakeholders.

561. If the Council of the CNMC deems that the existence of prohibited practices had not been sufficiently established after the investigations carried out by the Competition Directorate, the Council may declare the necessity of carrying out additional investigations in order to clarify the facts. In this context, the Competition Directorate will also prepare a draft resolution which shall include, when appropriate, a review of the facts according to new findings. The proposal will be notified to the affected parties, that can formulate any comments within fifteen days.

562. According to Article 37 of Regulation 261/2008, the Council of the CNMC, at any time during the resolution phase, may rule on the status of all interested persons which have proved a legitimate interest in the case in accordance with Article 4 of Act 39/2015. According to Article 51.3 LDC, the Council of the CNMC may also decide to hold a hearing, if requested by the parties or ex officio. This request has to mention all the persons interested in attending the hearing as well as their relationship with the interested parties in the case.

563. Article 38 of Regulation 261/2008 notes the contents of the fining decision. In this sense, the Councils' resolutions has to include the history of the case, the facts proven by the CNMC, the infringers, the legal basis for the decision taken as well as the legal qualification of the facts.

564. In accordance with Article 53.1 LDC, the Council of the CNMC has to declare, when appropriate, the existence of a conduct prohibited by the LDC and/or by Articles 101 and 102 TFEU or the existence of a conduct which, due to its small size and little relevance on the markets, are not able to significantly affect competition or result has not proven the existence of prohibited practices.

565. Similarly, under Article 53.2 LDC, the CNMC may order the cessation of the conduct prohibited within a certain time, impose structural or behavioural conditions or obligations, order the removal of the effects of the prohibited practices which are contrary to public interest, impose fines, file actions and take other measures in order to guarantee compliance with competition rules.

566. Before publishing the final decision, the resolution is sent to the interested parties. The parties then have the opportunity to request that certain parts of the documents have to be declared confidential before the publication is carried out. Additionally, the Spanish legislation on personal data protection[304] may apply and restrict the publication of data related to the identity of other involved persons, such as employees or directors.

304. *See* Organic Law 15/1999 of 13 December, on personal data protection.

Chapter 2. Voluntary Notifications and Clearance Decisions Merger Control

567. Merger control is regulated in Spain in Articles 7–10 and 44–60 LDC as well as in Articles 4–6 and 54–71 RDC.

568. As noted earlier, one of the major differences between the LDC and the 1989 Competition Act lies in the regulations on merger control: the latter raises the market share threshold, introduces a new simplified notification system for certain operations and adapts Spanish legislation on takeover bids to European rules. It also reinforces decision-making independence by attributing the final decision to the CNMC, while acknowledging the Government's right to veto CNMC resolutions in cases involving general interest.

569. Another important difference between them is that under the 1989 Competition Act concentration control procedures were defined at the regulatory level only, namely in the regulations adopted under Royal Decree 1443/2001 of 21 December implementing *Ley 16/1989, de 17 de julio, de Defensa de la Competencia*. In contrast, in the LDC the law-maker chose to set out the control procedures, to a large extent, in the act itself (subsequently enlarged upon at the regulatory level by Articles 4–6 and 54–71 RDC). The most prominent innovations included the notification requirement (Article 9 LDC) and the organization of the proceedings into two phases, as appropriate (Articles 57 and 58 LDC).[305]

§1. Preliminary Filing Obligations[306]

570. Further to the provisions of Article 7 LDC,[307] the CNMC must be notified in advance of operations that constitute economic concentrations. Such notifications must be submitted using the forms included in Annexes II and III RDC (Article 56.1 RDC).

571. Article 9.4 LDC provides that such notifications must be submitted (a) jointly by the parties participating in a merger, the creation of a joint venture or the

---

305. Cf. Alonso, R., in Menéndez, A. – Rojo, A., *Lecciones*, p. 323.

306. *See*, in detail, Folguera, J. – Vidal, P., 'Artículo 9 LDC', in Massaguer, J. *et altri*, *Comentario a la Ley de Defensa de la Competencia*, Civitas/Thomson Reuters, Cizur Menor, 3rd ed., 2012, pp. 381–394; Barrantes, B., 'Artículo 9', in Odriozola, M. (Dir.), *Derecho español de la Competencia*, Tomo I, Bosch, Barcelona, 2008, pp. 295–312, Viñuelas, M. – Gavela, A.- Hortalà, J., in Loma-Osorio, D., *Tratado*, pp. 423–433. *See also* Górriz, C., in Garcia-Cruces, J.A. (dir.). *Tratado*, pp. 392–396; Ortiz, L. *et altri*, *Manual de Derecho de la Competencia*, Tecnos, Madrid, 2008, pp. 356–359; Marcos, F. – Sánchez, A., 'El control de concentraciones en la Ley 15/2007, de 3 de julio, de Defensa de la Competencia', in Parejo, L. – Palomar, A., *Derecho de la Competencia. Estudios sobre la Ley 15/2007, de 3 de julio, de Defensa de la Competencia*, La Ley, 2008, pp. 111–117.

307. Regarding this provision, *see* Part I Chapter 3 §3 I above.

acquisition of the joint control of the whole or part of one or more undertakings; or (b) individually by a party acquiring the exclusive control of the whole or part of one or more undertakings.

572. Notification may be submitted at any time after the project or agreement is in place (Article 54.1 RDC) but necessarily prior to its implementation (Article 9.1 LDC). Moreover, the operation is contingent upon administrative authorization (Article 9.2 LDC), although this suspensory condition may be lifted by the CNMC Council (Articles 9.6 LDC and 58 RDC). The operation is not contingent upon authorization, however, if the concentration adopts the form of a takeover bid, although exercise of the voting rights associated with the shares purchased is subject to final approval of the operation by the competition authorities (Article 9.3 LDC).[308]

573. The complexity of any such notification and the data required of the parties submitting it led to the inclusion in the Act of certain mechanisms geared to facilitating directors' task, such as pre-notification and the admission of preliminary queries. The former is set out in Article 56.2 RDC, which provides that the party concerned may submit a draft notification to clarify questions of content or form. The latter is contained in Article 55.2 LDC and enlarged upon in Article 59 RDC, which provides that before submitting a notification on a concentration, the undertakings involved may ask whether it will be regarded as a concentration and whether it crosses the thresholds for mandatory notification laid down in the LDC.[309]

574. Article 55.3 LDC stipulates that where the *Dirección de Competencia* becomes aware of the possible existence of a concentration that is subject to control, it may initiate preliminary action to determine the existence or otherwise of the circumstances that would require notification according to Article 9 LDC. In the affirmative and in the absence of any notification, further to the provisions of Article 9.5 LDC, the CNMC may require the participating undertakings, ex officio, to submit the notification within twenty days. If it is not forthcoming within that deadline, the *Dirección de Competencia* may initiate merger control proceedings, likewise ex officio, without prejudice to the application of penalties or coercive fines provided for in Articles 61–70 LDC.[310]

---

308. Cf. Alonso, R., in Menéndez, A. – Rojo, A., *Lecciones*, p. 324. *See* in detail Viñuelas, M. – Gavela, A.- Hortalà, J., in Loma-Osorio, D., *Tratado*, pp. 433–438; Marcos, F. – Sánchez, A., in Parejo, L. – Palomar, A., *Derecho*, pp. 118–123.

309. On these preliminary queries, *see*, for all, Marcos, F. – Sánchez, A., in Parejo, L. – Palomar, A., *Derecho*, pp. 107–111.

310. *See* Alonso, R., in Menéndez, A. – Rojo, A., *Lecciones*, p. 324; Viñuelas, M. – Gavela, A.- Hortalà, J., in Loma-Osorio, D., *Tratado*, pp. 432–433.

I. Criteria and Thresholds[311]

575. Article 8 LDC defines the scope of Spanish legislation on merger control. In accordance with Article 8.1 LDC such legislation is applicable to any inter-undertaking concentration project or operation that may affect the domestic market and fulfils one or both of the following requirements.

576. a) The operation results in the acquisition or increase of 30% or greater share of the national or any duly defined regional market for the respective good or service.

577. However, Article 8.1 exempts concentrations from control proceedings, even when the aforementioned circumstances are present, when the undertakings or holdings acquired show a domestic turnover in the previous accounting year of less than EUR 10,000,000 and the participants do not, individually or jointly, have a share higher than 50% in any of the markets impacted, nationally or in a duly defined region.[312]

578. This means that the CNMC does not need to be notified of economically insignificant operations, even where the market share threshold is crossed.

579. b) The combined turnover from all operations in Spain of all participants in the previous accounting year exceeds EUR 240,000,000 and at least two of the participants have an individual domestic turnover of over EUR 60,000,000.

580. Article 8.2 LDC stipulates that Spanish legislation does not apply to concentrations with a 'European dimension' as defined in Council Regulation (EC) No 139/2004 of 20 January 2004 on the control of concentrations between undertakings (the EC Merger Regulation), unless the concentration is referred to the Spanish authorities by the European Commission.

581. Article 10.4 LDC, in turn, provides that merger control provisions are applicable to the creation or acquisition of cooperative joint ventures, although such operations are assessed in terms of the provisions of Articles 1 and 2 LDC.

II. Turnover Calculation

582. Article 5 RDC lays down the criteria for calculating the turnover thresholds stipulated in Article 8.1 b) LDC.

---

311. *See* BARRANTES, B., 'Artículo 8' in ODRIOZOLA, M. (Dir.), *Derecho español de la Competencia*, Tomo I, Bosch, Barcelona, 2008, pp. 270–295; GÓRRIZ, C., in GARCIA-CRUCES, J.A. (dir.), *Tratado*, pp. 366–371; VIÑUELAS, M. – GAVELA, A.- HORTALÀ, J., in LOMA-OSORIO, D., *Tratado*, pp. 415–422.

312. This '*de minimis*' rule was introduced by the Sustainable Economy Act 2/2011, of 4 March 2011, third final provision. Please note that regarding this '*de minimis*' rule, the law mentions the affected market and not the relevant one.

583. Domestic turnover is computed as ordinary sales to Spanish undertakings or consumers made in the previous accounting year by the undertakings involved in the merger, any discounts or rebates and the net value added tax and any other taxes directly related to the turnover. The turnover of undertakings totally or partially acquired or whose control is assigned after the closing date of the audited financial statements of the firms involved must be included in the turnover used for the intents and purposes of notifying the transaction.

584. Each undertaking's turnover is calculated by summing its own sales, the sales of the undertakings it controls solely or jointly, as well as the sales of its controlling undertaking or undertakings. The sum of all intra-group transactions is then subtracted from the above figure.

585. To avoid duplication, when an undertaking taken over was already controlled by one or several of the purchasers, only its own turnover is attributed to it.

586. When the concentration operation consists of the acquisition of a business division, unit or establishment, or in general a separate part of one or several undertakings, irrespective of whether it has an own legal personality, only the turnover attributable to that part of the target is used for this calculation.

587. Article 5.6 RDC provides that when two or more operations involving the same buyers and sellers take place in a given two year period, they are regarded as a single concentration performed on the date of the most recent operation. That provision aims to prevent undertakings from eluding the thresholds laid down in Article 8.1 b) LDC by dividing the operation into several smaller transactions.

588. Finally, Article 5.7 RDC lays down a series of specific rules for concentration operations involving investment funds, financial institutions and insurance undertakings.

III. Market Share Calculation

589. The criteria to be applied when calculating the market share set out in Article 8.1 a) LDC are listed in Article 4 RDC.

A. Definition of Market Shares

590. According to Article 4.1 RDC, the market share is the result of adding the market shares of the merging companies in the relevant market. The second paragraph of this same Article provides that it shall be considered that the market share has also been increased when the acquiring company was already controlling – before the merger – the acquired company. What matters is that after the economic concentration that has taken place there has been a change in the control. The same

Article foresees that an increment of the market share shall also be considered when a joint venture is created and the parent companies provide all or part of its business to the newly created entity.

591. In accordance with this provision it has been argued that it is irrelevant if the companies participating in the economic concentration already had a market share higher than 30% of the relevant market. What matters is that a market share of more than the 30% is acquired, or, when the acquiring company already had this market share, its market share has to be increased after the economic concentration.[313]

B. Relevant Market

592. The relevant market is not defined in the Spanish legislation.[314] It is generally admitted that only regarding the defined relevant market it is possible to calculate the market share of the companies involved in the economic concentration. The definition of the relevant market is carried out taking into account previous decisions of the CNMC, but this matter is discussed and criticized by several authors.[315] For the purposes of merger control rules, it has been argued that the relevant product market includes all the products and services that are substitutable from the consumers' point of view when taking into account their physical and technical characteristics, as well as their price, or the expected use with these products, their distribution system or the legal product definition.[316]

593. Due to the difficulties of defining the relevant market, Article 55.2 LDC foresees the possibility of asking the CNMC if a certain economic concentration exceeds the minimum thresholds for a compulsory notification *ex* Article 8 LDC. Also the former *Servicio de Defensa de la Competencia* argued that this mechanism foreseen in the law in order to ask *ex ante* the CNMC provides the possibility to determine if the threshold required for the mandatory notification is reached or not and that the European and Spanish precedents are useful in order to define the relevant market.[317] The Spanish Ministry of Economy has also argued that the market share is a good indicator of the potential power of the companies compared to the volume of sales and therefore it is related to the economic side of the regulation of

313. *See* Górriz, C., in in García-Cruces, J.A. (dir.), *Tratado*, p. 367.
314. It has been argued that the market share threshold should be removed because of its practical difficulties in order to define the relevant market. *See* Jiménez Laiglesia, J. M.: 'Propuesta de reforma del sistema de control de concentraciones', *in Documentos de Trabajo,* 56/2004, Fundación Alternativas, pp. 29–30.
315. Marcos, F. – Sánchez, A., 'El sistema de control de concentraciones empresariales en la nueva Ley de Defensa de la Competencia', en *IE Working Paper*, p. 8.
316. *Guía práctica de la Ley 15/2007, de 3 de julio, de Defensa de la Competencia y el Real Decreto 261/2008, de 22 de febrero, por el que se aprueba el Reglamento de Defensa de la Competencia, Uría Menéndez,* p. 67.
317. Barrantes, B., in Odriozola, M. (Dir.), *Derecho*, p. 273.

merger control and the possible effects of a certain merger on the markets. The Ministry of Economy added that Spanish and European precedents guide the definition of the relevant market.[318]

594. In its Decision related to the case *Shibsted/Milanuncios,*[319] the CNMC was aiming to 'define more specifically the relevant product market'. Thus, one could affirm that the authority tries to look for the more specific product market.

595. There are two judgments from the National High Court (*Audiencia Nacional*) which estimate the appeal against fines imposed in alleged gun jumping cases, annulling the decision of the authority, in which the product market definition taken into account by it differs from the product market definition taken into account by the notifying parties. The Court affirms that in cases in which the relevant product market definition has not been closed by the Spanish competition authority, it remains open to accept the market definition proposed by the notifying parties of the economic concentration, if this definition is 'reasonable'.[320] This 'reasonable' market definition can also be determined on the basis of the substitutability of the supply (not only of the demand).[321] The National High Court reminded also that the pre-notification of the concentration (Article 59 RDC) and the possibility of questioning the competition authority *ex* Article 55.2 LDC are not mandatory for the parties and the lack of use of these mechanisms cannot be interpreted as a negligence by the parties.[322]

C. Relevant Year

596. The LDC does not clarify the relevant year for the purpose of defining the market share. This improvement had been proposed in the White Paper before the current LDC was enacted.

597. In practice, the CNMC has analysed the market share during the precedent year of the notification. But since the ordinary reporting form added as Annex II RDC (section 6.1) requires the information related to the market shares of the last three financial years, it has been argued that also former years could be of a relevance when defining the market share.[323]

598. Other authors have argued that precedents in Spain are not clear and there have been cases in which the CNMC has taken into account the market share during the last fiscal year, the last calendar year or from date to date. The same authors

---

318. Ministerio de Economía, *Libro Blanco para la reforma del sistema español de defensa de la competencia*, 20 January 2005, p. 69.
319. CNMC Resolution of 5 June 2014 (Proceedings C/0573/14, *Schibsted/Milanuncios* case).
320. National High Court Judgment of 28 September 2012 (Appeal Number 566/2010).
321. National High Court Judgment of 6 June 2012 (Appeal Number 363/2010).
322. National High Court Judgment of 28 September 2012 (Appeal Number 566/2010).
323. Barrantes, B., in Odriozola, M. (Dir.), *Derecho*, p. 274.

affirm that the market share has to be determined retrospectively, taking always into account actual or estimated data of the past and not future sales expectations.[324]

599. However, there is one case in which the Competition Authority took into account the expected market share of the acquiring company in the near future.[325] In this case, the acquired companies had obtained the necessary licences to operate in the same markets as the acquirer and they already planned to start their activities within two years. The authority considered that it was certain that the acquirer would increase its market share but that the effective competition in the market would not be affected by the economic concentration. The competition authority affirmed in this case that a 'dynamic analysis' had to be carried out.

D. *Increasing Market Share in the Near Future Due to Contracts Already Signed*

600. With reference to the annual turnover, Article 5.1 RDC foresees that any acquisition or disposal of the control of all or part of companies carried out after the closing date of the audited accounts of the participating companies shall be reflected in the turnover used for the purposes of notification of the transaction concentration.

601. It has been argued that the market share threshold applies regardless of being a volatile market and that this threshold would be exceeded if this happens during the year the concentration is carried out and not in the last accounting year.[326]

IV. Other Relevant Notions

602. Not applicable.

324. Folguera, J. – Vidal, P., 'Artículo 8 LDC', in Massaguer, J. *et altri*, *Comentario a la Ley de Defensa de la Competencia*, Civitas/Thomson Reuters, Cizur Menor, 3rd ed., 2012, p. 377.
325. Report of the Servicio de Defensa de la Competencia of 26 March 2002, *Iberdrola/Guadalcín y Enron España*, Exp. N-227.
326. Barrantes, B., in Odriozola, M. (Dir.), *Derecho*, p. 275.

§2. STRUCTURE OF PROCEEDINGS

I. Preliminary Assessment and Full Investigation[327]

603. After the notification of the transaction, or falling this acting ex officio, the CNMC's *Dirección de Competencia* initiates a proceeding that may consist of one or two phases.

604. In the first phase (regulated by Articles 57 LDC and 62 and 63 RDC), the authority analyses the operation and drafts a report listing the assessment criteria laid down in Article 10 LDC as well as a proposed resolution. In light of the report, the CNMC Council may decide to: (a) authorize the transaction; (b) make authorization subject to the compliance with the commitments proposed by the parties concerned; (c) agree to initiate phase two of the process; (d) agree to refer the case to the European Commission for consideration under Article 22 of Regulation (EC) No. 139/2004 if the concentration has a European dimension; or (e) shelve the proceedings.

605. The second phase is regulated in Articles 58 LDC and 68 RDC. Further to Article 58.1 LDC, if a decision to proceed to phase two is forthcoming, the *Dirección de Competencia* issues a brief note on the details of the transaction, which is circulated to all parties potentially concerned as well as the Consumer Council. Any allegations in connection with the note must be submitted within ten days (Article 58.1 LDC). If, moreover, the transaction is likely to have a special impact on any given region, a report is requested from the respective regional competition authorities.

606. In this second phase of the proceedings, the *Dirección de Competencia* must draw up a 'statement of objections' identified in the concentration operation. The statement is circulated to all parties potentially concerned, who are invited to submit their allegations (Article 58.2 LDC, enlarged upon by Article 67 RDC). In view of the objections identified, the parties concerned may make commitments on their own initiative or in response to CNMC suggestions. Such commitments are open to scrutiny by third parties (Article 59 LDC, enlarged upon by Article 69 RDC). Such parties may also request a hearing before the CNMC Council (Article 58.3 LDC, enlarged upon by Article 68 RDC). Once the aforementioned proceedings are concluded, the *Dirección de Competencia* draws up a proposed final resolution for submission to the CNMC Council, whose final decision may entail: (a) authorizing the concentration; (b) making it subject to compliance with certain commitments proposed by the parties concerned or other conditions; (c) prohibit the concentration; or (d) shelve the proceedings under the circumstances laid down in

327. We follow the explanations of ALONSO, R., in MENÉNDEZ, A. – ROJO, A., *Lecciones*, pp. 324–325. *See also* in detail VIÑUELAS, M. – GAVELA, A.- HORTALÀ, J., in LOMA-OSORIO, D., *Tratado*, pp. 438–446. *See also* GÓRRIZ, C., in GARCIA-CRUCES, J.A. (dir.), *Tratado*, pp. 399–402; ORTIZ, L. *et altri*, *Manual*, pp. 359–367; MARCOS, F. – SÁNCHEZ, A., in PAREJO, L. – PALOMAR, A., *Derecho*, pp. 124–136.

the act (Article 58.4 LDC). As mentioned earlier, when adopting its resolution the CNMC must apply the criteria specified in Article 10.1 LDC.[328]

607. The proceedings reach conclusion when the CNMC Council's final resolution is reported to the Minister of the Economy and Competitiveness (Article 58.5 LDC), who is granted fifteen days to determine whether the Government will intervene (Article 36.3 LDC). Such intervention is only in order where the CNMC decides to prohibit or impose conditions on the concentration (Article 60.1 LDC) and only where it relates to matters related to the general interest in areas other than competition law (Article 60.3 LDC) such as: defence and national security, public health and safety, the free circulation of goods and services nationwide, environmental conservation, technological research and development, and maintenance of the objectives of sectorial regulation (Article 10.4 LDC). The Government's intervention may consist of either confirming the resolution issued by the CNMC Council or authorizing the concentration the concentration, subject to or exempt from conditions (Article 60.3 LDC). If the Government fails to adopt a decision by the established deadline, the CNMC's final resolution comes into effect and is applicable immediately thereafter (Article 60.4 LDC).[329]

II. Time Framework[330]

608. The maximum duration of merger control proceedings is laid down in Article 36 LDC.

609. More specifically, section 2 of that provision establishes the deadlines for the issue and service of notice of CNMC Council resolutions.

610. The maximum duration of the first phase is one month, counting from the date the CNMC resolution is notified in due form by the parties concerned (Article 36.2 a) LDC).

611. The second phase may last no longer than two months (Article 36.2 b) LDC). The *dies a quo* for this term is the date on which the CNMC Council decides to initiate this phase (Article 36.2 b) LDC).

612. Longer periods are envisioned when commitments are submitted, whether on the initiative of the parties concerned or at the CNMC's urging. In such cases, Article 59 LDC extends the maximum term for issuing the first phase resolution by ten days and the second phase resolution by fifteen. Article 69.1 RDC, in turn, enlarges on this rule by establishing the deadlines within which the parties signing the notification must submit such commitments to the *Dirección de Competencia*:

---

328. *See* Part I. §3. Concentrations. III. Substantive assessment criteria above.
329. *See*, about the Government intervention, VIÑUELAS, M. – GAVELA, A.- HORTALÀ, J., in LOMA-OSORIO, D., *Tratado*, pp. 449–452.
330. *See* VIÑUELAS, M. – GAVELA, A.- HORTALÀ, J., in LOMA-OSORIO, D., *Tratado*, pp. 456–459.

in the first phase, twenty days from the date of submission of the notification in due form and in the second, thirty-five days counting from the date of the CNMC Council's decision to initiate that phase of the proceedings.

613. The CNMC Council's second phase resolutions must be reported to the Minister of Economy and Competitiveness (Article 58.5 LDC). Where such resolutions prohibit a concentration or subordinate it to commitments or conditions, the Minister of Economy and Competitiveness is granted fifteen days from the date of receipt of the resolution to decide whether the Government will intervene (Article 36.3 LDC). The Government's decision must be adopted and notified within one month of the Minister of Economy and Competitiveness' resolution to raise the issue to the Council of Ministers (Article 36.4 LDC).

614. Article 37 LDC regulates circumstances in which time may not or must not be counted when calculating the final date of the deadline and those in which deadlines may be extended. When the party concerned is required to rectify shortcomings or submit documents or other information needed pursuant to the provisions of Article 55.4 and 55.5 LDC, the number of days lapsing between notification of the requirement and compliance therewith must not be counted. Requests for information from third parties or other public authorities may have a similar effect. However, a postponement of the deadlines by which proceedings must be concluded does not necessarily entail suspension of the proceedings themselves. Rather, this circumstance is established in the decision at issue.[331]

III. Rights of Defence

615. The rights of defence described in Chapter 1, §3 above are applicable to merger control proceedings.

§3. Clearance And Conditional Clearance

616. A concentration must be authorized when it is not liable to obstruct effective competition in all or part of the national market (Article 10.1 LDC). Otherwise, the concentration is to be prohibited, although it may be authorized subject to compliance with certain conditions (Articles 57.1 c) and 58.4 d) LDC).

331. *See* Viñuelas, M. – Gavela, A.- Hortalà, J., in Loma-Osorio, D., *Tratado*, p. 459.

I. Conditions and Undertakings[332]

A. Content

617. The existing LDC envisages authorizing a concentration subject to compliance with: (a) *commitments* submitted by the participants in the operation; or (b) *conditions* unilaterally imposed by the CNMC Council or the Government (Articles 57.2 b), 58.2 d) and 60.3 b) LDC). Unlike the EU regulations, which make no provision for the latter,[333] both possibilities were envisaged in the 1989 Competition Act, although commitments were only explicitly mentioned in connection with the first phase (Articles 15*ter* and 17.1 b)).

618. a) Commitments proposed by the parties involved and negotiated, as appropriate, with the *Dirección de Competencia*, may be submitted and agreed to either in the first (Article 57.2 b) LDC) or the second phase (Article 58.4 b) LDC). Such commitments should eliminate the obstacle to effective competition that the concentration operation might induce. The two keys to assessing if they are acceptable in that regard are suitability testing (to determine whether the commitments can remedy the competition problem) and feasibility testing (to determine whether they are readily applicable and able to ensure a permanent solution).

619. The brevity of the timeframes renders any analysis of the operations involving such proposals difficult. Commitments may therefore only be accepted in the first phase when the competition problem detected is clearly identifiable and readily remedied (Article 69.5 RDC). However, that does not mean that the competition problem need necessarily be minor. An operation subject to commitments may be authorized in the first phase, regardless of the magnitude of the competition problem detected, providing it is clearly identified and the commitment undertaken to remedy the problem is obviously able to do so.

620. Commitments, which may even be proposed in the pre-notification phase, are submitted in the form of a substantiated request. The *Dirección de Competencia* reviews the commitments submitted by the party concerned and may request amendments when the authority deems them insufficient to eliminate the obstacles to competition possibly deriving from the operation (Article 69.4 RDC). Moreover, information on commitments may be notified not only to the parties concerned, but

---

332. *See* Viñuelas, M. – Gavela, A.- Hortalà, J., in Loma-Osorio, D., *Tratado*, pp. 446–448 with later references.

333. *See* Arts 6.2 and 8.2 Council Regulation (EC) 139/2004 of 20 January 2004 on the control of concentrations between undertakings; and Arts 19, 20 and 20 bis Commission Regulation (EC) 802/2004 implementing Council Regulation (EC) 139/2004 on the control of concentrations between undertakings.

also to third operators with a view of evaluating their aptness for solving the competition problems raised by the specific transaction as well as its effects on the markets (Article 59.3 LDC). The *Dirección de Competencia*'s proposed decision must contain the final version of the proposed commitments (Article 69.7 RDC), irrespective of its own evaluation thereof.

621. Commitments are included in the report and proposed decision. Upon submission, the party concerned must substantiate any request for confidential treatment of the information and provide a non-confidential version thereof (Article 69.2 RDC). Confidentiality may be requested in respect of the information on the commitments included in the resolution as per the provisions of Article 61 RDC.

622. The most common types of commitments are structural (such as divestments, assignment of assets or spin-off of productive divisions) and behavioural (such as obligations with suppliers, customers or competitors, limitations to growth, contract safeguard clauses or third party access to infrastructure).

623. Commitments must be submitted together with a plan for their implementation, including terms, procedures, guarantees and any necessary measures to ensure compliance.

624. b) Unlike commitments, the possibility of subjecting authorization to conditions neither proposed by nor negotiated with the party concerned is a final alternative to prohibiting a concentration. This alternative may only be adopted by the CNMC Council and only in the second phase of the proceedings (Article 58.4 b) LDC) or by the Government, which may confirm, amend or even eliminate such conditions (Article 60 LDC).

625. In other words, conditions are imposed by the CNMC Council when it deems them able to solve the competition problems posed by the concentration, in the absence or presumed insufficiency of commitments.

626. c) The distinction between conditions and commitments lies solely in the voluntary or mandatory nature of the measures, but is irrelevant to the practical consequences, for in both cases authorization is contingent upon compliance with a series of obligations.

627. Article 67 d) LDC provides the CNMC with the power to impose coercive fines of up to EUR 12,000 per day in order to oblige the parties concerned to comply with the commitments or conditions set out in the CNMC Council's resolution or the Council of Ministers' decision. Such measures are without prejudice to any punitive fines that may be imposed or any other enforcement measures laid down in the existing legislation, including demerger orders, if appropriate (Article 41.2 LDC).

B. Timing

628. In the first phase, when the parties concerned submit commitments, the deadline for issuing the resolution is extended by ten days (Article 59.2 LDC). Commitments, including any amendments, must be submitted within twenty days of the date of notification of the concentration in due form (Article 69.1 a) RDC). The *Dirección de Competencia* is under no obligation to review commitments or amendments thereto proposed after that deadline, although nothing prevents it from doing so (Article 69.6 RDC).

629. In the second phase, when the parties concerned submit commitments, the deadline for issuing the resolutions is extended by fifteen days (Article 59.2 LDC). In this case such commitments and all amendments must be submitted within thirty-five days from the CNMC Council decision which initiates the second phase of the proceedings (Article 69.1 b) RDC).

§4. Relations with Other Merger Control Authorities

I. Other Authorities Within the Local Jurisdiction

630. The original wording of Article 17 LDC regulated the mechanisms for coordinating the former CNC with the sectorial regulation bodies in place at that time. That rule was repealed, however, with the entry into effect of Act 3/2013, *de 4 de junio de creación de la Comisión Nacional de los Mercados y la Competencia* (Act creating the CNMC) because all five former sectorial regulators now lie under the umbrella of the new supervisory body, the CNMC.[334]

631. Nonetheless, other authorities continue being active in concentration proceedings taking place in certain regulated industries.

632. Article 72 of *Real Decreto 2486/1998, de 20 de noviembre, por el que se aprueba el Reglamento de Ordenación y Supervisión de los Seguros Privados* (Royal Decree on the Regulation and Supervision of Private Insurance) regulates insurance undertaking mergers. Article 72.1 provides that such operations require Minister of the Economy and Finance (now Minister of the Economy and Competitiveness) authorization. Article 6 of *Real Decreto 345/2012, de 10 de febrero, por el que se desarrolla la estructura orgánica básica del Ministerio de Economía y Competitividad* (Royal Decree on the Basic Structure of the Ministry of the Economy and Competitiveness) stipulates that the *Dirección General de Seguros y Fondos de Pensiones* (DG of insurance and pension funds) fulfils the duties attributed to the ministry in connection with insurance undertaking mergers.

334. Namely, the *Comisión Nacional de la Energía, Comisión del Mercado de las Telecomunicaciones, Comité de Regulación Ferroviaria, Comisión de Regulación Económica Aeroportuaria* and *Comisión Nacional de Sector Postal* (energy, telecommunications, railways, airports and post).

633. In a similar sense, section 1 of the Twelfth Additional Provision to *Ley 10/2014, de 26 de junio, de ordenación, supervisión y solvencia de entidades de crédito* (Act on the rules, supervision and solvency of financial institutions) provides that bank mergers must be authorized by the Ministry of the Economy and Competitiveness. Prior administrative authorization is also required for mergers among credit unions (Article 10 of *Ley 13/1989, de 26 de mayo, de Cooperativas de Crédito*: Act on credit unions) and savings banks (Seventh Additional Provision to *Ley 26/2013, de 27 de diciembre, de cajas de ahorros y fundaciones bancarias*: Act on savings banks and bank foundations).

634. The relationship with the regional competition authorities in connection with merger control merits specific mention.[335] According to some provisions, the regions (*Comunidades Autónomas*) are not competent in concentration affairs (*see* Article 1.5 a) of *Ley 1/2002, de 21 de febrero, de Coordinación de las Competencias del Estado y las Comunidades Autónomas en materia de Defensa de la Competencia* (Act on coordinating national and regional competence in defence of competition), which reserves the application of concentration control rules for the central government, or Article 13 which by omission limits regional competition authorities' executive competence to proceedings associated with Articles 1 (collusive conduct), 2 (abusive conduct) and 3 (distortion of free competition through unfair practices) LDC).

635. Nonetheless, the issue is not entirely clear insofar as some regional competition authorities have drawn from the competence attributed thereto under their *Estatuto de Autonomía* (regional statutes) to claim exclusive competence for handling mergers that affect only the region in question.[336]

II. International Coordination

636. In the same sense as the competition authorities of all other Member States and the European Commission, the CNMC is a member of the European Competition Network.

637. If also forms part of European Competition Authorities, a discussion forum for the competition authorities in the European Economic Area (EEA) (the Member States of the European Union, the European Commission, the EFTA States – Norway, Iceland and Liechtenstein – and the EFTA Surveillance Authority).

---

335. *See* Rodríguez, J.A., 'Defensa de la Competencia y Comunidades Autónomas', in Beneyto, J.M. – Maillo, J., *La nueva Ley de Defensa de la Competencia. Análisis y comentarios*, Bosch, Barcelona, 2009, pp. 79–80.

336. *See* the position adopted by the Catalonian competition authority in the *Agabar/Cassa* case (Resolution of 18 January 2011, proceedings R. 1/2010).

Chapter 3. Challenging of the Administrative Decision

§1. Competent Courts

638. Final decisions of the Council of the CNMC, in which decision proposal of the Competition Directorate is ratified or when a proceeding is closed, may be appealed before Spain's National High Court (*Audiencia Nacional*).[337] Any person or undertaking with a legitimate right or interest in the decision is entitled to appeal the decision of the CNMC. Furthermore, in a second review, appeal is possible in certain cases before the Administrative Chamber of the Spanish Supreme Court (Third Chamber).[338]

§2. Time Limits

639. The decision of the CNMC can be appealed within two months since the notification of the Council decision.[339]

§3. Scope of Judicial Review

640. Reference is made in Article 48.1 LDC to the Act 29/1998, from 13 July, on administrative jurisdiction, which means that against decisions and acts of the President and Council of the CNMC only an administrative appeal may be filed.

337. *See* section three of the Seventh Additional Provision of Competition Act 15/2007 and Art. 48 of the same act foresee this possibility, mentioning that the Administrative Chamber of the National High Court is the competent one. *See also* Art. 11.1 h) of Act 29/1998, on administrative jurisdiction.
338. According to the amendments of the Administrative Jurisdiction Act 29/1998 of 13 July, which entered into force on 1 October 2015 (by Act 7/2015, of 1 July, in order to be able to go for a further appeal before the Supreme Court it will not be necessary any more that the amount exceeds EUR 600,000, rather that the matter presents some 'appeal interest' (*interés casacional*), e.g., when the case involves a lot of affected parties, when the public interest has been seriously damages, when the case involves an interpretation of EU law in a different way than the one pre-established by the European Court of Justice or when the appealed decision resolves an appeal against an act or decision of a regulatory or supervisory body or state agency whose decisions have to be challenged at the National High Court (*Audiencia Nacional*). *See* on this behalf Art. 88 of Law 29/1998 after the entering into force. The bill published in the Spanish Official State Bulletin (*Boletín Oficial del Estado*) on 22 July 2015, is available at http://www.boe.es/boe/dias/2015/07/22/pdfs/BOE-A-2015-8167.pdf (last time accessed: 7 February 2017).

    In its Report of 2012/2013 (last data included as of 30 September 2013), the CNC stated that since 1 September 2007, 76.9% of the appealed sanctioning decisions issued by the CNC were confirmed by the Administrative Chamber of the Spanish National High Court. In a second review, the Supreme Court has confirmed eleven decisions of the CNC and annulled only one decision, *see* in this regard the Judgment of the Supreme Court from 29 February 2012 (Appeal Number 3567/2010), confirming the annulment of the National High Court in its Judgment of 23 March 2010 (Case Number 624/07, *Iberdrola*).
339. *See* Art. 46.1 of Act 29/1998, on the Administrative Jurisdiction.

641. The CNMC is the administrative authority which was selected by the legislator in order to enforce competition law in Spain mainly due to its technical expertise. The judicial decision regarding the decision of the competition authority is based on its conformance or non-conformance with the law. Article 67.1 of Act 29/1998 notes that the judgment will take a decision on all controversial issues raised in the process.

642. Article 68 of Act 29/1998, foresees that the judgment may have an estimatory result (fully or partially), it may dismiss the appeal or even declare its inadmissibility. The judgment will dismiss the appeal in case the administrative decision respects the law (Article 70 of the mentioned act). Article 71 of the same act confirms that the appeal will be upheld in case the administrative act does not comply with the law and in this case the decision will be – totally or partially – annulled. This judgment can confirm the statement that an infringement of competition rules has taken place but revoke the imposition of a fine; it can confirm the existence of an infringement and the imposition of a fine but revoke the amount thereof; it can confirm that fines should be imposed taking into account the facts of a specific case but revoke the parameters of calculation of the imposed fine or fines; it can confirm that an infringement has occurred, the obligation to cease this illegal conduct, the amount of the fine but revoking other obligations imposed by the CNMC; it can also declare that an infringement had taken place when the CNMC terminated the case due to the lack of an infringement. In this case, the judge may impose the specific sanction(s) or refer the case to the CNMC in order to impose it/them.

Selected Bibliography

ALLENDESALAZAR, R. – VALLINA, R., 'Artículo 2 de la LDC: El abuso de posición dominante', in BACHES, S. (coord.), *La ley 15/2007, de Defensa de la Competencia. Balance de su aplicación*, La Ley, Madrid, 2010, pp. 165–211.

ALONSO, R., 'Lección 14. Derecho de la Competencia', in MENÉNDEZ, A. – ROJO, A., *Lecciones de Derecho Mercantil*, Volumen 1, Civitas Thomson Reuters, Madrid, 16ª ed. 2016, pp. 297–327.

BARRANTES, B., 'Artículo 10', in ODRIOZOLA, M. (Dir.), *Derecho español de la Competencia*, Tomo I, Bosch, Barcelona, 2008, pp. 312–369.

BARRANTES, B., 'Artículo 7', in ODRIOZOLA, M. (Dir.), *Derecho español de la Competencia*, Tomo I, Bosch, Barcelona, 2008, pp. 252–269.

BARRANTES, B., 'Artículo 8', in ODRIOZOLA, M. (Dir.), *Derecho español de la Competencia*, Tomo I, Bosch, Barcelona, 2008, pp. 270–295.

BARRANTES, B., 'Artículo 9', in ODRIOZOLA, M. (Dir.), *Derecho español de la Competencia*, Tomo I, Bosch, Barcelona, 2008, pp. 295–312.

BELLO, Mª.P., 'Control de concentraciones de empresas', in BELLO, Mª.P. – HERNÁNDEZ, F. (coord.), *Derecho de la libre competencia comunitario y español*, Thomson Aranzadi, Cizur Menor, 2009, pp. 333–420.

BERENGER, L. '¿La piedra de sísifo o el tejido de Penélope? Idas y venidas de la norma de la UE para la reclamación de daños en materia de competencia' in CASES, L. *Anuario de Defensa de la competencia* 2011–2012, 2012, pp. 55–84.

BORRELL, J.-R, 'Spanish Competition Policy: A Case of Government's Response to Domestically Perceived Problems', *The Antitrust Bulletin*, 1998, pp. 445–465.

CALVO, G. – RAMOS DE MOLINS, A., 'Derecho de la competencia y sectores regulados', in LOMA-OSORIO, D., *Tratado de Derecho de la Competencia*, Aranzadi, Madrid, 2013, pp. 589–654.

COSTAS, J., 'Prohibición de acuerdos colusorios', in BELLO, Mª.P. – HERNÁNDEZ, F. (coord.), *Derecho de la libre competencia comunitario y español*, Thomson Aranzadi, Cizur Menor, 2009, pp. 65–111.

COSTAS, J., 'Prohibición de falseamiento de la libre competencia por actos de competencia desleal', in BELLO, Mª.P. – HERNÁNDEZ, F. (coord.), *Derecho de la libre competencia comunitario y español*, Thomson Aranzadi, Cizur Menor, 2009, pp. 213–231.

DÍEZ, F., 'El abuso de posición dominante en el Derecho Comunitario y Español de Defensa de la Competencia', in GARCIA-CRUCES, J.A. (dir.), *Tratado de Derecho de la Competencia y de la Publicidad*, Tomo I, Tirant lo Blanch, Valencia, 2014, pp. 255–334.

Selected Bibliography

DÍEZ, F., 'El artículo 3 LDC: Falseamiento de la libre competencia por actos desleales', *Noticias de la Unión Europea*, 2012, No. 330, pp. 83–94.

DÍEZ, F., *La discriminación de precios en el derecho de competencia*, Thomson-Civitas, C. Madrid, 2003.

ESTRADA, A., 'Preseÿbusivfuturo del delito de alteración de precios' in *InDret. Revista para el análisis del Derecho,* nº 1, 2014, pp. 1-50, p. 7 ff, available at http://www.indret.com/pdf/1024.pdf (last time accessed: 7 February 2017).

FOLGUERA, J. – VIDAL, P., 'Artículo 10 LDC', in MASSAGUER, J. *et altri*, *Comentario a la Ley de Defensa de la Competencia*, Civitas/Thomson Reuters, Cizur Me^{no}r, 3rd ed., 2012, pp. 394-545.

FOLGUERA, J. – VIDAL, P., 'Artículo 7 LDC', in MASSAGUER, J. *et altri*, *Comentario a la Ley de Defensa de la Competencia*, Civitas/Thomson Reuters, Cizur Me^{no}r, 3rd ed., 2012, pp. 345–366.

FOLGUERA, J. – VIDAL, P., 'Artículo 8 LDC', in MASSAGUER, J. *et altri*, *Comentario a la Ley de Defensa de la Competencia*, Civitas/Thomson Reuters, Cizur Me^{no}r, 3rd ed., 2012, pp. 366–381.

FOLGUERA, J. – VIDAL, P., 'Artículo 9 LDC', in MASSAGUER, J. *et altri*, *Comentario a la Ley de Defensa de la Competencia*, Civitas/Thomson Reuters, Cizur Me^{no}r, 3rd ed., 2012, pp. 381–394.

GARCÍA, F., 'Fundamentos del Derecho de la libre competencia', in BELLO, Mª.P. – HERNÁNDEZ, F. (coord.), *Derecho de la libre competencia comunitario y español*, Thomson Aranzadi, Cizur Menor, 2009, pp. 37–64.

GONZÁLEZ-DÍAZ, F.E. – CARPI, J.M., 'La noción de concentración económica y la evaluación de sus efectos en los ordenamientos comunitario y español', in BENEYTO, J.M., *Tratado de Derecho de la Competencia,* Tomo 1, Bosch.

GÓRRIZ, C., 'Control de las concentraciones', in GARCIA-CRUCES, J.A. (dir.), *Tratado de Derecho de la Competencia y de la Publicidad*, Tomo I, Tirant lo Blanch, Valencia, 2014, pp. 335–419.

Guía práctica de la Ley 15/2007, de 3 de julio, de Defensa de la Competencia y el Real Decreto 261/2008, de 22 de febrero, por el que se aprueba el Reglamento de Defensa de la Competencia, Uría Menéndez.

GUILLÉN, J., 'La descentralización del Derecho de la Competencia en España', in GARCIA-CRUCES, J.A. (dir.), *Tratado de Derecho de la Competencia y de la Publicidad*, Tomo I, Tirant lo Blanch, Valencia, 2014, pp. 751–885.

GUTIERREZ, A., 'Comentario al 2 LDC', in MASSAGUER, J. *et altri*, *Comentario a la Ley de Defensa de la Competencia*, Civitas/Thomson Reuters, Cizur Me^{no}r, 3rd ed., 2012, pp. 174–218.

HERNÁNDEZ, F., 'Prohibición del abuso de posición dominante en el mercado', in BELLO, Mª.P. – HERNÁNDEZ, F. (coord.), *Derecho de la libre competencia comunitario y español*, Thomson Aranzadi, Cizur Menor, 2009, pp. 113–140.

HERNÁNDEZ, F., *Precios predatorios y derecho 'antitrust': Estudio comparado de los ordenamientos estadounidense, comunitario y español*, Marcial Pons, Madrid, 1997.

LAIGLESIA, J. M., 'Propuesta de reforma del sistema de control de concentraciones', *in Documentos de Trabajo,* 56/2004, Fundación Alternativas, pp. 29–30.

MARCOS, F., 'Damages Claims in the Spanish Sugar Cartel', in *Journal of Antitrust Enforcement,* Vol. 1, nº 3, 2015, pp. 205–225.

MARCOS, F. – SÁNCHEZ, A., 'El control de concentraciones en la Ley 15/2007, de 3 de julio, de Defensa de la Competencia', in PAREJO, L. – PALOMAR, A., *Derecho de la Competencia. Estudios sobre la Ley 15/2007, de 3 de julio, de Defensa de la Competencia*, La Ley, 2008, pp. 87–155.

MARCOS, F. – SÁNCHEZ, A., 'El sistema de control de concentraciones empresariales en la nueva Ley de Defensa de la Competencia', en *IE Working Paper*, 07–14.

MARCOS, F., 'Competition Law Private Litigation in the Spanish Courts (1999-2012)' in *Global Competition Litigation Review*, nº 4, 2013, pp. 167–211.

MARCOS, F., 'Indemnización de daños y perjuicios por boicot a raíÿbusivcártel del seguro de daños decenal (SDD): Notas a propósito de la sentencia del juzgado mercanti nº 12 de Madrid de 9 de mayo de 2014 (MUSAAT v. ASEFA, CASER y SCOR)' in *La Ley mercantil,* 29 July 2014, available at http://bit.ly/1klSXiM (last time accessed: 7 February 2017).

MARCOS, F., 'State Action Doctrine in Spain: Treatment of State Anticompetitive Restrictions', which is available (in Spanish) in http://bit.ly/1tO5nBX (last time accessed: 7 February 2017).

MARCOS, F., 'The Spanish Property Insurance Cartel' in *Connecticut Insurance Law Journal,* Vol. 18, nº 2, 2012, pp. 79–101.

MARCOS, F., 'The Spanish Property Insurance Cartel' in *Connecticut Insurance Law Journal*, nº 18, Spring 2012, pp. 509–529.

MASSAGUER, J., 'Comentario al art. 3 LDC', in MASSAGUER, J. *et altri*, *Comentario a la Ley de Defensa de la Competencia*, Civitas/Thomson Reuters, Cizur Me^no^r, 3rd ed., 2012, pp. 218–243.

Ministerio de Economía, *Libro Blanco para la reforma del sistema español de defensa de la competencia*, 20 January 2005.

MONTAÑÁ, M., 'Artículo 3' in ODRIOZOLA, M. (Dir.), *Derecho español de la Competencia*, Tomo I, Bosch, Barcelona, 2008, pp. 193–219.

NÚÑEZ, M., *El abuso anticompetitivo en precios. Rebajas y precios predatorios*, La Ley, 2012.

ORTIZ, I., 'La regla *de minimis* en el ámbito de los acuerdos restrictivos de la competencia', *Revist@ e-Mercatoria*, Volume 8, Number 2 (2009), pp. 1–39.

ORTIZ, L. *et altri*, *Manual de Derecho de la Competencia*, Tecnos, Madrid, 2008.

PELLISÉ, J., *La 'explotación abusiva' de una posición dominante (Arts.82 TCE y 6 LEDC)*, Civitas, Madrid, 2002.

PÉREZ, J.I., *et altri*, *Diagnosis of the White Paper for the Reform of the Regulatory Scheme of the Power Generation in Spain*, Instituto de Investigación Tecnológica (IIT), Universidad Pontificia Comillas de Madrid, 2005.

PÉREZ FERNÁNDEZ, P., 'The Difficult Relationship Between Restraints to the Attorney-Client Privilege and Compliance with the Law by Companies – Commentary on *Akzo Nobel Chemicals and others vs. Commission* (Case C-550/07)' in *European Criminal Law Review*, Vol. 1, nº 3, 2011, pp. 274–285.

PÉREZ FERNÁNDEZ, P., 'Repaso de las sanciones penales por ilícitos anticompetitivos en Europa', available at http://bit.ly/1Jj88V1 (last time accessed: 7 February 2017).

Selected Bibliography

QUINTANS, R., 'Órganos y procedimiento en el Derecho español de defensa de la Competencia', in BELLO, Mª.P. – HERNÁNDEZ, F. (coord.), *Derecho de la libre competencia comunitario y español*, Thomson Aranzadi, Cizur Menor, 2009, pp. 313 ff.

RODRÍGUEZ, J.A., 'Defensa de la Competencia y Comunidades Autónomas', in BENEYTO, J.M. – MAILLO, J., *La nueva Ley de Defensa de la Competencia. Análisis y comentarios*, Bosch, Barcelona, 2009, pp. 61–107.

RODRÍGUEZ, V. – ARANDA, B. – PASTOR, F., 'Abuso de posición de dominio', in LOMA-OSORIO, D., *Tratado de Derecho de la Competencia*, Aranzadi, Madrid, 2013, pp. 171–228.

RUIZ, J., 'Los descuentos y su problemática', in MARTÍNEZ S. – PETIBÒ, A. (dirs.), *El abuso de la posición de dominio*, Marcial Pons, Madrid, 2006, pp. 313–338.

SÁNCHEZ, A., 'Control de concentraciones', in BENEYTO, J.M. – MAILLO, J., *La nueva Ley de Defensa de la Competencia. Análisis y comentarios*, Bosch, Barcelona, 2009, pp. 189–231.

SANCHO, I., 'Ejercicio privado de las acciones basadas en el derecho comunitario y nacional de la competencia' in *InDret. Revista para el análisis del Derecho*, nº 1/2009.

SCHREIBER, T. & PÉREZ FERNÁNDEZ, P., 'Judgment of the Spanish Supreme Court in *Acor* (344/2012) June 8, 2012' in *Global Competition Litigation Review*, nº 1, 2013, pp. 37–41.

SIGNES, J.I. – FUENTES, M., 'Cuestiones horizontales a la aplicación de las disposiciones de competencia', in SIGNES, J.I. *et altri*, *Derecho de la competencia*, Civitas Thomson Reuters, Cizur Menor, 2013, pp. 77–104.

SIGNES, J.I., 'Fundamentos del Derecho de la Política de la Competencia', in SIGNES, J.I. *et altri*, *Derecho de la competencia*, Civitas Thomson Reuters, Cizur Menor, 2013, pp. 29–52.

TRONCOSO, M., 'El marco normativo de los ilícitos desleales de relevancia antitrust (Reflexiones en torno al art. 7 LDC)', in *Estudios jurídicos en homenaje al Profesor Aurelio Menéndez*, Tomo I, Civitas, Madrid, 1996, pp. 1034–1079.

VIÑUELAS, M. – GAVELA, A.- HORTALÀ, J., 'Concentraciones de empresas', in LOMA-OSORIO, D., *Tratado de Derecho de la Competencia*, Aranzadi, Madrid, 2013, pp. 347–474.

Index

The numbers here refer to paragraph numbers.

Index